Anxiety & Depression Workbook

FOR

DUMMIES®

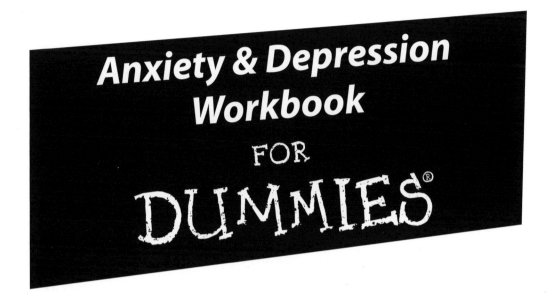

Anxiety & Depression Workbook

FOR DUMMIES®

**by Elaine Iljon Foreman, M.Sc., AFPBSs.,
Charles H. Elliott, PhD, and Laura L. Smith, PhD**

A John Wiley and Sons, Ltd, Publication

Anxiety & Depression Workbook For Dummies®

Published by
John Wiley & Sons, Ltd
The Atrium
Southern Gate
Chichester
West Sussex
PO19 8SQ
England

E-mail (for orders and customer service enquires): cs-books@wiley.co.uk

Visit our Home Page on www.wiley.com

Copyright © 2009 John Wiley & Sons, Ltd, Chichester, West Sussex, England

Published by John Wiley & Sons, Ltd, Chichester, West Sussex

For general information on our other products and services, please contact our Customer Care Department within the U.S. at 877-762-2974, outside the U.S. at 317-572-3993, or fax 317-572-4002.

For technical support, please visit www.wiley.com/techsupport.

Wiley also publishes its books in a variety of electronic formats. Some content that appears in print may not be available in electronic books.

British Library Cataloguing in Publication Data: A catalogue record for this book is available from the British Library

ISBN: 978-0-470-74200-6

Printed and bound in Great Britain by TJ International Ltd., Cornwall

10 9 8 7 6 5 4 3 2 1

About the Authors

Elaine Iljon Foreman M.Sc., AFPBSs., is a Chartered Clinical Psychologist and Associate Fellow of the British Psychological Society. She specialises in the treatment of fear of flying plus other anxiety- and depression-related problems. Elaine is a Consultant Specialist in Cognitive Behavioural Therapy, accredited with the British Association for Behavioural and Cognitive Psychotherapy, a Fellow of the Institute of Travel and Tourism, and chairs the UKCP Ethics Committee. Her highly specialised Freedom to Fly Treatment Programme for the fear of flying, and the Freedom from Fear approach for other depression- and anxiety-based problems have been developed over thirty years of clinical experience and ongoing research and development of cognitive behavioural therapy. She started research into the treatment of anxiety and depression in 1976 at the Middlesex Hospital Medical School and her continuing interest and success have brought invitations to present her findings in Europe, the Americas, Australia and the Far East. In addition she co-ordinates international research into the field of treatment for fear of flying. Her presentations and workshops are given both nationally and internationally on an ongoing basis to professional and self-help audiences.

Elaine's professional views are regularly sought by TV and radio in recognition of her innovative clinical research, and she regularly presents at international conferences, workshops, and publishes material in her specialist field. Her most recent publications are *Overcoming Anxiety For Dummies* and *Overcoming Depression For Dummies* co-authored with Charles Elliott and Laura Smith, and *Fly Away Fear, A Self-Help Guide to Overcoming Fear of Flying* co-authored with Lucas Van Gerwen, and published by Karnac in May 2008.

You can find out more about the Freedom to Fly organisation by visiting www.freedomtofly. biz. To request a Service Brochure detailing the range of services including workshops and psychological therapy, or to invite Elaine to speaking engagements and workshops, email elaine@freedomtofly.biz.

Charles H. Elliott, PhD, is a clinical psychologist and a member of the faculty at the Fielding Graduate Institute. He has a part-time private practice in Albuquerque, New Mexico, that specialises in the treatment of anxiety and depression. He is a Founding Fellow in the Academy of Cognitive Therapy, an internationally recognised organisation that certifies cognitive therapists for treating depression, anxiety, panic attacks and other emotional disorders. He has made numerous presentations nationally and internationally on new developments in assessment and therapy of emotional disorders. He is co-author of *Overcoming Depression For Dummies* (Wiley), *Overcoming Anxiety For Dummies* (Wiley), *Why Can't I Get What I Want?* (Davies-Black, 1998; A Behavioral Science Book Club Selection), *Why Can't I Be the Parent I Want to Be?* (New Harbinger Publications, 1999), and *Hollow Kids: Recapturing the Soul of a Generation Lost to the Self-Esteem Myth* (Prima, 2001).

Laura L. Smith, PhD, is a clinical psychologist at Presbyterian Behavioral Medicine, Albuquerque, New Mexico. At Presbyterian, she specialises in the assessment and treatment of both adults and children with anxiety and other mood disorders. She is an adjunct faculty member at the Fielding Graduate Institute. Formerly, she was the clinical supervisor for a regional educational cooperative. In addition, she has presented on new developments in cognitive therapy to both national and international audiences. Dr Smith is co-author of *Hollow Kids* (Prima, 2001) and *Why Can't I Be the Parent I Want to Be?* (New Harbinger Publications, 1999).

Dedication

From Elaine: To my parents, Helga and Nickie, my partner, Graham Kelly, and the Rocks who make up my world. You know who you are, and so, counting my blessings, do I!

From Laura and Charles: We dedicate this book to our kids: Alli, Brian, Grant, Nathan, Sara and Trevor. And to our granddaughter: Lauren Melodie. And finally to our parents: Edna Louise Smith, Joe Bond Elliott, Tea Elliott, William Thomas Smith (1914-1999), and Suzanne Wieder Elliott (1923–2004).

Authors' Acknowledgments

Elaine: The Trilogy is now complete, and all Dummies, most certainly including me, have clear guidance and support to overcome Anxiety (Wiley 2007), Depression (Wiley 2008), and their combination, with the publication of this Anxiety and Depression Workbook. The tumultuous times to which I've alluded in the two previous books are approaching conclusion. Strength can indeed come out of adversity. My gratitude goes to those caring, courageous souls who supported me so steadfastly, and continue to do so. Let's all of us go from strength to strength, be what we believe in, and live a life fulfilled.

Laura and Charles: We're no longer in denial. We're hopelessly addicted to this writing business. We no longer need to apologise to our family and friends for our neglect; they're used to it by now! We appreciate the efforts of our agents, Ed and Elizabeth Knappman who have encouraged our pursuits. Thanks to our editors at Wiley.

We have been privileged to hear the many stories of suffering, hurt, trauma, hope, recovery and resilience from our clients over the years. We respect and appreciate what they have taught us. This book would not be possible without their collective wisdom.

Publisher's Acknowledgments

We're proud of this book; please send us your comments through our Dummies online registration form located at www.dummies.com/register/.

Some of the people who helped bring this book to market include the following:

Acquisitions, Editorial, and Media Development

Acquisitions Editor: Nicole Hermitage

Project Editor: Rachael Chilvers

Development Editor: Brian Kramer

Content Editor: Jo Theedom

Copy Editor: Christine Lea

Technical Editor: Dr Cosmo Hallstrom

Executive Project Editor: Daniel Mersey

Cover Photos: Walter B. McKenzie/Getty Images

Cartoons: Ed McLachlan

Composition Services

Project Coordinator: Lynsey Stanford

Layout and Graphics: Samantha Allen, Reuben W. Davis, Jennifer Henry, Ronald Terry

Proofreaders: Caitie Copple, Melissa Cossell

Indexer: Ty Koontz

Contents at a Glance

Table of Contents

Foreword

*W*e should all understand anxiety and depression. Fundamentally, we all experience both from time to time, some of us more than others. This being so, where does the stigma, the mockery and the contempt come from? Mainly, I think, from a lack of understanding. People suffering from anxiety and depression are sometimes referred to as 'the worried well'. This is so far from the reality that it makes me feel depressed, and takes my breath away. People *suffering* from anxiety and depression are, in fact, the walking wounded. As such they deserve consideration, understanding and, above all, appropriate help.

I hear those who don't understand say: 'Surely these people, these sufferers from anxiety and depression, don't they just need to PULL THEMSELVES TOGETHER?' Those who suffer from anxiety and depression hear this phrase all too often. It carries with it criticism and an implied moral judgement; perhaps the problem in anxiety and depression is that people are weak, not trying hard enough, lacking in moral fibre and so on. Words like 'neurotic' are bandied about.

Pull yourself together? If only! As you will find out in this book, anxiety and depression are traps. People become stuck in particular counter-productive ways of thinking and behaving, and simply cannot see any way out. It is in the nature of anxiety and depression that, in their clinical forms, 'the solution becomes the problem'. The harder the sufferer tries, the more stuck they become. For example, when frightening and upsetting thoughts bother you, you try to push them out of your mind. What the person doesn't realise is that pushing the thoughts out of their mind is increasing their preoccupation. If you try not to think about something, you think it more. The anxious person avoids frightening situations so that they feel safer, but in doing so don't get a chance to discover that the things they fear don't really happen. The shy person doesn't say anything to others because they fear ridicule, but ends up believing that they have nothing to say. The depressed person withdraws from activities they find demanding, and in doing so never experiences feelings of success, achievement and approval.

Which brings us to the present book. The reality, if you suffer from anxiety and depression, is that you really do need to pull yourself together. The problem, of course, is knowing how to do this! I have never met an anxious or depressed person who didn't yearn to know how to get out of the trap they find themselves in. No one wants to have their life destroyed by feelings of fearfulness, worry and sadness. What is needed is some kind of guide on how to choose to change.

Cognitive behavioural therapy (CBT), which is the focus of this book, is the best established way of getting over anxiety and depression. Time after time the research shows that CBT is effective not only in the short term (drugs are too) but more importantly in the long term. That's because its effects are based on people learning new things about how to understand how they feel, why they feel that way, and why that feeling doesn't go away. If you know where your problems come from and why they persist, maybe you can learn to overcome them. Some people need therapy from a therapist (who, in CBT, is less of a doctor and more of a coach); others need a 'how to' guide. This book can be that guide, either with or without input from a therapist. For some people, sharing their understanding with someone who cares and can support them in their efforts to change is a great way forward.

Above all, cognitive behavioural therapy is about helping people to find out where they have become 'stuck' in how they think and react, and empowering them to see things in a different way and then go on to do things in a different way so that they can learn to live in a different, and better, way. For many people, this book will help them do that. For others, it will start something which needs some more help, including professional help. Whether you are someone who suffers from anxiety and depression, someone who lives with or is trying to help a sufferer, or simply want to know what its all about, then this book is a great way to start.

Paul Salkovskis

Professor of Clinical Psychology and Applied Science, Institute of Psychiatry, King's College London

Clinical Director, Centre for Anxiety Disorders and Trauma, South London and Maudsley Foundation Trust

Introduction

．．．

*A*re you finding life rough going? Do you worry too much? Are you often sad or down in the dumps? Do you have to drag yourself out of bed in the morning? Perhaps you avoid people more than you should. If so, you're probably dealing with some type of anxiety or depression. Depression and anxiety are serious problems – they can cloud your world view, distort thinking and even sap the joy and pleasure from life. Experiencing them can make life anything but plain sailing.

Everyone feels sad or worried from time to time. Unpleasant feelings are a normal part of life. But when depression or anxiety begins to interfere with your work, play and/or relationships, it's time to take action.

Good news! You can conquer these problems. And the *Anxiety & Depression Workbook For Dummies* will help. You can use this workbook on its own or alongside help from a qualified professional. Either way, numerous studies show that self-help efforts work – you can make a difference! Experts estimate that almost a quarter of the people in the world will experience significant problems with anxiety at some point in their lives. And between 15 and 20 per cent will have depression at some point. Unfortunately, many people suffer from both anxiety and depression, as the two are closely related. Over the years, we've known many clients, friends and family members who have had problems with anxiety or depression, but the good news is that most of them have found significant relief.

So if you struggle with anxiety, depression or both, you're certainly not alone. We join you in your battle by giving you research-based strategies and plenty of practice opportunities to help you defeat depression and overcome anxiety.

About This Book

Our purpose in writing this book is to give you a wide range of skills, tools and techniques for managing anxiety and depression. Although we touch on essential concepts about depression and anxiety, this book is action-oriented – in other words, you have the opportunity to actively apply our professional ideas to your life in meaningful ways, enabling you to make all the difference to your difficulties.

Today, you can find workbooks on almost any topic, from passing exams, DIY and home improvement, selling your home (after you've improved it!), doing your tax return and even improving your memory.

The purpose of any workbook is to lay out the basics of a topic and then provide numerous opportunities to apply and practise the new concepts to really get the hang of them. Typically, books concentrate more on explaining issues, and workbooks help you master new skills. In other words, the *Anxiety & Depression Workbook For Dummies* is one of the 'less talk, more action' variety. Don't be put off by the 'work' in this workbook, and please don't put this book back on the shelf quite yet! Decide to have a go, and we believe you'll be well rewarded for your work in the form of increased life satisfaction and reduced emotional distress. You'll even find that the work's pretty interesting when you get down to it, not least because you discover new ways to live your life and get what you want.

A Note to Depressed and Anxious Readers

Feeling depressed or anxious certainly is no joke. When you're feeling like this, you may find it quite difficult to see the funny side of anything. Nevertheless, we've chosen to add splashes of humour throughout this workbook. We understand that if you take this the wrong way, you may be offended, thinking that we appear to make light of what is a dark, difficult subject. But humour is an important coping tool and can make all the difference in enabling you to munch your way through and digest the messages, by making them more palatable.

How to Use This Book

Unlike most workbooks, you don't necessarily have to read and use the chapters of this book in order, from beginning to end. You can pick and choose which chapters to read and which exercises to do, and you can also choose where to start and stop. We give you sufficient information to carry out each of the exercises and improve your mood.

Please do write in this book – that's what it's for. Writing strengthens skills and commits you to taking action, so we strongly encourage you to do the work required for your recovery by writing out your answers in the forms and worksheets. Don't worry about handwriting or spelling – nobody's marking you on that.

Throughout this book, you'll see sections labelled My Reflections. When you come across a reflection space, we recommend that you take a little time to think about what you're feeling, what you've discovered and/or any new insights you've achieved. But guess what? This is *your* workbook – so you get to write down anything you want in My Reflections.

Foolish Assumptions

By the sheer fact that you've picked up this book, we assume, perhaps foolishly, that you want to do something about depression and/or anxiety – either your own, or that of someone close to you. We hope you already know a little about these topics, but if you want to know more, we suggest you read either or both of the companion books to this workbook: *Overcoming Anxiety For Dummies* and *Overcoming Depression For Dummies*, both by by Elaine Iljon Foreman, Charles H. Elliott and Laura L. Smith (Wiley). We admit we're slightly biased towards these books because we wrote them! Seriously, though, we've certainly put them to good effect in our lives. Chances are, they'll both broaden your understanding and increase your skills at working through emotional distress.

How This Book Is Organised

The *Anxiety & Depression Workbook For Dummies* is organised into seven parts, which we outline in the following sections.

Part 1: Recognising and Recording Anxiety and Depression

This part is all about helping you identify your problem and take the first small steps toward recovery. Chapter 1 helps you discover if you have any problems with anxiety or depression. The questionnaires in this chapter help you identify where these problems manifest in your world and what they do to your thoughts, behaviours, feelings and relationships. In Chapter 2, you go on a journey to the origins of your problems with anxiety and depression because knowing where it all began helps you realise that you're not to blame. Because change sometimes feels overwhelming, Chapter 3 addresses self-sabotage and helps you keep moving forward. Chapter 4 provides you with ways of keeping track of your moods and becoming more aware of your thoughts.

Part II: Understanding Your Thinking: Cognitive Therapy

The chapters in this part help you become a thought detective. In Chapter 5, you find out how to examine your thoughts for distortions; then, in Chapter 6, you take those distorted thoughts to task and restructure them.

Chapter 7 shows you how certain core beliefs darken and distort your view of yourself, your world and your future as surely as glasses with the wrong prescription lenses distort clear vision. We include techniques that enable you to swap your old, distorted lenses for ones that allow you to focus and see things more clearly and accurately. Finally, in Chapter 8, you have the opportunity to practise mindfulness and acceptance – two more techniques for effectively handling troubling thoughts.

Part III: Taking Action with Behaviour Therapy

Chapter 9 points out how you can take direct action against the natural tendency to avoid what makes you depressed or anxious. In Chapter 10, we get you up and moving by providing workbook-type exercises that encourage physical exercise. When you're depressed or anxious, few activities sound like fun, so Chapter 11 has worksheets for reintroducing pleasure into your life. Finally, Chapter 12 helps you tackle life problems that develop from your emotional distress.

Part IV: Feeling It Where It Hurts: Healing the Body

Addressing the physical side of distress is as important as addressing the mental or emotional side. Excessive stress associated with anxiety and depression produces hormones that can affect the body by increasing blood pressure and contributing to stomach problems, weight gain and heart disease. Therefore, relaxation techniques play an important role in alleviating anxiety and depression. In Chapter 13, you find a variety of exercises for reducing tension and stress. Because medication is an additional option for many people who are depressed or anxious, Chapter 14 guides you through the decision of whether or not taking medication is the right choice for you.

Part V: Revitalising Relationships

Depression and anxiety can spill over and damage your relationships. Good relationships offer support in dealing with emotional distress, while the opposite just make things worse. Chapter 15 helps you figure out if your relationships are suffering, and the worksheets and exercises in Chapter 16 guide you in improving the quality of your relationships.

Part VI: Life Beyond Anxiety and Depression

After people overcome their anxiety and depression, naturally they prefer to go on with their lives as though they'd never had a problem. Unfortunately, like the flu, you can succumb to depression or anxiety more than once. Chapter 17 tells you how to prepare for and deal with any setbacks, while Chapter 18 helps you develop positive habits that lead to a more joyful, meaningful, satisfying and connected life.

Part VII: The Part of Tens

This part contains a couple of our top ten lists when it comes to the subjects of anxiety and depression. Chapter 19 recommends ten resources for getting help in dealing with your depression and anxiety. If you're looking for a quick way out of a low mood, Chapter 20 is for you – it lists ten remedies that don't take a huge amount of effort.

Characters in This Book

Throughout this workbook, we use fictional characters to illustrate how you can complete the various worksheets and exercises. Although these characters aren't real people, they represent composites of various clients and others we've both known and worked with over the years. Any resemblance to an actual individual, whether alive or deceased, is unintended and coincidental. Despite their fictional nature, we believe you'll relate to them and find their experiences useful.

Icons Used in This Book

Throughout the book, icons in the margins alert you to important types of information:

This icon points to specific examples that show you the way through worksheets or exercises.

When you see this icon, you know it's time to roll up your sleeves and get down to work! It denotes a worksheet, form or exercise for you to complete.

We mark particularly noteworthy information with this icon; we hope you'll remember this information long after you finish the workbook.

This icon alerts you to especially useful insights and explanations.

When this icon appears, you need to take care; you may need professional help or should be on the lookout for possible trouble.

Where to Go from Here

The *Anxiety & Depression Workbook For Dummies* can help you deal with your depression and anxiety. It's pragmatic, concrete and goes straight to the point. As such, this workbook doesn't devote a lot of text to lengthy explanations or elaboration of basic concepts. You may therefore need something more in-depth if you want to find out more about specific types of depression and anxiety, available medications and alternative treatments. For that purpose, we strongly recommend that you consider reading one or both of the companion books, *Overcoming Depression For Dummies* and *Overcoming Anxiety For Dummies*. We wish you every success and much happiness as you sail along your journey of discovery, through both calm and turbulent waters, taking you and your life to better and better places.

Part I
Recognising and Recording Anxiety and Depression

'Well, just to come here at all is a start
to curing your anxiety complex, Mr Gumbottle.'

In this part . . .

We help you figure out how anxiety or depression affects your thinking, behaviour, feelings and bodily sensations. You discover how your problems began and work towards accepting that you're not to blame for having them. In case you feel stuck or unable to move forward, we give you strategies for overcoming obstacles. We also show you how to keep track of both your moods and the thoughts that accompany distressing feelings.

Chapter 1

Spotting the Signs of Anxiety and Depression

. . . .

In This Chapter

▶ Working out how depression and anxiety affect you

▶ Finding your personal starting point

▶ Knowing when to get more help

. . . .

*E*veryone feels sad or worried from time to time. Such emotions are both natural and unavoidable. People worry about their children, bills, aging parents, jobs and health. And most people have shed a tear or two watching a sad film or reading a news story about a poignant tragedy. That's normal. Sadness and worry are part of the everyday range of human emotion.

However, the intensity of these emotions and the distress they cause can vary enormously. When sadness or worry becomes much more extreme, you may start to realise that you're suffering from something that can be quite disturbing. When the intensity starts to affect your life, the emotions can increase from sadness and worry to anxiety and depression. Yet even then, a certain amount of these stronger emotions is also completely usual and quite natural for people to experience.

The intensity of anxiety or depression can increase still further, and you can reach a level where you have an anxiety disorder or clinical depression. In these states, you feel extremely low and sad most of the time, or your worries continuously dominate your mind. At this point, you may be experiencing a real problem with depression or anxiety.

Anxiety and depression can affect how you think, behave, feel and relate to others. The discussion and questionnaires in this chapter help you work out if, and even how much, depression and anxiety are affecting your life. And after you understand what's going on, you can then start doing something about it.

Don't panic if the questionnaires in this chapter indicate that you have a few symptoms of anxiety or depression. Rest assured, most people do. We let you know if you should be concerned.

If you have many symptoms, their effects are severe or your life seems out of control, you should consult your GP or a mental health professional. These questionnaires aren't meant to take the place of qualified mental health professionals, as these people are the only ones who can really diagnose your problem.

Dwelling on Negative Thoughts

If you were able to eavesdrop on the thoughts whirling round inside a depressed person's mind, you might hear 'I'm a failure', 'My future looks bleak', 'Things just keep getting worse' or 'I regret so many things in my life'.

On the other hand, the thoughts of an anxious person might be 'I'm going to look a right idiot when I give that talk', 'I never know what to say at parties', 'Motorways scare the hell out of me', 'I know that the chances of a plane crashing are tiny, but flying scares me' or 'I'll have a nervous breakdown if my editor doesn't like what I write'.

Thoughts affect the way you feel. And the very lowest, most miserable thoughts can lead to depression, while anxiety more often arises out of thoughts to do with being judged or coming to harm. And, of course, people often have both types of thoughts.

Do your thoughts dwell more on the melancholy, dispirited or on the scary, alarming aspects of life? Fill out the questionnaire in Worksheet 1-1 to find out if your thoughts reflect a problem more related to anxiety or to depression. Tick each item that you feel applies to you.

Worksheet 1-1	**Depressed and Anxious Thoughts Questionnaire**

❑ Things are going from bad to worse.

❑ I worry all the time.

❑ I'm just no good for anything.

❑ I can't think of anything that's worth saying.

❑ No one would miss me if I were dead.

❑ I think I'm a failure.

❑ Thoughts race through my mind, and I can't get rid of them.

❑ I don't really look forward to anything.

❑ I'm constantly on edge when I'm with new people.

❑ The world would be much better off without me.

❑ I'm tormented with thoughts about past traumatic events.

❑ I find it impossible to make decisions.

❑ I hate being the centre of attention.

❑ My life's just full of regrets.

❑ I can't stand making mistakes.

❑ I can't see any light at the end of the tunnel (except for the one that's the headlight of an oncoming train!).

❑ I constantly worry about my health.

❑ I'm deeply ashamed of myself.

❑ I always go overboard in my preparations.

The preceding thoughts can occur to someone who's either depressed, anxious or both. The odd-numbered items point more towards depression and the even-numbered items to anxiety. This questionnaire isn't a test that you pass or fail. The more items you tick, the more cause you have for concern. And if you tick more than eight to ten items, do seriously consider doing something about these difficulties. On the other hand, even if you tick only one item, but you fervently believe it, you still may be suffering from anxiety or depression and may well benefit from help.

If you have any thoughts of suicide or utter hopelessness, consult your doctor or a mental health professional immediately.

Recognising What You Do When You're Anxious or Blue

If you follow a depressed or anxious person, you're likely to see some behavioural signs of their emotional turmoil. That's because depression and anxiety, while experienced on the inside, affect what people do in the outside world. For example, a depressed person may look tired, move slowly or withdraw from friends and family; an anxious person may avoid socialising or speak in a quavering voice.

Complete the questionnaire in Worksheet 1-2 to see if your behaviour indicates that you may have a problem with anxiety and/or depression. Tick each statement that applies to you.

Worksheet 1-2	**The Troubled Behaviour Questionnaire**

❑ I've been crying for no obvious reason.

❑ I pace around when I'm worried.

❑ Sometimes I can't make myself get out of bed.

❑ I avoid going into crowded areas.

❑ I can't seem to make myself exercise.

❑ I avoid risks because I'm afraid of failure.

❑ Recently, I've stopped doing things for fun.

❑ I always play it safe.

❑ I've been missing work lately because I just don't feel motivated.

❑ I'm really fidgety.

❑ I'm doing everything more slowly, for no apparent reason.

❑ I avoid people or places that remind me of any previous bad experience.

❑ I no longer care what I look like.

❑ I spend too much time trying to make myself look good.

❑ I've lost my sense of humour and seldom laugh.

❑ My hands shake when I'm nervous.

❑ I've been letting things slide that really do require my attention.

❑ I feel I absolutely must repeat certain actions (such as hand-washing, checking locks, arranging things in a certain way and so on).

Like Worksheet 1-1, there's no pass or fail here – it's not a test. Interpret the results by understanding that the more items you tick, the greater the problem. Even-numbered items reflect anxiety, and odd-numbered items largely indicate depression. And of course, like many people, you may have symptoms of both types of problem.

Sizing Up Stress

Depression and anxiety inevitably are accompanied by physical symptoms. Some people primarily experience changes in appetite, sleep, energy or pain, while experiencing few problematic thoughts. Symptoms of both anxiety and depression can directly affect your body. Though others can't see what you're feeling, they may well notice behavioural changes, like those covered in the preceding section.

The following questionnaire, Worksheet 1-3, helps you see if your body is trying to tell you something about your emotional state.

Worksheet 1-3   The Sensations of Sadness and Stress Questionnaire

❑ I've lost my appetite.

❑ My palms are constantly sweaty.

❑ I wake up very early in the morning and can't go back to sleep.

❑ I've been experiencing a lot of nausea and diarrhoea.

❑ I've been sleeping a lot more than usual.

❑ I feel shaky all over.

❑ I've been having lots of aches and pains for no good reason.

❑ My chest feels tight when I'm nervous.

❑ I seem to have no energy lately.

❑ My heart races when I'm tense.

❑ I've been constipated a lot more often than usual.

❑ I feel I can't catch my breath.

❑ I'm always hungry and can't stop eating.

❑ My hands often feel cold and clammy.

❑ I'm just not interested in sex.

❑ Sometimes I breathe very rapidly and end up hyperventilating.

❑ Every move I make takes more effort lately.

❑ I get dizzy easily.

The symptoms in this questionnaire can also be due to various physical illnesses, taking both over-the-counter and prescription drugs, or even drinking too much alcohol or very strong coffee. Be sure to consult your GP if you're experiencing any of the symptoms in The Sensations of Sadness and Stress Questionnaire. It's important to go for a check-up if you experience noticeable changes in your body.

Although physical sensations overlap in anxiety and depression, even-numbered items in the questionnaire above are most consistent with anxiety, and the odd-numbered items usually affect those with depression. No cut-off point identifies if you have a problem. The more statements you tick, the greater your problem.

Relating to Relationship Problems

When you're feeling low, distressed or anxious for any length of time, the chances are your relationships with other people suffer. Although you may think that your depression or anxiety affects only you, it has an impact on your friends, family, colleagues and acquaintances.

Go through Worksheet 1-4 to see if your feelings and emotions are having a negative effect on your relationships. Tick all statements that apply to you.

Worksheet 1-4	The Disrupted Relationship Questionnaire

❑ I don't feel sociable.

❑ I get edgy when I meet new people.

❑ I don't feel like talking to anyone.

❑ I'm super-sensitive to all criticism.

❑ I'm more irritable than usual with others.

❑ I worry about saying the wrong things.

❑ I don't feel close to anyone.

❑ I worry about being abandoned.

❑ I don't feel like going out anywhere, with anyone, any more.

❑ I'm troubled by disturbing fantasies of people I care about getting hurt.

❑ I've withdrawn from everyone.

❑ I feel uneasy when lots of people are around, so I stay away from anywhere crowded.

❑ I feel emotionally numb when I'm with people.

❑ I'm always uncomfortable in the spotlight.

❑ I feel that I don't deserve friendship and love.

❑ Receiving compliments makes me uncomfortable.

No cut-off score identifies if you're anxious or depressed. But the more items you tick, the more your relationships are being affected by your anxiety, depression or both. Odd-numbered items usually indicate problems with depression; even-numbered items particularly reflect anxiety.

Do be aware that many people are a bit shy or introverted. You can easily feel a little anxious when meeting new people or may feel uncomfortable in the spotlight. These feelings aren't necessarily anything to be concerned about. However, they can become a problem if you then avoid social activities or meeting new people.

Producing Your Personal Problems Profile

The Personal Problems Profile provides you with an overview of your troubling symptoms. (If you skipped the questionnaires in the previous sections of this chapter, do go back and take the time to complete them. You need your answers to complete this exercise.) This section helps you identify the ways in which anxiety and depression affect you. One good thing about creating a profile is that you can monitor changes in your symptoms as you work through the rest of this book.

Bill, a middle-aged engineer, doesn't consider himself depressed or bothered by any emotional problems. But when he sees his GP, Bill complains of fatigue, recent weight gain and a noticeable loss of his sex drive. After ruling out physical causes, the doctor suggests that he may be depressed. 'Funny you should say that,' Bill replies. 'My girlfriend's just bought me the *Anxiety & Depression Workbook For Dummies.* She also said she thought I was depressed. Maybe I'll take a look at the book.'

When Bill fills out his Personal Problems Profile (see Worksheet 1-5), he comes up with the following top ten symptoms and notes if they indicate anxiety or depression (with an *A* or *D*).

Worksheet 1-5	Bill's Personal Problems Profile
1.	I seem to have no energy lately. (D)
2.	Recently it seems every move I make takes so much more effort. (D)
3.	I'm just not interested in sex. (D)
4.	I'm always hungry and can't stop eating. (D)
5.	I don't feel like being sociable. (D)
6.	I don't really look forward to anything. (D)
7.	I find it impossible to make decisions. (D)
8.	I constantly worry about my health (A)
9.	I feel shaky all over. (A)
10.	Sometimes I can't make myself get out of bed. (D)

As you can see, Bill suffers primarily from symptoms of depression, and most of them are physical in nature. Filling out his Personal Problems Profile helps Bill see that he probably does have depression, even though he wasn't actually aware of it. He reflects on his discovery (see Worksheet 1-6).

Worksheet 1-6	Bill's Reflections

I can see I do have some of the signs of depression. I didn't realise that before. My depression particularly takes the form of physical symptoms. It's affecting my energy, sex drive and appetite. It's also making me withdraw from my girlfriend. That's pretty obvious, given my loss of sex drive and that I'm no longer keen to be with her. I also seem to have a few symptoms of anxiety, and I think I've always had these sorts of feelings. I guess it's high time I finally did something about this.

Right! That's what Bill's decided. And you've chosen to read the *Anxiety & Depression Workbook For Dummies.* But please remember, this isn't just a book. It's a *work* book! Realistically, merely reading it is insufficient – you're unlikely to feel better unless you *do* something, that is, some work! And you're likely to find that the activities really aren't that difficult. Of course, you can skip a few of the exercises. But the more exercises you do, the sooner you start feeling better. Strange as it may seem, simply writing things down can actually do a world of good. The simple act of writing actually helps you remember, clarifies your thinking and increases your focus and reflection.

So now, it's time for you to complete your own Personal Problems Profile in Worksheet 1-7. Look back at the questionnaires earlier in this chapter and underline your most troubling thoughts, feelings, behaviours and relationship issues. Then, choose no more than ten of the most significant items that you've underlined and write them in the My Personal Problems Profile.

Put an *A* by the symptoms that are most indicative of anxiety (even-numbered items in the preceding questionnaires) and a *D* next to those that mainly reflect depression (odd-numbered items).

Worksheet 1-7	My Personal Problems Profile
1.	
2.	
3.	
4.	
5.	
6.	
7.	
8.	
9.	
10.	

Look over your list. Do your symptoms primarily involve anxiety, depression or are they an equal mix of both? And do they seem to mostly affect your thoughts, feelings, behaviours or relationships? Take some time to consider your profile. What conclusions can you draw? Record them in Worksheet 1-8.

Worksheet 1-8	My Reflections

Choosing Your Challenge

Parts II through V of this workbook cover the areas of thoughts, feelings/emotions, behaviours and relationships. An obvious way of deciding which area to start with is to choose the one that causes you the most problems. Alternatively, you can work through them all in the order we present them. Whichever way you choose to start, you should know that all these areas are interrelated. For example, if you have anxious thoughts about being judged, you're likely to avoid the spotlight (behaviour). And you could very well experience butterflies (feelings). In addition, you may also be super-sensitive to criticism from others (relationships).

We generally find that most people prefer to start by tackling the problem area that best fits their personal style. In other words, some people are 'doers', others are 'thinkers', still others are 'feelers' and some are 'relaters'. Use the Personal Style Questionnaire in Worksheet 1-9 to identify your preferred style.

Worksheet 1-9	Personal Style Questionnaire

Thinkers

❑ I like facts and numbers.

❑ I tend to be a very logical person.

❑ I'm a planner.

❑ I like to think through problems.

❑ I carefully weigh the costs and benefits before I act.

Doers

❑ I can't stand sitting around and thinking.

❑ I like to take action on problems.

❑ I like accomplishing things each day.

❑ I get a kick out of overcoming obstacles.

❑ I act first and think later.

Feelers

❑ I'm a very sensuous person.

❑ I really love my creature comforts.

❑ I love massages and hot baths.

❑ Music and art are very important to me.

❑ I'm very in touch with my feelings.

Relaters

❑ I'm a people person.

❑ I'd rather be with people than do anything else.

❑ I care deeply about other people's feelings.

❑ I'm very empathetic.

❑ Relationships are more important to me than accomplishments.

Are you predominately a thinker, doer, feeler or relater? If you ticked substantially more items in one area than the others, you may want to start working in the section of this book that corresponds to that style:

✔ Thinker: Part II, Thought Therapy

✔ Doer: Part III, Behaviour Therapy

✔ Feeler: Part IV, Physical Feelings

✔ Relater: Part V, Relationship Therapy

Knowing When to Get More Help

Self-help tools are likely to be useful for everyone who puts effort into them. Many people find they can overcome minor to moderate emotional problems by working with books like this one. Nevertheless, some difficulties require professional help, perhaps because your anxiety or depression is especially serious or because your problems are simply too complex to be addressed by self-help methods.

Work through The Serious Symptom Checklist in Worksheet 1-10 to find out whether you should seriously consider seeking treatment from a mental health professional.

Ticking any one item from the list below means that you should strongly consider seeking professional help. Please realise that no such list can be all-inclusive. If you're really unsure whether you need help, do see a mental health professional for an assessment.

Worksheet 1-10	The Serious Symptom Checklist

❑ I have thoughts about killing myself.

❑ I feel hopeless.

❑ My sleep has been seriously disturbed for more than two weeks (both sleeping too little or too much).

❑ I've gained or lost more than a few pounds without trying to do so.

❑ I'm ignoring major responsibilities in my life such as going to work or paying the bills.

❑ I'm hearing voices when no one is around.

❑ I'm seeing things that aren't there.

❑ My drug use and/or drinking are interfering with my life.

❑ My thoughts race, and I can't slow them down.

❑ Someone I trust and care about has said I need help.

❑ I've been getting into numerous fights or arguments.

❑ I've been making really poor decisions lately (such as buying expensive or really unnecessary things, or getting involved in questionable business schemes).

❑ Lately, I've felt that people are out to get me.

❑ I haven't been able to get myself to leave the house except for absolute essentials.

❑ I'm taking risks that I never did before.

❑ Suddenly I feel like I'm a special person who's capable of extraordinary things.

❑ I'm spending considerably more time everyday than I should repeating actions such as hand-washing, arranging things and checking and rechecking things (appliances, locks and so on).

❑ I have highly disturbing flashbacks or nightmares about past trauma that I can't seem to forget about.

If you ticked one or more of the preceding statements and you're beginning to think that perhaps you need help, where should you go? Many people start with their GP, which is a pretty good idea because your doctor can determine if your problems actually have a physical cause. If physical problems have been ruled out or treated and you still need help, you can:

- ✔ Find out if you can self-refer or if you need a GP letter to see your local Community Mental Health Resource Centre.

- ✔ Phone the Samaritans on 08457-909090 in the UK (local call rates) or in the Republic of Ireland, dial 1850-609090 (local call rates). Many Samaritan branches also offer local branch telephone numbers. You can also use the Samaritans textphones (for the deaf or hard of hearing): Dial 08457-909192 in the UK.

- ✔ Ask trusted friends or family for recommendations.

- ✔ NHS Direct is available by phone 24 hours a day, 7 days per week. The phone number is 0845-4647.

- ✔ If you have private health insurance, phone your insurance company and ask for recommendations.

Before or during your first session, talk to the mental health professional and ask if you'll receive a scientifically validated treatment for anxiety or depression. Unfortunately, some practitioners lack necessary training in therapies that have been shown by scientific studies to be effective. Also make sure that whoever you see is a qualified mental health practitioner.

At this point, take a moment and pat yourself on the back! Regardless of whether this is the first chapter you've read, we reckon you've made a pretty good start. And do take heart from the fact that every minute you spend working your way through this workbook is likely to substantially increase your chances of improving your mood.

Chapter 2

Digging Down to the Roots of Your Worries

In This Chapter
▶ Considering your biology, genetics and health
▶ Studying your history
▶ Seeking out stressors

*I*f you're reading this book, you probably feel a little anxious or depressed. Chapter 1 gives you many tools for taking an inventory of your anxiety and depression. But you may not know where these feelings come from.

Exploring some of the origins of your feelings – including the influences of biology and genetics, personal history or current stress – can be helpful in improving your situation. This chapter helps you see the deeper and wider picture, which can be a bit like becoming aware of the submerged, normally invisible part of an iceberg, or the forest surrounding a single tree. Understanding what underpins your emotions can enable you to cut loose from the self-blame and guilt (see Chapter 5) that may be dragging you down.

In this chapter, we review the major causes of depression and anxiety: biology, personal history and stress. Many of our clients come to us believing that they're to blame for being overwhelmed by emotional distress. When these clients discover the factors that contribute to their problems' origins, they usually feel less guilty. Getting rid of that guilt frees up energy that they can then use to make important changes. So if less guilt and more energy sound good to you, read on!

Exploring Physical Contributors

Feeling depressed or anxious can have roots in your genes and your physical health. Your feelings can be impacted by any medication or drugs you're taking. This section gives you a quick snapshot of possible physical contributors to your feelings of sadness or worry.

Uncovering your biological history

Feelings can have a biological basis. Was Uncle Paul often down in the dumps? Did Auntie Herta follow you around sweeping up the cake crumbs, wiping each mouthful of chocolate off your face and maintaining a perfect show-home with never a thing out of place? Perhaps your grandmother always kept herself to herself, had few friends and seldom participated in family life. Have your parents told you anything about their grandparents? You may wonder why these questions are important. The answer is that depression and anxiety tend to run in families. So your genes may be influencing quite a bit of your emotional distress (you can think of them as 'blue' genes!).

If you have relatives or friends who know and are open to talking about your family history, have a chat with them. Ask if any relatives, on either side of your family, suffered from anxiety or depression. You may want to review the symptoms we cover in Chapter 1. No magic number of anxious or depressed relatives proves that genetics underlie your symptoms. However, the more family members with similar problems, the more likely you've inherited a tendency for depression or anxiety. Record what you find out.

Members of my family with anxiety or depression (brothers, sisters, cousins, parents, uncles, aunts, grandparents and great-grandparents):

_____

_____

_____

_____

_____

Considering drugs and other chemicals

In addition to genetics, any drugs you are taking (legal or illegal, prescribed or over-the-counter) as well as any illness or health conditions can affect your anxiety or depression. Drugs have many side effects. Sometimes solving your problem is as simple as identifying what you're storing in your medicine cabinet. Almost any medication you're taking can influence your emotions negatively. Read the information leaflets. Is depression or anxiety listed within the side effects?

If you've thrown out the leaflets, check with your pharmacist or your GP to see if your medication may be causing part of your problem. Or research the drugs online; most manufacturers of over-the-counter and prescription drugs provide extensive information online. Whatever you find out, only stop taking a medication *after* consulting a medical professional.

Mood-altering illegal drugs like marijuana, cocaine, heroin and amphetamines may make you feel good in the short term. However, in the long run, they almost all worsen your mood problems. If you're experiencing problems to do with drugs, consult a professional or check out the numerous self-help organisations relating to that particular substance.

Alcohol can also contribute to depression or anxiety. Some people find that even moderate amounts of alcohol worsen their mood problems. Alcohol also interacts with a wide variety of prescribed and over-the-counter drugs, either amplifying the effects that the alcohol has (a little going a long way is not necessarily a good thing) or the alcohol may even block the medication's effect. The nicotine in tobacco is well-recognised as a mood-altering drug.

Noting physical illnesses

Physical illnesses and medical conditions can also produce symptoms of anxiety or depression. Not only can they cause mood problems, but also worrying about them can contribute to your distress. If you've been diagnosed with an illness, or any medical condition, check with your doctor to see if your depression or anxiety relates to it. Be aware that both anxiety and depression can have an impact on the course of illnesses and other medical conditions.

Looking Back at Your Life

Any sadness or anxiety you're feeling at the moment may have its roots in the past. Exploring your personal history can provide clues as to the origins of your problems. So try answering the family history questions that appear in Worksheet 2-2.

The questions in Worksheet 2-2 get you to examine your childhood and ask yourself about your parents, your relationship with them and your early experiences. Some of the memories may evoke powerful emotions. If you do feel overwhelmed, consider stopping the exercise and consulting a mental health professional for guidance and support.

Filling out this form is a lot easier after you see a completed example. So consider Brian. Brian goes to his GP and complains of some upsetting physical symptoms: lack of energy and increased appetite. He doesn't know that he is, in fact, depressed, let alone why. His GP refers him to a psychologist who suggests Brian fills out an Early Life form (Worksheet 2-1) to explore his childhood experiences.

Worksheet 2-1	**Brian's Early Life**

Questions about Mother (or Other Primary Carer)

1. **What was your mother like?**

   She was self-centred and seldom thought much about what my sister and I needed. When things didn't go her way, she'd explode. She was domineering and incredibly uptight. My mother was a perfectionist who constantly went on about the 'right way' or the 'wrong way' to do things. She always played the martyr.

2. **How did your mother discipline you?**

   Mostly she just shouted at us. Sometimes she'd stop us going out, but we'd talk our way out of it. I didn't get into trouble much, because I made sure she didn't catch me breaking the rules.

3. **Was your mother warm or cold towards you?**

   It's rather strange — on the one hand she was really warm sometimes. But at other times it almost felt like she couldn't care less about me.

4. **Was she either exceptionally critical or supportive?**

   Again, she was inconsistent. She could be both. Sometimes, she'd be really encouraging, yet at other times, I felt like she tore me to pieces. I just never knew what to expect.

5. **How did she spend time with you?**

   This seems odd, but I just don't remember doing much of anything with her. She was quite a leading light in the school's Parent Teacher Association. Funny, now that I come to think of it, the things she did always seemed to be more about her than about me.

6. **Were there special circumstances that affected the care she gave (for example, illness, death, divorce, travel-related absences and so on)?**

   She had a miscarriage when I was about 6 years old. She was pretty depressed for several years after that.

7. **Does anything else important about her come to mind – positive or negative?**

   She never seemed especially happy or satisfied with her life. I remember her getting furious with my father quite a few times. But they never spoke about it – at least not in front of us children.

Questions about Father (or Other Important Carer)

1. **What was your father like?**

   Everybody adored him. He loved making people laugh. But actually, I never really knew him very well. He was so open and outgoing when we were out, but quite morose and withdrawn at home.

2. **How did your father discipline you?**

   He mostly stayed out of the discipline area. But sometimes he'd explode over nothing.

3. **Was your father warm or cold towards you?**

   He was quite warm, but looking back, it feels like it was pretty superficial. He never said, 'I love you,' and seldom praised me.

4. **Was he either exceptionally critical or supportive?**

   Neither really. He didn't pay a lot of attention to me. He was always much closer to my sister than to me. I always had the feeling I wasn't good enough to deserve his attention.

5. **How did he spend time with you?**

   When I was little, he'd play-fight and muck around with me. He increasingly worked longer and longer hours, and wasn't really around that much.

6. **Were there special circumstances that affected the care he gave (for example, illness, death, divorce, travel-related absences and so on)?**

   Nothing really. I think to everyone else we seemed like a pretty typical family with no particular problems.

7. **Does anything else important about him come to mind – positive or negative?**

   Whenever he tried to teach me to do anything, he'd be really impatient and become furious if I didn't get the hang of it right away.

Other Questions about Childhood

1. **What are your earliest memories?**

   I don't remember much from when I was little. My grandfather used to take us fishing. That was fun. I remember my father and my grandparents having a big fight over money. That was scary.

2. **Did you have siblings or other people at home who influenced you? And if so, in which way(s) did they influence you?**

   I looked up to my older sister, but she didn't want anything to do with me after she went to secondary school. I think she was the favourite – at least in my Dad's eyes. I never felt like I was as good as her.

3. **What do you remember about primary school? (Were you happy? What did you think about yourself? How did you do in school? What were your friendships? Were there any important events?)**

   I remember being really shy. But I was a model pupil. I had a few quite good friends, but they were mostly misfits, like me.

4. **What do you remember about middle school? (Were you happy? What did you think about yourself? How did you do in school? What were your friendships like? Were there any important events?)**

   I was even shyer then. I felt clumsy and awkward all the time. I didn't get invited to parties much. I wasn't very happy. Sometimes if I got really upset, my mother would do some of my homework for me. But then she'd make me feel guilty about it.

5. **What do you remember about secondary school? (Were you happy? What did you think about yourself? How did you do in school? What were your friendships like? Were there any important events?)**

   I made some new male friends, then, and started going out with girls. I was pretty miserable when a girl dumped me. I remember staying in my room for hours on end. I realise now that I didn't know how to handle my emotions very well – when I didn't know what else to do, I'd just withdraw. I worked just hard enough to get Bs, but I know I could have done much better in school.

6. **What are the major events of your adulthood, including traumas and setbacks, as well as successes and achievements?**

   I left school and was accepted onto an apprenticeship. I got married, and we had a couple of kids. My divorce after 14 years of marriage came as a bit of a shock, but I got through it okay.

7. **What did this exercise teach you about the origins of your anxiety or depression?**

   When I think back on my childhood, I realise it wasn't all that happy. My dad didn't seem to care much about me. My mother cared more, but she was like an emotional roller-coaster. I just shut down, and I think I've had that tendency my whole life. Maybe I'm shutting down now, too; it's what I do when I'm unhappy. I guess I realise that blaming myself for my problems won't get me any-where. It sort of makes sense that I shut down whenever I face possible rejection, criticism or when someone gets angry with me.

After completing the Early Life worksheet, Brian has a better understanding of why he copes with stress the way he does. He's identified at least one reason why he shuts down when facing certain types of situations. The exercise isn't about blame and fault-finding; rather answering the questions points Brian towards a path for a new beginning. Eventually, he can forgive himself for being the way he is. (Chapter 8 has more about coming to terms with yourself and your life.)

Now, complete your own Early Life form in Worksheet 2-2. This is an important exercise; take as much time as you need. If you happen to be receiving counselling or psychotherapy, your counsellor will no doubt find this information useful and informative.

Start by reflecting on your childhood. You can stimulate your memory by talking to relatives or by looking through old photo albums. Then move on to answer the questions about your parents or carers as well as the questions about your childhood and adolescence. Don't worry about getting all the details right – just do the best you can. Memories aren't always completely accurate, but, in powerful ways, they impact on the way you feel today.

This exercise is certainly not designed to place blame on your parents or other important people in your life. These people indeed may have made significant contributions to your problems, and that's useful to know. But they also developed their own problems, just as you did. While understanding helps, blame and fault-finding certainly don't!

Worksheet 2-2 **My Early Life**

Questions about Mother (or Other Primary Carer)

1. **What was your mother like?**

_____

_____

_____

_____

2. **How did your mother discipline you?**

_____

_____

_____

_____

3. **Was your mother warm or cold towards you?**

_____

_____

_____

_____

4. **Was she either exceptionally critical or supportive?**

_____

_____

_____

_____

5. How did she spend time with you?

_____

_____

_____

_____

6. Were there special circumstances that affected the care she gave (for example, illness, death, divorce, travel-related absences and so on)?

_____

_____

_____

_____

7. Does anything else important about her come to mind – positive or negative?

_____

_____

_____

_____

**Questions about Father (or Other Important Carer)**

1. What was your father like?

_____

_____

_____

_____

2. How did your father discipline you?

_____

_____

_____

_____

3. Was your father warm or cold?

_____

_____

_____

_____

4. **Was he either exceptionally critical or supportive?**

_____

_____

_____

_____

5. **How did he spend time with you?**

_____

_____

_____

_____

6. **Were there special circumstances that affected the care he gave (for example, illness, death, divorce, travel-related absences and so on)?**

_____

_____

_____

_____

7. **Does anything else important about him come to mind – positive or negative?**

_____

_____

_____

_____

Other Questions about Childhood

1. **What are your earliest memories?**

_____

_____

_____

_____

2. **Did you have siblings or other people at home who influenced you? And if so, in which way(s) did they influence you?**

_____

_____

_____

_____

3. What do you remember about primary school? (Were you happy? What did you
   think about yourself? How did you do in school? What were your friendships like?
   Were there any important events?)

   _____

   _____

   _____

   _____

4. What do you remember about middle school? (Were you happy? What did you think
   about yourself? How did you do in school? What were your friendships like? Were
   there any important events?)

   _____

   _____

   _____

   _____

5. What do you remember about secondary school? (Were you happy? What did you
   think about yourself? How did you do in school? What were your friendships like?
   Were there any important events?)

   _____

   _____

   _____

   _____

6. What are the major events of your adulthood, both good and bad?

   _____

   _____

   _____

   _____

7. What does this exercise teach you about the origins of your anxiety and/or
   depression?

   _____

   _____

   _____

   _____

Identifying Your Sources of Stress

In the search for triggers of your anxiety or depression, you need to review your world. Open your eyes. Look around. What's going on in your life that worsens your mood? From daily traffic hassles to major losses, stressful events deplete your coping resources and even harm your health.

Divine where your stress comes from by using Worksheet 2-3 to identify your major sources of stress. You can't make your world less stressful, unless you first identify the sources of the stress.

Worksheet 2-3   **Divining Stress Sources**

In the past year or so, I have (tick all that apply):

❑ Lost someone who I care about through death, divorce or prolonged separation. Specify:

_____

_____

_____

_____

❑ Experienced a serious physical injury or suffered a severe illness. Specify:

_____

_____

_____

_____

❑ Had serious financial difficulties or made a major purchase (such as a new house or car). Specify:

_____

_____

_____

_____

❑ Had significant arguments or ongoing conflicts with anyone. Specify:

_____

_____

_____

_____

❑ Experienced problems at work, such as new responsibilities, longer hours, poor management or bullying. Specify:

_____

_____

_____

_____

❑ Made any major changes in my life, such as starting a new job, retiring, or beginning or ending a significant relationship. Specify:

_____

_____

_____

_____

❑ Taken major responsibility for the care of a parent or child? Specify:

_____

_____

_____

_____

❑ Experienced daily commuting hassles, disturbing noises or poor living conditions? Specify:

_____

_____

_____

_____

You may notice that a few of the items in Worksheet 2-3 have positive aspects to them. For example, retirement or the purchase of a new home may be exciting. However, all major changes, whether positive or negative, contribute to significant stress.

Drawing Conclusions

You didn't ask for depression or anxiety, but your distress is understandable after you examine the three major contributors: biology/genetics, your personal history and the stresses in your world.

Take a moment to summarise in Worksheet 2-4 what you believe are the most important roots and contributors to your depression and/or anxiety.

Worksheet 2-4   **My Most Important Contributors**

---

1. **Physical contributors (genetics, drugs, illness):**

_____

_____

_____

_____

2. **My personal history:**

_____

_____

_____

_____

3. **The stresses in my world:**

_____

_____

_____

_____

As you review your summary, avoid blaming yourself for your depression and/or anxiety. And yet at the same time, remember that you are responsible for doing something about your distress – no one can do that work for you. Focus on the payoff. Perhaps even better than winning the lottery, working on your emotional distress rewards you with lifelong benefits.

Chapter 3

Overcoming Obstacles to Change

• •

In This Chapter

▶ Meeting and beating self-defeating beliefs

▶ Weighing the pros and cons of your beliefs

▶ Identifying ways you sabotage yourself

▶ Envisaging a new story for your life

• •

*Y*ou don't want to feel depressed or anxious. But at times you may believe that you have no choice but to feel that way. You want to do something about your distress, but you may feel overwhelmed and incapable. The truth is that you *can* do something about your predicament. While certain situations may indeed be outside of your control, other situations you can do something about, but only if you can understand and overcome the obstacles thrown up by your mind that are preventing you from taking action and moving forward.

In this chapter, we help you uncover assumptions and beliefs you may have that make tackling your problems difficult. After you identify the beliefs that stand in your way, we show you how to shift these obstacles from your path. We also help you discover if you are inadvertently self-sabotaging. We show you how to stop creating obstacles for yourself and impeding your progress.

Defeating Self-Defeating Beliefs

People view change differently. Some see any change as frightening. Others think they don't deserve to be happy in the first place, so they make no attempt to change their lives in order to improve their situation. *Assumptions* such as these can keep you stuck in a depressed or anxious state by stifling your motivation to change. Unfortunately, most people aren't aware of when and how their underlying assumptions can scupper even the most serious and sincere efforts to change.

We designed the worksheets in this section to help you discover if you're setting up self-defeating beliefs that act as obstacles on your route to change. We then show you how you can triumph over these beliefs by carefully and honestly analysing whether each one is helping or hindering you.

Recognising redundant beliefs

People resist change for a variety of reasons. Sometimes they resist because they're afraid or feel they don't deserve something better. Perhaps they view themselves as helpless to do anything about their circumstances. You may not even be aware that you're holding these types of beliefs – beliefs that inevitably interfere with your progress towards change.

Complete the following three worksheets to identify if any of these barriers exist in your mind. Tick each statement in Worksheets 3-1, 3-2 and 3-3 that you feel applies to you. You can fill in the blank lines with an idea or two of your own if you want to.

Worksheet 3-1   **Fear of Change**

❑ If I take a risk, I'm likely to fail.

❑ If I reach out to others, I'll get rejected.

❑ Whenever I try something new, I always mess it up.

❑ Every time I get my hopes up, I'm disappointed.

❑ If I work on my problems, I'll just make things worse.

❑ I'd prefer to not try instead of failing.

❑ I can't see myself as a success.

❑ I'm too anxious and depressed to succeed.

❑

❑

Worksheet 3-2   **Beliefs of Worthlessness**

❑ I don't deserve to be happy.

❑ I don't expect much out of my life.

❑ I'm less worthy than other people.

❑ I feel guilty asking anyone for help, so I'd rather not ask.

❑ There's something fundamentally wrong with me; that's why I'm upset.

❑ I don't feel I'm as good as other people.

❑ I'm uncomfortable when people are nice to me.

❑ I feel like other people deserve a lot more than I do.

❑

❑

Worksheet 3-3   **Unfair, Unjust Beliefs**

❑ I often think about how unfair life has been to me.

❑ I feel helpless to deal with my problems.

❑ I can't stop thinking about the ways I've been mistreated.

❑ I feel angry about all the bad things that have happened to me.

❑ Other people don't understand how difficult my life has been.

❑ Anyone with my life couldn't help but complain.

❑ Practically no one can appreciate how much I've suffered.

❑ Doing something about my problems would somehow discount the importance of the trauma I've been through.

❑

❑

After you complete Worksheets 3-1, 3-2 and 3-3, look for patterns and clusters of similar responses. Did any of the worksheets really seem to ring a bell for you?

- ✔ If you ticked two or more items relating to Fear of Change in Worksheet 3-1, you probably are scared at the thought of changing.

- ✔ If you ticked two or more items describing Beliefs of Worthlessness in Worksheet 3-2, you may feel that you don't deserve the good things that may come your way if you were to change.

- ✔ If you ticked two or more items to do with Unfair, Unjust Beliefs in Worksheet 3-3, you may dwell so much on how you're suffering that you have trouble tapping into the resources you do have for making changes.

- ✔ If you ticked two or more items from two or more worksheets, you probably have several things you need to work on.

Holding any of the self-defeating beliefs outlined in Worksheets 3-1, 3-2 or 3-3 doesn't mean you're thinking that way by choice. People may develop these ideas when they are children or after they experience traumatic events at any time in their lives. And some potentially self-defeating beliefs can well contain a degree of truth, For example:

- ✔ Life is often unfair.

- ✔ It's perfectly reasonable to feel a little angry at times.

- ✔ You most definitely can't always succeed.

However, we believe that everybody really does deserve to feel happy – even including you! You can succeed in the things you do, and you can move past the bad things that have happened to you. Even if you've experienced horrific trauma, moving on doesn't diminish the significance of what you experienced. Getting better simply makes you more powerful and allows you to live again.

Yasmin, a mother of three, worries all the time. As a child, she was sexually abused by a babysitter. Now, she tends to be overly protective of her own children. Lately, she's been sleeping poorly; her youngest child has asthma, and Yasmin finds herself listening to the child's breathing throughout the night. She panics when her middle child is late from school. Her oldest son is an exchange student in another country and rarely calls home, so images of him being hurt or kidnapped float through Yasmin's mind throughout the day. Her doctor is concerned about her rising blood pressure, so Yasmin decides to work on her anxiety and stress. She completes Worksheets 3-1, 3-2 and 3-3 and discovers she has a variety of self-defeating beliefs. Fear of Change and Underlying Undeserving Beliefs predominate. She then fills in Worksheet 3-4, her Top Three Self-Defeating Beliefs.

Worksheet 3-4	Yasmin's Top Three Self-Defeating Beliefs
1.	Whenever I try something new, I always mess it up.
2.	Every time I get my hopes up, I'm disappointed.
3.	I feel guilty asking anyone for help, so I'd rather not.

Next, Yasmin jots down her reflections on all the self-defeating beliefs she's identified and summarised (see Worksheet 3-5).

Worksheet 3-5	Yasmin's Reflections

I can see that I do have some of these self-defeating beliefs. I suppose I've always thought that this is just the way my life is. But coming to think about it, I can see how these beliefs could get in the way of doing something about my problems. Nothing is going to change if I hold on tightly to these assumptions. But what on earth can I do about them?

In the following section, 'Beating obstructive beliefs', Yasmin finds answers to the questions she asks in Worksheet 3-5, by seeing what she can do about her problematic beliefs. But before reading her solution, write your own top three self-defeating beliefs in Worksheet 3-6. Go back to the three self-defeating belief worksheets (Worksheets 3-1, 3-2 and 3-3) and look through all the items you ticked. Then write down the three beliefs that seem to be the most troubling and the most likely to prevent you making changes.

Worksheet 3-6	My Top Three Self-Defeating Beliefs Summary
1.	
2.	
3.	

In Worksheet 3-7, jot down your reflections about these beliefs. What have you learned? Do you think these beliefs are helping you or getting in your way? Write down anything that comes to mind.

Worksheet 3-7	My Reflections

_____

_____

_____

_____

Beating obstructive beliefs

Completing the exercises in the preceding section gives you an idea of which self-defeating beliefs may be getting in your way. If you've tried to make changes in the past and failed, one or more of these beliefs is very likely responsible. Unfortunately, you can't get rid of such problematic beliefs by just sweeping them out of the door. Dealing with these beliefs is much more than knowing what they are and firmly declaring that you no longer believe in them. You need to restructure your way of thinking. Fortunately, this section offers some tools to help you do exactly that.

Changing beliefs requires that you appreciate and understand the extent to which your assumptions cause you grief. If you've only just discovered what your beliefs are, you can't expect yourself to fully understand the pros and cons of your beliefs. You need to explore the advantages and disadvantages of each belief in order to achieve this insight.

Yasmin (see the preceding section for more on her story) fills out Worksheet 3-8, which explores the advantages and disadvantages of her top three self-defeating beliefs, as a way of better understanding how her self-defeating beliefs affect her. She starts by writing down the reasons her self-defeating beliefs feel both good and are of benefit to her. Next, she records the problems each belief causes – how it stands in her way. Finally, she reviews both lists very carefully and writes down her conclusions. She fills out this form for each belief in her top three self-defeating beliefs (although Worksheet 3-8 only shows analyses of two of Yasmin's beliefs).

Worksheet 3-8   Yasmin's Advantages and Disadvantages Analysis

---

Self-Defeating Belief 1: Whenever I try something new, I always mess it up.

Advantages of This Belief	*Disadvantages of This Belief*
If I don't try, then I don't risk failing.	Of course, I can never succeed either.
It saves me the wasted effort. And let's face it, change is a lot of work.	Having this belief means I always feel miserable.
I don't know why, but change is scary. This belief protects me from having to deal with that fear.	I miss out on opportunities by clinging to this belief. It's just possible that even if I do fail, I could end up learning something useful for my life. This view really does keep me stuck.

Self-Defeating Belief 2: I feel guilty asking anyone for help, so I'd rather not.

Advantages of This Belief	*Disadvantages of This Belief*
I don't expect anyone to help me, so that way I don't end up disappointed.	I don't get the chance to share my worries with anyone.
People don't have to worry about me leaning on them.	I don't get as close to people as I could.
At least I don't bother anyone, because they never know when I'm upset.	When I'm really upset, I go quiet. So because I've said nothing, people think I'm angry when I'm not. Realistically, everyone does need a little help from others. I'm at a disadvantage when I don't seek it.

After analysing the advantages and disadvantages of her self-defeating beliefs, Yasmin takes some time to reflect. She reconsiders whether the advantages she listed really are advantageous, and concludes that her original self-defeating beliefs are actually doing more harm than good. She then writes down her reflections in Worksheet 3-9.

Worksheet 3-9	Yasmin's Reflections

I realise that when I don't try, I still don't succeed — so it's the equivalent of failing. Not trying therefore isn't really an advantage. And yes, change may be a lot of work and seem scary and overwhelming, but let's face it, right now I'm utterly miserable. When I think about it, I get a lot of satisfaction from helping others. So logically, they won't mind helping me from time to time. I could use some help. It also could feel really nice getting close to people. On balance, my self-defeating beliefs are keeping me stuck.

Clearly, Yasmin can see that her assumptions about change are keeping her in limbo. Now that she's completed the exercises and disputed her original assumptions, she can start moving forward. Because she's aware of these self-defeating beliefs, she can be on the lookout for them popping up again. She can be ready to remind herself of their considerable disadvantages (see Chapters 5 and 6 for more about beliefs).

Now it's your turn.

1. **In Worksheet 3-10, write down each of your top three self-defeating beliefs (see Worksheet 3-6).**

2. **List all the reasons that each belief feels right, true and useful to you on the left side of Worksheet 3-10.**

3. **Consider the other side of the argument for each belief and each reason you provide in Step 2. On the right side of the worksheet, make a list of all the ways in which your beliefs may actually be harmful.**

Worksheet 3-10	Advantages and Disadvantages Analysis

Self-Defeating Belief 1: _____

Advantages of This Belief	*Disadvantages of This Belief*

Self-Defeating Belief 2: _____

Advantages of This Belief	Disadvantages of This Belief

Self-Defeating Belief 3: _____

Advantages of This Belief	Disadvantages of This Belief

Now, look over the pros and cons you list for each self-defeating belief in Worksheet 3-10. Think about the advantages again. Ask yourself whether each reason is really helping you. We predict that your advantages aren't really all that advantageous when you take time to consider them. Weigh up the pros and the cons of holding on to your beliefs and write down your reflections in Worksheet 3-11.

Worksheet 3-11   **My Reflections**

\
\
\
\
\

If you get stuck on any of these exercises – or if you see more advantages than disadvantages to your self-defeating beliefs – consider talking about your feelings with a counsellor, or perhaps a close friend who has overcome similar problems, in order to get some further help and advice.

Spotting Self-Sabotage

Overcoming anxiety or depression can be tough, sometimes even frightening work. (Even positive change can be scary!) As a result, people tend to resist, avoid or procrastinate about working on their problems. So you do need to be on the lookout for self-sabotage. *Self-sabotage* consists of the things you do to keep from addressing and correcting your problems. It appears in various forms and guises.

Some people indulge in self-sabotage by telling themselves that change is impossible. Others defeat themselves by finding reasons to put off working on their issues. What are your reasons for avoiding making changes?

Complete Worksheet 3-12 to see if you're falling into the self-sabotage trap. Tick any statements that sound familiar. If you want to, add your own self-sabotaging statements.

Worksheet 3-12   **Self-Sabotaging Statements**

❑ I feel my situation is hopeless.

❑ I'll never be okay given my history.

❑ I'm waiting until just the right time to change. But somehow it never comes.

❑ I want a guarantee that I'll get better before I'm willing to risk changing.

❑ I have a load of excuses for why I don't deal with my problems.

❑ I find it hard to stick with anything if it doesn't work immediately.

❑ Sometimes I get confused or feel out of it when I try tackling my issues.

❑ If I don't succeed 100 per cent, I'm very critical of myself.

❑ If I do something well, it's hard for me to give myself credit for it.

❑ I want immediate results, or else I just can't be bothered.

❑ I dwell so much on my past failures that it's hard to try something new.

❑ My depression or anxiety is biological, so I can't do anything about it.

❑

❑

Thoughts like the preceding ones can easily bog you down and prevent active efforts to change. Remember that almost everyone engages in at least a little self-sabotage, whether consciously or not. So don't make matters worse by beating yourself up when you become aware that you're self-sabotaging. Self-criticism merely increases self-sabotage.

Instead, monitor your self-sabotaging thoughts. When you feel them getting in your way, fight back and argue against them using the Self-Sabotage Diary we present in the next section.

Stopping self-sabotage

Throughout this book, we ask you to write down your thoughts, feelings, beliefs and life events. We return to the activity of writing again and again because it's an invaluable tool for battling problematic emotions, sorting out issues, achieving important insights and solving problems. In this section, we invite you to monitor and record your (probably) unintentional acts and thoughts of self-sabotage in a diary. But first, see what Maureen writes in her Self-Sabotage Diary (Worksheet 3-13).

Maureen's a busy, highly successful professional at the top of her career. None of her colleagues are aware that she suffers from considerable anxiety and depression. She worries that others will discover that she doesn't deserve her professional success. She realises that, for the last decade, she has neglected friends and family in pursuit of her career. Now, she feels lonely and despondent; success hasn't brought her the happiness she expected, and her anxiety and depression have only increased. Maureen sees a psychologist, and together they identify her self-sabotaging tendencies. She keeps a diary in which she records her acts of self-sabotage and responses to them. Worksheet 3-13 shows five days from Maureen's diary.

Worksheet 3-13	Maureen's Self-Sabotage Diary	
Day	*Example of Self-Sabotage*	*Response to Self-Sabotage*
Sunday	It was raining today, so I didn't feel like going to the gym like my psychologist suggested.	Obviously, not a helpful thing to do. The weather's just an excuse. Everyone makes excuses sometimes, but I want to try and push through them next time.
Monday	I scraped my car on a pole in the car park. I was so upset — it wrecked my whole day. I just hate myself when I make a mess of things.	I suppose having a go at myself isn't particularly useful. I need to accept myself, warts and all, if I'm ever going to get anywhere.

(continued)

Worksheet 3-13 *(continued)*

Day	*Example of Self-Sabotage*	*Response to Self-Sabotage*
Tuesday	I promised I'd do a worksheet for my therapy. But somehow I was just too busy.	Hey! Look at that! Another excuse! Honestly, it only takes ten minutes. I'll watch out for that one.
Wednesday	One of my clients complimented me on my work. But I felt uncomfy accepting the compliment, so I gave someone else the credit.	That didn't do me any favours! I tend to discount positive things that happen to me. No wonder my self-esteem sometimes suffers.
Thursday	My homework today was to ask a friend over for coffee. When I thought about phoning, I felt panicky, tongue-tied and confused – so I didn't!	Whenever I try to do something difficult, I seem to get so anxious I can't think straight. I must work on slowing down, giving myself more time and space, relax a bit – and then have another go. (Which chapter has those relaxation exercises?)

Now, it's time for you to record your own Self-Sabotage Diary. Keep your diary with you and fill it in when you spot these thoughts. If that's not possible, fill it in during the evening, before bedtime. Remember to take your time.

1. **In the middle column of Worksheet 3-14, write down any thought or action you noticed on that day that you feel limits your efforts to overcome your anxiety or depression.**

   If you get stuck identifying examples of self-sabotaging behaviour and thought, review Worksheet 3-12 for examples.

2. **In the right-hand column, write down how helpful (if at all) you think the self-sabotage may have been, plus any arguments you can find against self-sabotage.**

3. **Keep your diary up for at least a week – or for quite a bit longer if you continue to see lots of self-sabotage.**

Criticising yourself for any self-sabotage you notice only leads to more sabotage. Stop the cycle! You really can choose to get off your bike and just dismount!

Worksheet 3-14	My Self-Sabotage Diary	
Day	*Example of Self-Sabotage*	*Response to Self-Sabotage*
Sunday		
Monday		
Tuesday		
Wednesday		
Thursday		
Friday		
Saturday		

Photocopy Worksheet 3-14 so you always have a clean copy on hand – or download extra copies at www.dummies.com/go/adwb.

Surmounting self-sabotaging scenarios

Your mind (like everyone else's) creates stories – about yourself, your life and your world. If you feel stuck, your stories are probably flavoured with themes of failure. For example, you may have a long-running play in your mind with you as its central character. That character has a series of mishaps, failures and missed opportunities. If this sounds familiar, you're probably ready for a rewrite.

Try creating a new story – a life scenario – about you and your life that allows you ultimately to succeed. But remember, besides a successful conclusion, the new story does need to include realistic struggles and difficulty. After all, life isn't a fairy tale.

To the outside world, Maureen is successful. But inside, she feels like a fraud. Worksheet 3-15 describes how she currently characterises her life story.

Worksheet 3-15   **Maureen's Current Life Scenario**

Though I have money and some prestige, I really don't deserve it. I'm sure I'm not as talented as I should be for the position I have. No one likes me because I'm irritable. I have no friends or close family. I'm different to other people. I'll never really fit in. I'm going to die alone, lonely and I'll soon be forgotten. My life actually means nothing.

Maureen struggles writing her new script. When she finishes, she reads her new story every day for a month. Although it takes a while before she starts believing it, gradually she begins to see her life in a new light. Worksheet 3-16 gives her revised story.

Worksheet 3-16   **Maureen's New Life Scenario**

I have a good job, and I actually worked very hard to get it. I don't need to discount my accomplishments. Yes, I do get irritable sometimes, and who doesn't? Besides, I'm capable of learning new behaviours, and I'm working on my irritability. I don't have many friends because I'm a workaholic. This will be a struggle for me, but I see myself cutting back a little on my work and making new friends. I'm going to put more meaning into my life. As a start, I'm exploring opportunities for voluntary work.

Your turn! Do the following to begin rewriting your story of self-sabotage.

1. **Write your current life script in Worksheet 3-17.**

   Describe how you see yourself today and your prediction for the future. How do you view your accomplishments, relationships and failures?

2. **Write a new life scenario in Worksheet 3-18.**

   Describe your thoughts on hope, change and possibilities, as well as struggles and challenges.

3. **Read your new life scenario every day over the next month.** Carry it in your wallet or handbag, so it's easily accessible.

   Revise and add to your new life scenario as you like.

Worksheet 3-17   **My Current Life Scenario**

_____

_____

_____

_____

_____

Worksheet 3-18	My New Life Scenario

_____

_____

_____

_____

_____

Chapter 4

Monitoring Your Moods

· ·

In This Chapter

▶ Listening to your body

▶ Figuring out your feelings

▶ Connecting events and feelings

▶ Monitoring thoughts, events and feelings

· ·

The first step in the process of change is to become aware. In this chapter, we provide guidance, enabling you to observe the relationship between your feelings, your thoughts and the events in your life.

First, you find out how to monitor your body's response to events. This information helps you become more aware of the physical components of depression and anxiety. Next, you keep track of your feelings. Some people aren't very good at identifying their feelings, so we help you by providing a list of feeling words. Then you observe how events, feelings and bodily sensations go hand in hand . . . in hand. Finally, we show you how to become aware of the way that thoughts are connected to feelings, events and bodily sensations. The rewarding process of feeling better starts with understanding these connections.

Getting in Touch with Your Body's Signals

Your heart may race or your hands may sweat when you feel anxious. Changes in appetite and sleep may occur alongside feelings of sadness and depression. These physical reactions signal that something important is going on internally. Monitoring your bodily sensations gives you an early warning that a storm of emotional distress is brewing.

James is surprised when his doctor diagnoses him with depression, accompanied by some anxiety. His friends tell him he's 'out of touch with his feelings'. James begins to understand his body's signals through a process of monitoring physical sensations on a daily basis. He fills out the Body Responses Record, Worksheet 4-1. He makes a note of the times he experiences physical discomfort and writes down what was going on at the time.

Worksheet 4-1	James's Body Responses Record	
Body's Response	*How Did My Body Feel?*	*When did it happen? What was I doing?*
Muscle tightness	Pain in my shoulders and back.	Monday morning. I was going over the new project with my boss.

(continued)

Worksheet 4-1 *(continued)*

Body's Response	How Did My Body Feel?	When did it happen? What was I doing?
Stomach symptoms	Growling tummy; just embarrassing.	Sitting in the theatre.
Fatigue	My body feels heavy. Like trying to wade through quick sand.	Lately, I've felt this way every day.
Headaches	None this week.	
Posture	I noticed I'm walking around stooped over. And I've been slumped at my desk.	Mostly after lunch on Thursday and Friday.
Leg spasms when lying down	Unable to settle down and get comfortable. Difficulty falling asleep and consequent tiredness.	When I went to bed earlier than usual on Monday and Saturday.
Other: dizziness, sweating, lightness, tingling, constriction in throat or chest	Feeling light-headed, with a sense of unreality; spaced out.	Saturday morning settling down to pay the bills.

After filling out his Body Responses Record, James takes some time to reflect on the exercise (see Worksheet 4-2).

Worksheet 4-2 **James's Reflections**

I can see that my body seems to react quite strongly to what's going on in my life. I really wasn't aware of that before. These sensations aren't very pleasant. So perhaps my GP's right that I'm depressed. Amazing how just talking to my boss makes me feel really stressed and quite shaky. It affected my sleep as well. Looks like I'm also worried about finances. Funny, I haven't wanted to admit that. Now that I know all this, I really want to do something to get myself to a better place.

Over the course of a week, fill out your own Body Responses Record (see Worksheet 4-3) and note your reflections on the exercise (see Worksheet 4-4).

1. **Once or twice a day, review each of the body responses in the left-hand column.**

2. **If you experienced a reaction in a given category, elaborate and specify how your body reacted (in the middle column).**

3. **Record when the body response happened and what was going on at the time.**

   This information can help you make the links between events and responses.

4. After completing the record, take some time to think about what you've written.

Note down your reflections in Worksheet 4-4.

Worksheet 4-3	My Body Responses Record	
Body Response	*How did my body feel?*	*When did this happen?* *What was I doing?*
Muscle tightness		
Breathing		
Stomach symptoms		
Fatigue		
Headaches		
Posture		
Restless legs		
Other: dizziness, lightness, tingling, constriction in throat or chest, light-headed and/or disoriented		

Visit www.dummies.com/go/adwb to obtain extra copies of this form. Print out a few and keep one in your bag or briefcase, so you have it on hand whenever you experience unpleasant physical sensations.

Worksheet 4-4	My Reflections

Matching Mind and Body

After you become more aware of your body's signals, you can begin to link up your mental and physical states. Feeling words connect and label these combined states. If you're not used to describing your feelings, take some time to look over the list of words in the following chart. Think about if they apply to you. Read through the list slowly and spend time thinking back over how you feel each day – don't rush the process.

Rate your feelings every day for a week using the Daily Unpleasant Emotions List in Worksheet 4-5. See Chapter 18 for exercises relating to positive emotions.

1. **Each day, circle all the feeling words that describe your emotions.**

2. **At the end of the week, look back over your list and identify your most prevalent feelings.**

   Use Worksheet 4-6 to reflect on the exercise.

Worksheet 4-5		Daily Unpleasant Emotions List		
Day	**Sadness**	**Fear**	**Shame**	**Anger**
Sunday	Despondent, miserable, hopeless, gloomy, grief, joyless, dispirited, dejected, sad	Panicky, nervous, tense, afraid, timid, terrified, apprehensive, worried	Guilty, regretful, remorseful, embarrassed, in disgrace	Furious, resentful, irritable, outraged, bitter, indignant, mad, annoyed
Monday	Despondent, miserable, hopeless, gloomy, grief, joyless, dispirited, dejected, sad	Panicky, nervous, tense, afraid, timid, terrified, apprehensive, worried	Guilty, regretful, remorseful, embarrassed, in disgrace	Furious, resentful, irritable, outraged, bitter, indignant, mad, annoyed
Tuesday	Despondent, miserable, hopeless, gloomy, grief, joyless, dispirited, dejected, sad	Panicky, nervous, tense, afraid, timid, terrified, apprehensive, worried	Guilty, regretful, remorseful, embarrassed, in disgrace	Furious, resentful, irritable, outraged, bitter, indignant, mad, annoyed

Day	Sadness	Fear	Shame	Anger
Wednesday	Despondent, miserable, hopeless, gloomy, grief, joyless, dispirited, dejected, sad	Panicky, nervous, tense, afraid, timid, terrified, apprehensive, worried	Guilty, regretful, remorseful, embarrassed, in disgrace	Furious, resentful, irritable, outraged, bitter, indignant, mad, annoyed
Thursday	Despondent, miserable, hopeless, gloomy, grief, joyless, dispirited, dejected, sad	Panicky, nervous, tense, afraid, timid, terrified, apprehensive, worried	Guilty, regretful, remorseful, embarrassed, in disgrace	Furious, resentful, irritable, outraged, bitter, indignant, mad, annoyed
Friday	Despondent, miserable, hopeless, gloomy, grief, joyless, dispirited, dejected, sad	Panicky, nervous, tense, afraid, timid, terrified, apprehensive, worried	Guilty, regretful, remorseful, embarrassed, in disgrace	Furious, resentful, irritable, outraged, bitter, indignant, mad, annoyed
Saturday	Despondent, miserable, hopeless, gloomy, grief, joyless, dispirited, dejected, sad	Panicky, nervous, tense, afraid, timid, terrified, apprehensive, worried	Guilty, regretful, remorseful, embarrassed, in disgrace	Furious, resentful, irritable, outraged, bitter, indignant, mad, annoyed

Worksheet 4-6	**My Reflections**

_____

_____

_____

_____

_____

Making Connections between Events, Feelings and Sensations

As you work through this chapter, you become more aware of how your body reacts to events in your life. And by using the Daily Unpleasant Emotions List in the previous section, you have feeling words to label your mental and physical states. Now you can begin to link your body sensations and feeling words to the events that trigger them.

Fleur is worried and anxious practically all the time. She suspects that her worries are mainly to do with her children, but at times she hasn't a clue as to where her anxiety is coming from. So, she fills in a Mood Diary. She pays special attention to her body's signals and writes them down whenever she feels something unpleasant. She then searches for a feeling word that captures her emotion. She rates the emotions and sensations on a scale of 1 (almost undetectable) to 100 (maximum). She then asks herself what was going on when she became aware of her distress. Worksheet 4-7 is a sample of Fleur's Mood Diary – a record of four days on which she noticed moods she would have preferred not to have.

Worksheet 4-7	Fleur's Mood Diary	
Day	*Feelings and Sensations (Rated 1–100)*	*Concurrent Events*
Sunday	Apprehension, tightness in my chest (70)	I was thinking about going to work tomorrow morning.
Tuesday	Anger, trembling (85)	My secretary made a mess of my appointments.
Thursday	Worry, tightness in my chest (60)	My middle child has a cold. I'm worried she'll have an asthma attack.

Fleur keeps track of her moods over a period of a few weeks. After studying her complete Mood Diary, she comes to a few conclusions (see Worksheet 4-8).

Worksheet 4-8	Fleur's Reflections
Well, I'm surprised. I thought that all I worried about was the kids. Actually, my job can really wind me up at times. Conflict isn't easy for me either. I'd better do something about that. My shyness gets in my way, too. I didn't realise how often I have these feelings.	

Now it's your turn. Fill in a Mood Diary (see Worksheet 4-9). This exercise can provide you with invaluable information about patterns and issues that consistently cause you distress. This knowledge helps you see what needs to change in your life. The exercise also lays a foundation for changing your thinking, which we get into in Part II of this book.

1. **Over the next week, pay attention to your body's signals.**

   Write down whenever you feel something unpleasant.

2. **Find a feeling word that captures your emotion and make a note of it.**

   You can refer to the Daily Unpleasant Emotions List (Worksheet 4-5) for help finding the right feeling words.

3. **Rate your feeling on a scale of intensity from 1 (hardly at all) to 100 (full on).**

4. **Ask yourself what was going on when you started noticing your emotions and body's signals.**

The event, or *trigger,* can be something happening in your world, or even a thought or image going through your mind. Be concrete and specific; don't write something overly general such as 'I hate my work'. Instead, ask yourself what actually happened at work that you didn't like.

5. **Look over your Mood Diary to see if you can draw any conclusions or come up with any new insights into where your body signals come from.**

   Write a few sentences of reflection in Worksheet 4-10.

Worksheet 4-9	My Mood Diary	
Day	*Feelings and Sensations (Rated 1–100)*	*Concurrent Events*
Sunday		
Monday		
Tuesday		
Wednesday		
Thursday		
Friday		
Saturday		

Visit www.dummies.com/go/adwb for extra copies of this form. For maximum benefit, continue filling them out for several weeks.

Worksheet 4-10	My Reflections

Becoming a Thought Detective

Imagine yourself manoeuvring in a car park on a rainy winter night. You're tired, and the next thing you know, CRUNCH! You've reversed into that stupid metal pole. What's your reaction? Do you have angry thoughts like 'Who the dot dot dot put that stupid thing there!?' Do you feel anxious and worried about the costs of repair, and what it will do to your No Claims bonus? Or do you feel really upset and furious with yourself because you can't believe you were that careless?

Most people feel upset for a bit after scraping the car. But if your thoughts are really intense or persist for ages, they can provide clues about your negative thinking habits. These habits dictate how you interpret the accident and thus the way you feel about it. If you feel terribly worried, you probably tend to have lots of anxious thoughts. If you heavily criticise yourself, you may be prone to depressive thoughts.

Thought Catchers are tools that show you how feelings, events and thoughts connect – they lay it all out for you. What are you saying to yourself when you feel upset? See how Mandy, James and Fleur complete their Thought Catchers before you try a few for yourself.

Mandy reverses her car into a pole one night. She and her psychologist have agreed that she completes a Thought Catcher for the week, writing down whenever she notices upsetting feelings. So later that night, she completes a Thought Catcher about the incident (see Worksheet 4-11).

Worksheet 4-11	Mandy's Thought Catcher	
Feelings and Sensations (Rated 1–100)	**Corresponding Events**	**Thoughts/Interpretations**
Despair (70); nauseous	Dented my back bumper	I can't believe I did that. I'm such an idiot! Everyone at work will notice.
Tense (90); tightness through my back and shoulders	I don't have time to deal with this. I'll have to call the insurance company, get a couple of repair estimates and alternative transportation. arrange I'm already way behind on the current project at work. Now, no way will I complete it on time.	

Strange as it may seem, James also reverses his car into that same pole, though not until the following night. He too fills out a Thought Catcher about the incident (see Worksheet 4-12) – having read about them in the *Anxiety & Depression Workbook For Dummies,* of course!

Worksheet 4-12	James's Thought Catcher	
Feelings and Sensations (Rated 1–100)	*Corresponding Events*	*Thoughts/Interpretations*
Rage (80); flushed face and rapid breathing	I hit that stupid pole with my new sports car.	There's not one good reason why anyone would put a pole there! I should sue whoever owns the car park.
Sad (65); tired	This is just too awful. I've only had that car for three months. Cars are never the same after you've bashed them. It's not fair how horrible things keep happening to me.	

You may find this really hard to believe, but Fleur happens to be in that same car park a week later. Somehow cars seem drawn to that pole. Sure enough – CRUNCH! Like Mandy and James, Fleur completes a Thought Catcher (see Worksheet 4-13) following her encounter with that pesky pole.

Worksheet 4-13	Fleur's Thought Catcher	
Feelings and Sensations (Rated 1–100)	*Corresponding Events*	*Thoughts/Interpretations*
Panic (95); terrified, sweaty, rapid shallow breathing, dizzy	I rammed my car into a pole.	At first I thought I might have run into someone's car and could have hurt somebody. I never know how to handle things like this. I'll probably lose my driver's license or my insurance company will drop me. My husband will be furious with me. I can't stand it when he's mad at me.

Three different people, one identical event. You can clearly see how their thoughts contribute to the way they feel. All three of them look at this event in their own unique way and feel differently as a result.

✔ Mandy worries about the consequences of the accident and blames herself. Because of the way she interprets the event, Mandy's at risk for anxiety and depression.

✔ James gets really angry and exaggerates/catastrophises about the bump. He tends to have problems with both anger and depression.

✔ Fleur panics about the disagreement with the pole. Her reaction arises out of her frequent struggles with feelings of anxiety and panic.

Sometimes people say they really don't know what's going on in their heads when they feel distressed. They know how they feel and they know what happened, but they simply have no idea what they're thinking. You too may experience this problem. If so, ask yourself the questions in Worksheet 4-14 about an event that accompanied your difficult feelings.

Worksheet 4-14	The Thought Query Quiz

1. What meaning does the event have for me in my life?

_____

_____

_____

2. Will this event affect my future in any way?

_____

_____

_____

3. What bothers me about the event?

_____

_____

_____

4. Does the event say something about me as a person?

_____

_____

_____

5. What passed through my mind when I experienced the event?

_____

_____

_____

_____

Thought Catchers give you important information about the way your mind interprets events and your related feelings. That's why we recommend that you use them regularly, on an ongoing basis. See Part II for methods of changing your way of thinking and improving your mood.

The Thought Catcher demonstrates how the way you think about events influences the way you feel. Sad feelings inevitably accompany thoughts about loss, low self-worth or rejection. Anxious or worried feelings go along with thoughts about danger, vulnerability or horrible outcomes. Complete your own Thought Catcher in Worksheet 4-15, by following these instructions:

1. **Pay attention to your body's signals and write them down whenever you feel something unpleasant.**

2. **Search for a feeling word that captures your emotion and jot that down, too.**

   Refer to the Daily Unpleasant Emotions List (Worksheet 4-5) for help.

3. **Rate your feeling on a scale of intensity from 1 (almost undetectable) to 100 (maximum).**

4. **Ask yourself what was going on when you started noticing your emotions and body's signals.**

   The concurrent event can be something happening in your world, but it can also be a thought or image that runs through your mind. Be concrete and specific; don't write something overly general.

5. **Record your thoughts in the Thoughts/Interpretations column.**

   Describe how you perceive, interpret or think about the event. Refer to the Thought Query Quiz (Worksheet 4-14) if you experience any difficulty figuring out your thoughts about the event.

Worksheet 4-15	My Thought Catcher	
Feelings and Sensations (Rated 1–100)	*Corresponding Events*	*Thoughts/Interpretations*

(continued)

Worksheet 4-15 *(continued)*

Feelings and Sensations (Rated 1–100)	Corresponding Events	Thoughts/Interpretations

Visit www.dummies.com/go/adwb to download extra copies of this form.

Do you notice any patterns to the types of thoughts you have? Are these thoughts associated with certain types of feelings? Take the time to reflect on this exercise using Worksheet 4-16.

Worksheet 4-16   **My Reflections**

_____

_____

_____

_____

_____

Part II
Understanding Your Thinking: Cognitive Therapy

'I wouldn't let fear of water
bother you too much, Mr Lemming.'

In this part . . .

*W*e help you understand the link between your thoughts and feelings through cognitive therapy, a well established, research-based approach for the treatment of depression and anxiety. We reveal how distorted thinking can make you more upset than you need to be, and we show you how to identify and re-structure your negative thoughts, enabling you to both see and think clearly.

Finally, we help you uncover the deep, core beliefs and assumptions that may be responsible for many of your distorted thoughts. These beliefs can act like cracked or dirty lenses that you see yourself and your world through, so we help you remove and replace them with new, accurate lenses to enable you to see things more clearly.

Chapter 5

Viewing Things Differently

● ●

● ●

*I*n this chapter, we lay out the principles of *cognitive behavioural therapy*, or CBT. The basis of CBT asserts that the way you think about or interpret events substantially influences the way you feel, both about the events and about a whole load of other things. The great thing about the *cognitive* bit of CBT is that changing the way you think means that you can then change the way you feel. Part III focuses more on the behaviour bit of CBT, but the same principle applies: changing how you behave leads to changes in what you think and feel.

Everyone at times has some distortions in thinking. When your thinking is distorted, it doesn't accurately reflect, predict or describe what's going on. Have you ever been woken up by a loud noise in the night and felt terrified? You may have been quite sure in those first few moments that the sound was an attempted burglary. Fortunately this rarely turns out to be the case. The noise was far more likely made by the wind, the fridge or creaking floor-boards. But when you hear a strange noise in the night, your fear is very real. Your thoughts, while understandable, are often distorted. A Scottish traditional prayer sums up night-time fears very neatly, asking the Good Lord to deliver us from 'ghoulies and ghosties and long-leggedy beasties and things that go bump in the night'.

Distorted thinking can be disproportionately positive as well as negative. For example, you may feel really attached to something you've owned for years. By now it may objectively be pretty old and tatty-looking – but to you, given all it means, it's beautiful. However, if you're really honest with yourself, you have to admit your perception is distorted. Likewise, if you've ever been in love, you may remember what the person looked like when viewed solely through rose-coloured spectacles.

Distorted thinking becomes a problem when it leads to depression and anxiety. Three key types of distortions are:

✔ Incoming information reality distortions

✔ Self-judging reality distortions

✔ Self-blaming reality distortions

Although this chapter makes distinctions among various types of distorted thinking, in reality, they often overlap or exist in groups. So one single thought can be influenced by reality distortions, plus distortions involving self-judging and self-blame. The examples in this chapter show you how multiple distortions combine.

Identifying Incoming Information Reality Distortions

Reality distortions warp your perceptions of your world and events occurring around you. You may be unaware of the reality distortions influencing your thinking, but give it a bit of thought, and you'll probably start recognising some.

Reality distortions are the various ways in which the mind distorts the information coming into it. For example, suppose a depressed man gets a mediocre annual performance review at work. He may well magnify and over-generalise this event, turning it into a total catastrophe and taking the mediocre result to mean than he's a totally worthless person. Without the distortion, the reality is simply that his performance at that particular time was considered average but acceptable, notwithstanding the fact that he would have been much happier with a more positive rating.

The following exercise shows you the many ways in which reality distortions can initially affect your thinking and subsequently influence the way you feel.

1. **Read the description of each type of reality distortion and the accompanying examples in Worksheet 5-1.**

2. **Think about when your thoughts may have been influenced by a reality distortion.**

3. **Write down specific thoughts that you've had that may actually belong to each type of reality distortion.** If you can't think of an example for each type of reality distortion, don't be concerned. Later in this chapter, we provide additional exercises to show you how all the distortions work.

Worksheet 5-1	**Identifying Reality Distortions**

1. **Magnifying and minimising:** Particularly when you're depressed or anxious, your mind is likely to exaggerate the awfulness of unpleasant events while also minimising the extent and importance of anything positive about yourself, your world or your future. For example, you may think, 'I can't face doing my tax return. I really can't stand it!' Being totally honest with yourself, you do have to admit that difficult though it may be, your tax return pales in significance when you consider the experience of suddenly facing a serious health problem.

_____

_____

_____

_____

2. **Selective attention:** Your mind homes in on things that are frightening or worrying, while tending to blindly ignore more positive information. The not-too-surprising result? The world looks considerably more worrying than reality suggests. For example, suppose your annual performance review rates you highly in most areas but has one area in which you score below average. You may well focus exclusively on the below-average rating and end up believing that the whole review was in fact mediocre at best.

_____

_____

_____

_____

3. **Black and white, all-or-nothing thinking:** Your mind looks at both events and at yourself, seeing everything as either all good or totally awful, with nothing in between. Thus, a single poor score or below average performance means complete failure. Think about teenagers who develop spots and then conclude that they look totally horrible. The problem with such polarised thinking is that it sets you up for inevitable experiences of failure, disappointment and self-criticism.

_____

_____

_____

_____

4. **Dismissing evidence:** Your mind discards evidence that may contradict its negative thoughts. For example, suppose you're preparing a talk and have the thought that during the presentation, you'll be so terrified you'll completely dry up and be unable to talk. Your mind just doesn't want to remember the fact that you've given numerous previous presentations before – or the evidence that you've never once been so scared that you couldn't talk.

_____

_____

_____

_____

5. **Overgeneralising:** You look at a single unpleasant occurrence and decide that this is what always happens, all the time, and that it will continue to do so. For example, a wife tells her husband that she's furious because he's always late. In reality, he's late only about 20 per cent of the time. (Words like *always* and *never* are clues to over-generalisation.)

_____

_____

_____

_____

6. **Mind reading:** You assume that you know what others are thinking without checking it out. Thus, when your manager walks past without saying hello, you automatically think, 'She's really angry with me. What have I done wrong this time?' Yet the reality is that your manager is merely distracted, and that's why she hasn't greeted you.

_____

_____

_____

_____

7. **Emotional reasoning:** You treat feelings as facts. For example, if you're feeling guilty, you conclude that you must have done something wrong. Or if you don't feel like doing something, such as working on your depression, you assume that means you're unable to. And if you're afraid of something, it must be dangerous merely because you fear it.

_____

_____

_____

8. **Crystal ball gazing:** You're sure something will turn out badly, despite having no real evidence on which to base your prediction. For example, you have an argument with your partner and believe that your partner is bound to leave you. Or, you avoid driving on motorways because you're convinced that you'll be involved in an accident.

Using a Thought Catcher to Record Reality Distortions

Monitoring your thoughts and looking out for any distortions in them by using a Thought Catcher enables you to then change your thinking, which in turn leads to improving your mood. However, before working on your own Thought Catcher, have a look at those of Brian (see Worksheet 5-2) and Shona (see Worksheet 5-3) to see what happens when they monitor their thoughts and check them out for reality distortions.

Worksheet 5-2	Brian's Thought Catcher		
Feelings and Sensations Rated 1–100	*Concurrent Events*	*Thoughts/Interpretations*	*Reality Distortions*
Hopeless(70), anxious (65), tightness in my chest	The manager's announced we have to increase our productivity.	I hate this job. Bet the manager knows it, and that he hates me. Things just go from bad to worse. I'll never reach the new targets.	Magnifying, mind reading, all-or-nothing thinking, over generalising, crystal ball gazing.

Worksheet 5-3	Shona's Thought Catcher		
Feelings and Sensations Rated 1–100	*Concurrent Events*	*Thoughts/Interpretations*	*Reality Distortions*
Sad (75); overwhelming heaviness and fatigue	We've been gazumped again. The estate agent did say there are plenty of better ones coming up.	I'll never find a place that's as good. Silver linings are only for other people.	Over-generalising, all-or-nothing thinking, dismissing evidence

Feelings and Sensations Rated 1–100	Concurrent Events	Thoughts/Interpretations	Reality Distortions
Panic (90); racing heart, shaky, nauseous	Jack's 20 minutes' late home from school.	He's never usually this late; Something awful's happened. I can feel it in the pit of my stomach.	Emotional reasoning, crystal ball gazing
Nervous (70); queasy tummy	Getting the house ready for the party.	No one's going to come. I know they came to the last one, but that's only because they felt they had to. And though they said they enjoyed it, I just know they were only being polite.	Crystal ball gazing, mind reading, dismissing

Now that you've seen a couple of examples of information reality distortions at work, take the challenge of seeing if you can spot the reality distortions in different situations. Worksheet 5-4 presents a partially completed Thought Catcher consisting of typical experiences and thoughts. Look through the feelings and sensations, events and the thoughts and interpretations of those events. Identify which reality distortions you think apply. Our answers appear later in this section, so don't peek just yet!

Worksheet 5-4   Thought Catcher for Information Reality Distortions

Scenario	Feelings and Sensations Rated 1–100	Concurrent Events	Thoughts/ Interpretations	Reality Distortions
1.	Miserable (65); embarrassed (75); tired	My partner commented that I've put on weight.	It's true! I've completely let myself go. At this rate, I'll probably die of a heart attack. I feel so out of control. It's obvious I've got no willpower whatsoever.	

(continued)

Worksheet 5-4 (continued)

Scenario	Feelings and Sensations Rated 1–100	Concurrent Events	Thoughts/ Interpretations	Reality Distortions
2.	Apprehensive (70); unreal, tense	I've been promoted to head of my department.	I'm being set up to fail, so they can then get rid of me. Though the pay's better, the job's only vacant because no one will touch it with a barge pole.	
3.	Bitter (80); gloomy (65); muscle tension, back pain	Some yob has scraped a key down the side of my car.	This type of thing's always happening to me. It'll cost an absolute bomb to fix.	

Here are our answers to the Thought Catcher for Information Reality Distortions exercise. If your answers are slightly different, it makes no odds, as the point of the exercise is just to spot distortions. Sometimes the precise distortions involved are indeed debatable.

✔ **Scenario 1:** Magnifying, crystal ball gazing, all-or-nothing thinking, emotional reasoning

✔ **Scenario 2:** Dismissing evidence, mind reading, selective attention

✔ **Scenario 3:** Magnifying, overgeneralising, crystal ball gazing

Monitor your own thoughts and look for possible information reality distortions. This process helps you to see that some of your unwanted, difficult feelings actually come from the way your mind misinterprets events in your world. You now get to create your own Thought Catcher using Worksheet 5-5. For more detailed information about Thought Catchers, see Chapter 4.

1. **Pay attention to your body's signals and whenever you feel something unpleasant, write down what you feel.**

2. **Look for a feeling word that captures the emotion you're feeling and make a note of it in the Feelings and Sensations column.**

   Refer to the Daily Unpleasant Emotions List in Chapter 4 for a comprehensive list of feeling words to get you started.

3. **Rate your feeling on a scale of intensity from 1 (almost undetectable) to 100 (maximum).**

4. **Ask yourself what was going on when you started noticing your emotions and your body's signals, and record that event in the Concurrent Events column.**

   The event can be something happening in your world or it can come in the form of a thought or image that runs through your mind. Be concrete and specific when recording events. Don't write something overly general such as 'I hate my work'; instead, ask yourself what your boss did, or didn't do, that you disliked, or what is it in particular about your work that upsets you.

5. **Record your thoughts about the event in the appropriate column.**

   Describe how you perceive, interpret or think about the event. Refer to The Thought Query Questionnaire in Chapter 4 if you experience any difficulty identifying your thoughts about the event.

6. **Using the reality distortions information from Worksheet 5-1, record the distortions you believe are operating.**

Worksheet 5-5	Thought Tracker Reality Distortion		
Feelings and Sensations Rated 1–100	*Concurrent Events*	*Thoughts/Interpretations*	*Reality Distortions*

For extra copies of this form, visit www.dummies.com/go/adwb.

In working through the exercise in Worksheet 5-5, were you able to find incoming information reality distortions in your thinking? If so, we expect you'll begin questioning if your thoughts about events are always accurate. With that doubt comes the possibility of seeing things a little differently – more realistically, actually. Record your reflections in Worksheet 5-6. We hope we're beginning to shake up your thinking (see Chapter 6 for a variety of strategies for replacing distorted thinking with more accurate perceptions).

Worksheet 5-6	My Reflections

_____

_____

_____

_____

Going to Battle against Self-Judging Reality Distortions

Self-judging reality distortions twist the way you view yourself and your behaviour. Depressed and anxious minds tend to be harshly critical, judgemental and self-derogatory. Why is that a problem? Because self-judging is a form of self-sabotage (see Chapter 3). Although you may think otherwise, self-criticism doesn't motivate you to do anything positive or productive; rather, it only makes you feel worse and leaves you with less energy for changing.

Self-judging reality distortions come in three different forms:

- ✔ Musts, oughts and shoulds
- ✔ Critical comparisons
- ✔ Loathsome labels

Shoulding on yourself

Psychologist Dr Albert Ellis, founder of CBT, neatly captured some of the ways people beat themselves up – terming them 'shoulding on yourself'. Does that describe what you've been doing? Well, take heart, you're not the only one! *Shoulding* involves putting yourself down by telling yourself that you should be different or act differently in some way. It can refer to past, present or future actions. Musts, oughts and shoulds distort accurate self-views and turns them into self-criticisms.

To identify your own shoulds, complete Worksheet 5-7, putting a tick next to each thought that has run through your mind over the past few months.

Worksheet 5-7	Shoulding on Yourself

❑ I should have known better.

❑ I mustn't eat so much.

❑ I ought to be a better person.

❑ I really ought to be more careful.

❑ I mustn't have distorted thoughts!

❑ I shouldn't be so crabby.

❑ I mustn't make so many mistakes.

❑ I ought to exercise more.

❑ I should be nicer to people.

❑ I shouldn't get so upset about things.

So what's wrong with these thoughts? (We can almost hear you thinking, 'But I *SHOULD* eat less, be a better person or not get so upset about things!') Well, where is it written in stone that you must/ought/should act or think in certain ways? Shoulding is a form of criticism that makes you feel bad and creates feelings of guilt and shame – and guilt and shame don't motivate positive behaviour. The bottom line is that shoulding and telling yourself you 'ought to' doesn't help.

The alternative to this type of thinking is recognising that although doing things differently may be good, you refuse to engage in harsh self-judgement. Before you get to creating your own should alternatives, read Iain's statements in Worksheet 5-8 and see how he develops alternatives.

Worksheet 5-8	Iain's Should Alternative Exercise
Should Statement	*Should Alternative Statement*
I shouldn't get upset so often.	I wish I didn't get upset so often, but I do. And I'm trying to master relaxation as an alternative.
I shouldn't get in bad moods so often.	I don't like bad moods, but they're tough to change. I do want to work on them, but I don't need to beat myself up when they happen.
I shouldn't let myself get out of shape.	I'd prefer to get into better shape. It's difficult to find the time to exercise. I'll try to make more time for taking care of myself.
I should spend more time on the exercises in this workbook.	I do want to spend more time on these exercises, but every bit that I do is worth something.
I shouldn't make mistakes.	I prefer not to make mistakes, but I'm human, after all.

Review any items you endorsed from the Shoulding on Yourself checklist in Worksheet 5-7 and also listen to your self-talk. Then fill out the Should Alternative Exercise in Worksheet 5-9 by following these instructions:

1. **Tune into what you're telling yourself when you feel upset.**

2. **Listen for any time that you tell yourself 'I should' or 'I shouldn't' – as well as any time you use words such as 'must' or 'ought'.**

3. **Record those statements in the left-hand column.**

4. **Come up with alternative perspectives for each should statement and write them in the right-hand column.**

    Words like 'prefer', 'would like to', 'wish' and 'would be better if' make good alternatives to 'should'.

Worksheet 5-9	My Should Alternative Exercise
Should Statement	*Should Alternative Statement*

Making critical comparisons

Are you the wealthiest, best-looking or brightest person in the world? Strange that! Us neither. There's always someone who has more of something than you do. Even if you're the best at something, that doesn't mean you're the best at everything. People have strengths and weaknesses, and if you do think you're the best at everything, you have a problem that's quite different from anxiety or depression.

Everyone compares themselves to others sometimes. But anxious and depressed people tend to rate themselves more negatively and place more value on those comparisons.

To identify your negative personal comparisons, tick each item in Worksheet 5-10 that you sometimes find you make comparisons on between yourself and others.

Worksheet 5-10	Critical Comparisons

❑ Finances or wealth

❑ Looks and appearance

❑ Intelligence

❑ Popularity

❑ Relationships

❑ Fame

❑ Gadgets (boys' toys, usually)

❑ House

❑ Car

❑ Clothes

❑ Status

❑ Age

❑ Knowledge

Essentially, the fewer comparisons you make, the better. But comparisons are so tempting because they do contain a kernel of truth. The reality is that there's always someone richer, younger or more successful than you. Comparisons may be unavoidable, but they only become problematic when you conclude that because you're not the best, you aren't good enough.

What's the alternative to making critical comparisons that distort the way you see yourself? Like should alternative statements (see 'Shoulding on yourself'), comparison alternatives are all about looking at an issue from a different, less judgemental perspective. Before creating your own alternative statements, take a look at Worksheet 5-11 for an example.

Worksheet 5-11	Dimitri's Comparison Alternative Exercise
Critical Comparison	*Comparison Alternative*
My friend Joe has done a lot better than I have in his career.	Well, he has. But I've done fine. I spend a lot of time with my family, and that's my real priority.
When we went to the Cup Final party, I was really jealous of that 60-inch plasma TV. Our TV looks pretty paltry in comparison.	There was nothing wrong with my TV before that party. I don't even watch that much TV.
I went to the gym and noticed that everyone was more fit than I am.	Of course, most of the really unfit people don't even go to the gym. I'm in better shape than I was a month ago; that's progress, and that's what matters.
I read an article on retirement and got anxious when I realised that I don't have as much in savings as a lot of people do.	Having kids was more expensive than I thought it would be, but I wouldn't trade them for the world. After Trevor's uni expenses are paid for, we'll prioritise saving.

Review the items you checked on your Critical Comparisons quiz (see Worksheet 5-10) and listen to your self-dialogue. Then fill out the Comparison Alternative Exercise in Worksheet 5-12 by following these instructions:

1. **Tune into what you're telling yourself when you feel upset and listen for any time that you critically compare yourself to others.**

2. **List those statements in the left-hand column.**

3. **Come up with alternative perspectives and record them in the right-hand column.**

Because only one person in the world is at the top on any given issue or activity, try to accept that you are average, normal or even occasionally below average at many things. Comparing yourself to the very top only leaves you disappointed, so appreciate your own strengths, weaknesses and chosen priorities.

Worksheet 5-12	My Comparison Alternative Exercise
Critical Comparison	*Comparison Alternative*

Banishing loathsome self-labels

Sticks and stones *can* break your bones, and words *can* really hurt you. The final self-judging reality distortion amounts to calling yourself names. Labelling yourself in this way is so easy – and when you do, you inevitably feel worse.

To pinpoint the loathsome labels you give yourself, complete Worksheet 5-13. Tick the words that you use to describe yourself when things go wrong.

Worksheet 5-13	Loathsome Self-Labels

❑ Loser

❑ Pathetic

❑ Misfit

❑ Twit

❑ Clot

❑ Clumsy

❑ Fat pig

❏ Failure

❏ Nerd

❏ Pathetic

❏ Stupid

❏ Useless

❏ Mad

❏ Crazy

❏ Idiot

❏ Jerk

❏ Imbecile

❏ Fool

❏ Moron

Labels erode your self-worth. They always involve overgeneralisation and black and white thinking (see the section 'Identifying Incoming Information Reality Distortions' earlier in this chapter). Labels represent concepts that hold no redeeming value; they don't help you, and they often lead to increased emotional distress. So what should you do when these labels drift through your mind? See Worksheet 5-14 for examples of self-labels and new ways of looking at them.

Worksheet 5-14	Alternatives to Labels	
Event	*Corresponding Label*	*Alternative to Label*
I spilled a drink at a restaurant.	I'm such a clumsy clot!	I've seen other people spill drinks. Good grief, it's not a big deal.
I started to cry when I was talking about my mother's illness.	I'm pathetic and pitiful.	There's nothing wrong with showing some emotion.
My voice started to shake during a meeting at work.	I'm a loser.	I was talking about something very important to me. At times like that, I do get a little tense. I wish I didn't, but that doesn't make me a failure.
I didn't get into my first choice of university.	I'm a failure.	It was very competitive. I did get my third choice. Sure, I'd have preferred the other one, but I can still succeed in my chosen career.
I can't seem to lose weight.	I'm a fat pig!	My GP said that after reaching 50, metabolic changes make it harder to lose weight. I have put on some extra weight, and I don't like it, but it doesn't help to call myself a pig.

If you stop calling yourself inaccurate, hurtful names, and replace the labels with more reasonable perspectives, you'll feel better. Therefore, we recommend that you complete the Alternative Label Exercise in Worksheet 5-15 each time you hear a destructive label in your mind:

1. **Tune into what you're telling yourself when you feel upset and listen for any time that you describe yourself with a hurtful label.**

2. **Write the triggering event in the left-hand column.**

3. **Write the label you're putting on yourself in the middle column.**

4. **Come up with alternative perspectives to the labels and record them in the right-hand column.**

    In creating label replacements, try to accept any part of the event that has truth in it, such as having gained some weight, but look at the issue more realistically. Try to be self-forgiving. Because labels tend to be magnified, your alternative thoughts should be specific and look for positive possibilities.

If you have trouble coming up with alternatives to your loathsome labels, don't worry. Jump to Chapter 6 for lots of ideas for challenging negative self-talk.

Worksheet 5-15	My Alternative Label Exercise	
Event	*Corresponding Label*	*Alternative to Label*

After you identify some alternatives to those loathsome labels, take a few minutes to reflect on what self-labelling has been doing to you and how it feels to change (see Worksheet 5-16).

Worksheet 5-16	**My Reflections**

_____

_____

_____

_____

Stopping the Self-Blame Reality Distortion

When sadness or anxiety clouds your thinking, you're likely to add to your distress by assuming full responsibility for your misery. You may accuse yourself of being inept, incapable or inadequate – and therefore fully culpable for all your suffering. When the self-blame reality distortion is at work, you attribute all fault and blame to yourself. Doing so leads you to become bogged down with shame and self-loathing.

In this section, we give you a tool for identifying if you use the self-blame reality distortion. After you begin to understand that your problem isn't completely your fault, you can take action on the portion for which you own responsibility. The Rating Responsibility Exercise helps you see that most problems have many causes and that you only own a portion of the responsibility. Accepting these facts can help you lessen the guilt and shame you feel. After you understand the range of causes of a problem, you're more ready to do something productive about it.

Rowena blames herself for her recent divorce and believes that she is almost entirely responsible for her husband leaving the marriage for another woman. Rowena considers herself boring and unattractive, and she berates herself for not seeing the signs early enough to prevent what happened. Rowena decides to take the Rating Responsibility Exercise (see Worksheet 5-17), focusing on the blame she places on herself for her divorce.

Worksheet 5-17	**Rowena's Rating Responsibility Exercise**

I blame myself for: My recent divorce

I rate the blame at: 95 per cent

All Possible Causes of Your Problem	*Percentage of Responsibility*
My husband's roving eye.	10%: He does have a roving eye!
My husband's hostility.	15%: He's a difficult man.
Diana's conniving, manipulative plan to steal him.	20%: She was after him for months, no doubt about it.
The strain of our financial problems.	10%: This didn't help.
My husband's grief over losing his mother, father and brother over the last year and a half.	10%: He could never talk about these losses, and I know they got to him.

(continued)

Worksheet 5-17 *(continued)*

I blame myself for: My recent divorce

I rate the blame at: 95 per cent

All Possible Causes of Your Problem	Percentage of Responsibility
The stress of our daughter's tumour. She's recovered now, but my husband still worries.	10%: Again, he couldn't talk about it.
I gained ten pounds during our marriage.	5%: I know I'm not that overweight.
My husband can easily find women more attractive than me.	5%: Yeah, but I do look better than many women my age.
We had stopped talking to each other about our days at work.	10%: I probably should have paid more attention to that issue.
Random events.	5%: I'm sure there are things I'm not taking into account.

My re-rated level of responsibility is: 20 per cent

As you can see, Rowena initially puts 95 per cent of the blame for the divorce on herself. At the end, she reassesses her level of responsibility because she's able to see things a bit more objectively. She re-rates the level of blame she ascribes to herself and identifies that 20 per cent seems more appropriate – she's only partly responsible. This knowledge helps her to feel less guilty and self-disparaging.

After seeing the Rating Responsibility Exercise in action, you're ready to evaluate the level of responsibility you feel you carry. In other words, you're figuring out how much of the problem is you. Complete your Rating Responsibility Exercise in Worksheet 5-18 by following these steps:

1. **Name a problem you're blaming yourself for.**

   Write this at the top of the worksheet.

2. **Using a percentage from 1 to 100, rate how much blame you put on yourself for this problem.**

   At the top of the worksheet, write this percentage under the problem you've identified.

3. **In the left-hand column, list all imaginable causes of your problem.**

4. **In the right-hand column, using a number from 1 to 100, estimate the percentage of actual responsibility for this problem that each cause in the left-hand column owns.**

   Make note of your own contributions to the problem.

5. **Re-rate the percentage of responsibility you have for the problem you identified.**

Worksheet 5-18	My Rating Responsibility Exercise

I blame myself for: _____

I rate the blame at: _____

All Possible Causes of Your Problem	Percentage of Responsibility

My re-rated level of responsibility is: _____

Some people deny any and all responsibility for problems they encounter. They usually find a convenient scapegoat such as a mother, father, significant other, society or event to blame for all their woes. Failing to accept any responsibility for your troubles makes you see yourself as helpless and the world as unfair and unjust (check out Chapter 3 for more information about such self-sabotaging beliefs). You don't want to fall into that trap – read the next section to see how to avoid it.

Giving It a Go: Problem Solving

In this section, you face your problem and take action to change it. By assessing your responsibility and determining what you can do about your problem, you avoid immersing yourself in self-loathing and harsh self-blame. This approach allows you to take responsibility for an appropriate portion of the problem and do what you can with it.

If your responsibility involves something that's over and done with, no action is possible. But you can still try to let go of the shame that leads nowhere and does nothing to help you. And you may be able to do some things to prevent a similar problem in the future.

Rowena reviews her Rating Responsibility Exercise (see Worksheet 5-17) and notices that she owns partial responsibility for some of the problems that led to her divorce. She lists those contributions and then plans steps for productive action on the Action Strategy Worksheet, shown in Worksheet 5-19.

Worksheet 5-19   **Rowena's Action Strategy Worksheet**

The problem: My divorce.

My Specific Contributions to the Problem	Specific Actions I Can Take
I am ten pounds overweight.	I can lose ten pounds by increasing my exercise and watching my diet. It won't help this divorce, but my counsellor said exercise will lift my spirits, and I'll be healthier.
I'm not the most attractive woman in the world.	I can't do a lot about my appearance other than realise it's not that important. I don't want a man who wants me just for the way I look anyway.
I ignored our lack of communication in the marriage.	When I find another relationship, I need to pay attention to how we talk and any other problems that crop up. I don't want to bury my head in the sand.

After completing your Rating Responsibility Exercise in Worksheet 5-18, the next step is to create an action strategy to determine how you can begin solving your problem. By identifying productive actions to address the problem, you can move forward and stop berating yourself. Follow these steps to create an action strategy in Worksheet 5-20:

1. **Name the problem you're blaming yourself for and write it at the top of the worksheet.**

2. **In the left-hand column, list the specific contributions you've identified that you have some control over.**

   In other words, record anything you did that may have led to the problem or made it worse.

3. **In the right-hand column, list any steps you can take now or in the future that may be useful in solving this problem.**

Worksheet 5-20 | **My Action Strategy Worksheet**

*The problem:*_____

My Specific Contributions to the Problem	*Specific Actions I Can Take*

As you finish this chapter, take the time to reflect on what you've discovered about your patterns of thinking and how they affect your view of yourself. Write down your feelings, thoughts and insights in Worksheet 5-21.

Worksheet 5-21 | **My Reflections**

_____
_____
_____

Chapter 6

Challenging and Changing Thoughts

● ●

In This Chapter

▶ Investigating thoughts

▶ Taking thoughts to task

▶ Repairing and replacing thoughts

● ●

*M*ost people simply assume that thoughts they have about themselves and the world are true. But thoughts don't always reflect reality, just as distorting mirrors don't reflect the way you really look. In Chapter 5, we help you identify the distortions in your thoughts.

In this chapter, you become a thought detective. But you won't need all the usual paraphernalia – just the tools and instructions we provide in this chapter . . . and an open mind. We show you how to take your thoughts to task. If you find them guilty (and we think you will), you find out how to restructure them.

Weighing Up the Evidence

We base the following technique – called Taking Your Thoughts to Task – on the principles of cognitive therapy, which later merged with behaviour therapy, to become cognitive behavioural therapy, or CBT. *Cognitive therapy* was founded in the late 1950s by Dr Aaron T. Beck. He demonstrated that changing the way people think changes the way they feel. Many studies attest to the fact that cognitive therapy works very well to overcome anxiety and depression. Therefore, we recommend that you regularly practise the exercises in this section until you find yourself starting to think and feel differently – and then carry on for a little while longer. If you want to find out more about CBT, take a look at *Cognitive Behavioural Therapy For Dummies* by Rob Willson and Rhena Branch (Wiley).

Before being taken to task, the accused must first be caught. So we provide a Thought Catcher to do just that. Thought Catchers show you the connections between feelings, events and thoughts, and then help you weigh up the evidence for and against. We give you examples of Thought Catchers in this section, but for more information, go to Chapter 4.

When you've caught your thought in the Thought Catcher, the next step in the process of Taking Your Thoughts to Task is that of Weighing up the Evidence. This involves examining the thought you caught in your Thought Catcher and bringing it to trial. You play the roles of prosecution, judge – and jury! As the defence solicitor, you present the evidence that supports the validity or accuracy of the thought. In other words, the defence claims that your thought is accurate, not unduly negative, and so can't be blamed for upsetting you. You then play the role of prosecutor, presenting a case demonstrating that the thought is actually guilty of distortion, and therefore has caused you unnecessary emotional distress. When the thought goes on trial, you weigh up the evidence just like a jury. You then play at being the judge. If you find the thought guilty, we give you ways to restructure it.

You're very unlikely to acquit a thought. If you do consistently judge that your suspicious thoughts seem justified and accurate, you should see a mental health professional. You may need a fresh perspective to help sort out your troubles.

Most people learn better through stories and examples than through laborious explanations. With that in mind, we help you master the process of Taking the Thought to Task by presenting a case example in the next section. Then we give you the chance to take your own thoughts to task, and put them on trial. If you need more help, we follow up your practice session with some more case examples in the section 'Looking at further show trials'.

Examining a trial case

Jeremy is a good-looking 23-year-old personal trainer who takes pride in his healthy lifestyle. People admire his strength and athleticism. He's conspicuous at the gym, both for his physique and for always wearing colourful long-sleeved sweatshirts. Jeremy receives more than his share of attention from women, but he never gets involved because he has a secret: he was seriously burned as a child, and his chest and arms are severely scarred. Jeremy has never had a serious relationship; he believes any woman seeing his scars would recoil in disgust. Rather than risk rejection and ridicule, he keeps his secret to himself, shuns T-shirts and vests, and never goes swimming.

Jeremy finds himself very attracted to a young woman he meets at the gym, and the feelings are obviously mutual. She asks him out for coffee, and he panics and prevaricates. However, the combination of fear and yearning motivate him to seek help, and he manages to tell his counsellor about his lifelong secret. Jeremy's counsellor suggests that he start examining his thoughts using a Thought Catcher (see Worksheet 6-1) and then take his thoughts to task, by putting them on trial, in order to weigh up the evidence.

Worksheet 6-1	Jeremy's Thought Catcher	
Feelings and Sensations (Rated 1–100, with 0 being no disturbing feelings to 100 meaning extremely distressing ones)	*Corresponding Events*	*Thoughts/Interpretations*
Anxiety (85), fear (95); shaking hands, flushed face	Mona suggests we go for a cappuccino.	If we get on well, she might want to see more of me. I can't take that risk! I couldn't stand to see the look of repulsion on her face. No way, no how!
Anxiety (75), shame (85), bitterness (85); sweaty, sinking feeling in the pit of my stomach	The new manager suggests we have the staff Christmas party with a Caribbean Beach theme to get to know each other better.	If I make excuses, I may be marginalised and not part of the team. I'll look ridiculous in long sleeves at a beach party. But on the other hand, my colleagues are bound to react badly if they see my arms and chest, and I'll feel terrible — it will be too awful for words. It's not fair that I have to go through life like this.

After filling out his Thought Catcher, Jeremy and his counsellor start identifying his most negative, negative thoughts. He realises that two negative thoughts give him the most pain:

1. I couldn't stand to see the look of repulsion on Mona's face.

2. It's not fair that I was burned and have to go through life this way.

Next, his counsellor suggests that Jeremy put the first of these thoughts on trial using Worksheet 6-2. In the first column, he finds all the evidence he can to support the case that the thought is true. In the next column, Jeremy then presents the prosecution's case, to demonstrate the thought's inaccuracies.

Worksheet 6-2	Jeremy's Taking the Thought to Task Worksheet
Suspect negative thought: I couldn't stand it if Mona found my body unattractive.	
Defence: Evidence Supporting the Thought	**Prosecution: Evidence Disproving the Thought**
People find scarring repulsive.	The hospital staff haven't seemed a bit phased.
I remember the look of shock on people's faces from before.	My family doesn't seem uncomfortable or put off.
My mother wept when she saw my scars.	
After one of my many operations, I was told I'd just have to learn to live with the remaining scars.	
If I ever wear short sleeves on a really hot day, I'm sure people look at me and are talking about me.	

So far, the defence clearly has the upper hand. Jeremy's pretty convinced that his thought is a true reflection of reality; it's just the way things are. He can't imagine seeing things differently. The counsellor congratulates him on a good start, but asks him to consider the questions in Worksheet 6-3 and write down his reflections on those questions (see Worksheet 6-4).

Worksheet 6-3	Prosecution Questions: Challenging the Thought

1. Is this thought illogical or distorted in any way? (See Chapter 5 for a list of misleading misperceptions that indicate distortions in thoughts.)

2. Is this event really as horrible as I'm letting myself believe it is?

3. Were there any times in my life when this thought wouldn't have held true?

(continued)

Worksheet 6-3 *(continued)*
---

4. Do I know of friends or acquaintances who have experienced similar events but for whom this thought wouldn't apply?

5. Am I ignoring any evidence that may dispute this thought?

6. Is this thought really helping me?

7. Have I ever coped with something like this before and got through it okay?

8. What would happen if I just started acting as though the thought weren't true?

Worksheet 6-4 **Jeremy's Reflections**

These questions are a little tricky. But let's see. Are there any distortions in the thought? Well, while I would really dislike being rejected, it probably won't kill me. Perhaps I'm magnifying the awfulness somewhat. I've seen attractive women who are with guys who aren't exactly Adonis personified. I was in that burn support group, and I admit there were some people who had developed really good relationships. So I suppose it's possible she may not be repulsed. And the thought is doing me more harm than good because it keeps me from ever considering a relationship. Maybe it's worth testing out if it's true or not.

After Jeremy reflects on the list of questions for the prosecution in Worksheet 6-3, his counsellor advises him to take another look at his Taking the Thought to Task Worksheet and try to add more evidence and logic to the prosecution side of his case (see Worksheet 6-5).

Worksheet 6-5 **Jeremy's Taking the Thought to Task Worksheet – Revised**

Suspect negative thought: I couldn't stand it if Mona found my body unattractive.

Defence: Evidence Supporting the Thought	*Prosecution: Evidence Disproving the Thought*
People are repulsed by burn scars.	Actually, there are quite a few people I know who haven't been shocked or repulsed by my scars. That thought is overgeneralising.
I vividly remember how shocked some people looked when I was younger.	My family seems to have got used to my scars. If they can, it's certainly possible that others could — especially if they cared about me.

Defence: Evidence Supporting the Thought	Prosecution: Evidence Disproving the Thought
I remember my mother crying when she saw how badly I was burned.	Just because she cried doesn't mean she can't stand looking at me or hugging me. Maybe she was just so upset and sorry for me.
After one of my many operations, I was told I'd just have to learn to live with the remaining scars.	Just because I do have to live with them doesn't mean I can't have a relationship. This thought is distorted both by magnifying and overgeneralising.
If I ever wear short sleeves on a really hot day, I'm sure people look at me and are talking about me.	I suppose it could just be that they are noticing my physique. I have worked hard on that. I'm mind-reading if I assume I know they're saying horrible things about me.
	I know many people from the burns unit and from my support group who have great relationships – which often began after their accidents.
	Anyone who really likes and cares about me will surely see below the surface. And if they are that superficial – then I'm not interested in them!
	If I don't have a go, I'll never know. And then I'll never find a partner. This thought really isn't helping me much to improve the quality of my life.
	If she does reject me, how does that mean everyone else will? And think of the pain I've handled to date – I must be pretty tough after all!

At this point, Jeremy carefully reviews the case presented in Worksheet 6-5. He finds his thought is a pretty clear example of a classic negative thought, and that it's causing him grief. He and his counsellor agree to work on alternative thoughts for his most disturbing negative ones (see the section 'Restructuring Your Thoughts after the Verdict' later in this chapter). Jeremy proceeds to put his other negative thoughts on trial and eventually restructures them all.

Putting your thoughts on trial

You guessed it; now it's your turn to weigh the evidence. Don't be concerned if you find yourself struggling initially to identify if each thought is negative. This important exercise takes practice. (And if you're still confused after examining your own thoughts, we provide several more examples of how this process works.) The first step is to fill in a Thought Catcher (see Worksheet 6-6):

1. **Pay attention to your body's signals and write down any you feel are unpleasant.**

2. **Search for a feeling word that captures your emotion and jot it down in Worksheet 6-6.** Refer to the Daily Unpleasant Emotions List in Chapter 4 for help finding the right feeling words.

3. **Rate your feeling on a scale of intensity from 1 (almost undetectable) to 100 (maximum).**

4. **Ask yourself what was going on when you started noticing both your emotions and your body's signals.** While the corresponding event may be something happening around you, it can also be a remembered thought or image that runs through your mind. Be concrete and specific; don't write something vague like 'I hate my work'. Instead, ask yourself what happened at work that you didn't like.

5. **Record your thoughts in the Thoughts/Interpretations column of the worksheet.** Describe how you perceive, interpret or think about the event. Refer to The Thought Query Quiz in Chapter 4 if you experience any difficulty deciphering your thoughts about the event.

6. **Review your thoughts and write down the one(s) that evokes the greatest amount of emotion – your most troubling negative thoughts.**

Worksheet 6-6	My Thought Catcher	
Feelings and Sensations (Rated 1–100)	*Corresponding Events*	*Thoughts/Interpretations*

My most troubling negative thoughts:

1. _____

2. _____

You can find this worksheet on the Internet at www.dummies.com/go/adwb. Download as many copies as you need and frequently practise this exercise. Over time, you're likely to start changing the way you think and, therefore, the way you feel. Just remind yourself of the three Ts – Things Take Time.

The Thought Catcher prepares you for the next step, which is putting your own thoughts on trial, and weighing up the evidence. This process does take some planning and preparation. Choose a negative thought and consider the questions in Worksheet 6-3. Reflect on your answers in Worksheet 6-7.

Worksheet 6-7	My Reflections

Now you're ready to put the first disturbing thought on trial, and then move on to the next.

1. **In Worksheet 6-8, identify one of your most upsetting negative thoughts and write it down.**

2. **In the left-hand column, write down everything you can to support the validity of that negative thought.** In other words, defend that thought as best you can.

3. **In the right-hand column, note down all the reasons, evidence and logic that refute and dispute the accuracy or truth of the thought.**

Worksheet 6-8	My Putting Thoughts on Trial Worksheet
Suspect Negative Thought:	
Defence: Evidence Supporting the Thought	*Prosecution: Evidence Disproving the Thought*

(continued)

Worksheet 6-8 *(continued)*

Defence: Evidence Supporting the Thought	*Prosecution: Evidence Disproving the Thought*

You can download extra copies of this form at `www.dummies.com/go/adwb`. You're likely to need practice to develop the skill of weighing up the evidence in order to reap the full benefit from this exercise.

After you've put your thought on trial, it's time to reach your verdict. Decide for yourself whether or not your thought is a negative one – and guilty of causing you unwarranted emotional distress such as anxiety, depression or other difficult feelings. Even if you conclude that your thought has some grain of truth, you're likely to discover that the thought is doing you more harm than good.

When weighing the evidence, don't judge your thought as negative or guilty only on the basis of 'beyond a reasonable doubt'. Rather, we suggest you decide on the 'balance of evidence'. So without any legal-speak, in plain English, your thought is a negative, inaccurate one if the evidence weighs heaviest on that side.

Looking at further show trials

Here are a few more examples. Because the Thought Catcher also appears in chapters 4 and 5, we start with the accused thought here, which comes from the most negative thoughts revealed at the end of completing a Thought Catcher worksheet (see 'Putting your thoughts on trial').

Colin: Down the slippery slope

Over the years, Colin, a 58-year-old secondary school teacher, has been golfing abroad with the lads twice a year on 'boys only' getaways. Despite being in their fifties, they still behave as they always did when away from the WAGs. However, Colin finds that his arthritis has been steadily worsening. He tries to ignore the pain but eventually has to see his doctor because the pain is becoming unbearable. His doctor refers him to an orthopaedic specialist who tells Colin he needs a hip replacement. Colin begins to get depressed after this consultation. However, he fills in a Thought Catcher and identifies the negative thoughts: 'I'll never be really happy again. My quality of life will just go steadily downhill from here.' He then proceeds to take his thought to task and puts it on trial. Worksheet 6-9 shows how he weighs up the evidence.

Worksheet 6-9	Colin's Putting Thoughts on Trial Worksheet

Suspect negative thought: I'll never be happy again – life will just go downhill from now on.

Defence: Evidence Supporting the Thought	Prosecution: Evidence Disproving the Thought
This hip replacement is really the beginning of the end.	Loads of people have hip replacements without additional health problems. This thought is distorted through exaggeration and by crystal ball gazing.
I'm happiest when I'm outdoors. If I have to give up golf, I'll never be happy again.	Rubbish! I enjoy films, meals out and reading thrillers. I'm filtering out these other pleasures.
I'm going to experience chronic pain for the rest of my life. I can't possibly have any fun.	This conclusion's unwarranted right now – it's distorted through crystal ball gazing and exaggeration. I should check this with the doctor first. I know there are good pain management courses. And I know other people with arthritis who enjoy excellent quality of life.
No one wants to be with someone who's a wimp and a whinger.	So who says I have to behave like one? Bet they'll respect me when they see how hard I'm trying to improve and help myself. Anyway, that distortion's more crystal ball gazing.
I won't be able to get to my bedroom upstairs anymore.	Yet another crystal ball gazing distortion! The literature says most people have full, active lives after a hip replacement.
I should've exercised more. I ought to have watched my weight better.	There's a 'should' and an 'ought' – since when is any of this written in stone? 'Shoulds' and 'oughts' change nothing.
I'll bet it won't be long before I'm wheelchair bound.	What a distortion. Good old crystal ball gazing again. I do that a lot.

(continued)

Worksheet 6-9 *(continued)*

Defence: Evidence Supporting the Thought	Prosecution: Evidence Disproving the Thought
	Realistically, I can expect some discomfort after surgery, and rehab could take a while. But chances are, if I do my physio programme, I'll feel enormously better than I do now.
	Come on! Get a grip! My uncle who is in his eighties had a hip replacement, and he's back to training three times a week at the gym!

Colin carefully considers the evidence. His verdict: you're a negative thought! Gotcha! He now realises the thought, 'I'll never be happy again – life will just go downhill from now on' is far from being accurate and certainly doesn't help him cope with his reality.

Emma: Filled with anxiety

Emma, a 37-year-old accountant, regularly puts in a 50-hour week. As a divorced single parent, she struggles to find a satisfactory work/life balance. She's also a perfectionist and expects to be able to handle everything. Understandably, Emma is often troubled by anxiety. She worries about keeping up with her job and being a good mother to her two children. So when Emma's son brings home a mediocre school report, a serious depression begins. She loses her temper, yells at her son and berates herself for being a terrible mother. Emma completes a Thought Catcher and then puts her most negative thoughts on trial (see Worksheet 6-10).

Worksheet 6-10   Emma's Putting Thoughts on Trial Worksheet

Suspect negative thought: I'm an abject failure as a mother; my son's going to drop out or be slung out of school.

Defence: Evidence Supporting the Thought	Prosecution: Evidence Disproving the Thought
How obvious can you get! That report card proves how badly he's doing.	Hang on a second. That was ONE report, in ONE subject. And it was only that his standard was lower than he'd achieved previously – he didn't blow it completely. Overall, he's done okay. I can see I'm exaggerating here.
I screamed at him – I shouldn't have done that. It's proof I'm a rotten mum.	I'm not the only parent who loses their temper occasionally. Usually I'm pretty laid back. Shoulding on myself isn't going to help me.

Defence: Evidence Supporting the Thought	*Prosecution: Evidence Disproving the Thought*
If I were really a good mother, I should have known he needed assistance with his schoolwork.	Perhaps the teacher shares some of the responsibility for not alerting me earlier if there was a problem. I even asked, after all!
I made my son cry when I yelled at him. Bet he hates me. Just what kind of a mother is that?	Hang on a sec. Children often cry when adults shout. But that doesn't mean he'll never ever get over it. Mind reading?
I missed the last Parents' Evening because of my work commitments.	I made a point of catching the relevant teachers by phone and also dropped off a note asking them to be in touch if they had any concerns.
Other mothers volunteer for playground duty. That's what good mums do.	How can I be at work earning money to support the family and be in the playground as well? Let's face it, which is better for my son's long-term future? That's an example of critical comparisons.
I've been putting my work before my family.	That's clearly not so. When my children really need me – like when they're ill – I always take time off. I'm overgeneralising here.
I don't know what to do to help him.	I suppose I'll work that out with the teacher.
	If he really were on the verge of being slung out, his other subjects would also be suffering.
	Until now he's always been in the top ten in class. I just need to find out what's going on.
	The evidence shows I do loads of things with my son. And no one, least of all me, can expect me to be Superwoman!

Weighing up the evidence is one of the most effective tools for combating anxiety, depression and other unpleasant emotions. If you have trouble with the exercise, spend more time going over the questions in Worksheet 6-3. Reviewing Chapter 5 and re-reading the examples in this chapter may be helpful as well. If you still struggle, we recommend you consult a clinical psychologist who's proficient in cognitive behavioural therapy.

Restructuring Your Thoughts after the Verdict

Hopefully, the prosecution presents a convincing case against your negative thoughts, and you begin to see that many of your thoughts are actually distorting reality and causing distress. So now what?

In this section, we show you how to restructure each of your negative thoughts. Restructuring your thoughts decreases feelings of depression and anxiety because a restructured thought offers a balanced, realistic appraisal of your problem. This new thought is a comparatively quick and easy rejoinder to negative, distorted thinking.

You can use a number of different techniques to develop effective restructured thoughts. The strategies we outline in the following sections help you untangle distortions and straighten out your thinking. With these strategies, you discover how to replace your negative thoughts with more helpful, realistic restructured ones. We provide four alternative strategies. So if one doesn't work, just try another.

Being your own best friend

This strategy is surprisingly simple. Imagine that a good friend of yours is going through the same kind of problem as you are. Your friend has thoughts similar to yours about the problem. Now imagine your friend sitting opposite you. You feel empathy, and you want to help.

What can you say? How do you suggest your friend thinks about this situation? It's important that you evaluate your friend's problem honestly. Simply trying to make your friend feel better by negating or underplaying the issue just won't work. You must provide your friend with a reasonable way to think about the problem.

The essence of this powerful, yet surprisingly simple, technique is that the advice you would give a friend is the advice you can, and then do, give yourself. The strategy works by helping you get a little distance from your problem. Viewing thoughts and feelings from a distance helps you be more objective.

As a variation on this technique, you can also turn the tables and imagine the advice your friend (a real or imaginary person) your very 'bestest' friend in the whole wide world might provide. Conjure up what your friend looks and sounds like, as well as what words he or she might say. Play a scene in your mind in which you're scared or sad and your friend is encouraging you and showing you realistic, alternative ways of looking at things. This technique, known as *compassionate mind therapy,* is one of the more recent developments within CBT that Paul Gilbert of Derby University has developed.

The following example shows you how you can use the techniques of compassionate mind therapy, or being your own best friend, to help you discover new, more realistic views of challenging situations.

Emma (see 'Emma: Filled with anxiety' earlier in this chapter) has put her most negative thought on trial, weighed the evidence and found it guilty. Now she tries to restructure that thought by being her own best friend. She thinks about her actual best friend, Louise, and imagines a situation in which Louise asks Emma's advice for a problem about Louise's son (see Worksheet 6-11).

Emma's/Louise's most negative thought:

I'm an abject failure as a mother; my son's going to drop out or be slung out of school.

Worksheet 6-11   Emma Being Her Own Best Friend (Louise)

Well, Louise, I know you feel like a failure, but your son only came home with two C's and three B's. That's not exactly catastrophic. So you haven't spent that much time with him lately? You've been pretty tied up with work. That happens. Why beat yourself up about it? Talk to his teacher and see what you can do to help. Stop sounding like a helpless victim. Face it, he's already 16. Hasn't he got some part in his own success and failure? Why is it all down to you?

Emma reviews her imaginary discussion with Louise. She finds to her surprise that her own perspective changes when she hears the advice she gives Louise, instead of buying into her own negative automatic thoughts. Next, she distills this perspective into a single restructured alternative thought (see Worksheet 6-12).

Worksheet 6-12   Emma's Restructured Alternative Thought

The evidence shows my son isn't falling to bits and that I'm not a failure. Realistically, all I can do is see how I can assist — the rest is up to him.

Take one of your most negative thoughts and address it directly using Compassionate Mind Therapy.

1. **Write down one of your most negative or distressing thoughts identified by your Thought Catcher (see Worksheet 6-6).**

2. **Imagine the very best, warmest, wisest being or spirit you possible can.** What does this person look like and sound like? What does this person say to you about your negative thought?

3. **Write the advice you imagine receiving from this person in Worksheet 6-13.**

4. **Clear your mind and think of someone you know and respect.** Imagine that this friend has a problem very similar to your own and has similar thoughts about the problem.

5. **Imagine you're talking with your friend about a better way to think about and deal with the problem.**

6. **Write down the advice you would give your friend in Worksheet 6-14.**

7. **Look over the advice in Worksheets 6-13 and 6-14.** Try to restructure your negative thought into a more balanced alternative in Worksheet 6-15.

My most negative thought:

Worksheet 6-13   **Being Your Own Best Friend**

Worksheet 6-14   **Giving the Problem and Solution to Your Best Friend**

Worksheet 6-15   **My Restructured Alternative Thought**

Looking back when time is on your side

What bothers you today seldom has the same impact a few days, weeks or months later. For example, have you ever felt really upset by any of the following?

- ✔ Being cut up in traffic
- ✔ Being embarrassed
- ✔ Locking yourself out of your car
- ✔ Forgetting someone's name
- ✔ A minor illness or injury
- ✔ Spilling something
- ✔ For women (well, mostly women anyway): a ladder in your tights
- ✔ For men (again, for the most part): cutting your face when shaving
- ✔ A bad hair day
- ✔ A parking ticket
- ✔ Being late

These events often give rise to very negative thoughts and highly distressing feelings. Yet on later reflection, you rarely feel that same intensity of emotion. That's because most upsetting events honestly aren't all that important – when you view them in the wider context of your whole life. Here's an example of looking back when time is on your side.

Joe has just moved to a new area. He used to be a keen cricketer but hasn't played for some years. Now that he's divorced, he'd love to get back into it. He knows about a local team but is afraid to put himself forward. What if they don't want him? He's been putting off joining for months because of how scary the whole endeavour seems. Now the season is almost starting, and though he has been working on his fitness, he still feels daunted.

Joe uses a Thought Catcher (see 'Weighing Up the Evidence' at the beginning of this chapter) and identifies his most negative thought: 'I'll make an idiot of myself – I'll probably drop catches AND be out for a duck when I bat.' Joe re-examines the thought from the perspective of having time on his side. He asks himself how he'll look back on his current situation at various times in the future (see Worksheet 6-16). He rates the emotional upset and effect on his life that he feels right now and then he re-rates the impact on his life at the conclusion of the exercise.

Worksheet 6-16 **Joe Puts Time on His Side**

If I really make a fool out of myself, I'll probably feel pretty awful. The impact on my life will feel like 30 or even 40 on a scale of 0–100. I'll still feel embarrassed a week later, and probably see it quite often in my imagination. In six months though, I doubt I'll think about it much at all. And in a year I'll have almost completely forgotten about it. So overall, the effect on my life will likely be around 1.

After working through how powerful his negative thought will seem in the future, Joe feels ready to develop a more realistic alternative thought (see Worksheet 6-17).

Worksheet 6-17 **Joe's Restructured Alternative Thought**

Even if I do look like a twit, it's hardly going to be a life-changing event. I may as well just give it a go. Who knows, I might even make some new friends. There'll be some players worse than me and some better. That's the nature of being in a club.

Putting time on your side doesn't deal with all your thoughts and problems, but it works wonders with quite a few. Joe could also have looked for obvious distortions in his negative thought, such as selective attention and magnifying (see Chapter 5). He also could have taken the negative thought to task (see the previous section 'Putting your thoughts on trial'). Try various strategies to restructure your thoughts in order to find what works best for you and your particular negative thought or thoughts.

Take one of your most distressing negative thoughts. Using the technique of putting time on your side, construct an effective alternative.

1. **Select one of your most upsetting negative thoughts that you catch in your Thought Catcher (see Worksheet 6-6).**

2. **In Worksheet 6-18, rate how much the thought upsets you and impacts on your life at the moment.** Use a scale of 1 to 100, with 100 representing the highest imaginable impact. Write down any feelings you can imagine yourself having.

3. **Think about how your thoughts are likely to change in one week from now.**

4. **Think about how your thoughts are likely to change in six months.**

5. **Think about how your thoughts are likely to change in a year.**

6. **Re-rate how much impact you'll feel as a whole.** Describe your feelings one year later.

7. **In Worksheet 6-19, write down a balanced alternative restructured thought, based on any new perspectives you discover using this strategy.**

My most negative thought:

_____

Worksheet 6-18	Looking Back with Time on My Side

_____
_____
_____

Worksheet 6-19	My Restructured Alternative Thought

_____
_____
_____

Moving from probabilities to possibilities

When you're anxious, worried or depressed, your mind frequently makes catastrophic predictions about the future. People worry both about horrible things that haven't happened, and that bad things that did happen are bound to recur. The fears are diverse as could be, ranging from plane crashes to contamination by germs, and from facing heights to being horribly embarrassed. People predict that practically anything they do will result in horror, misery or unhappiness. Yet such worries typically way overestimate actual probability. Many people do this quite often – even more so when upset.

Predicting negative outcomes can prevent you from taking action. To restructure your thoughts, you first need to identify your negative predictions. You can then re-evaluate your actual risk. The following example illustrates this technique.

Grace's boss, Freya, goes off on maternity leave. Grace is asked to cover Freya's post in her absence. This involves considerable additional responsibility. She does a great job. Soon after the birth, Freya decides she isn't coming back to work. Grace is invited to apply for Freya's job, but now she's beset by doubts and anxiety. She predicts that she won't be offered the job, and if she is, then she won't be able to hack it. She just can't see herself as a manager. Her most undermining thoughts are, 'I'm not the supervisory type – I'm a follower, not a leader. I can't do this.'

Grace restructures her negative predictions using Worksheet 6-20 to identify and test out her predictions.

Worksheet 6-20   **Grace's Restructured Negative Prediction**

1. **How many times have you predicted this outcome and how many times has it actually happened to you?**

   There are other challenges in my life that I thought I couldn't do. I didn't think I'd get through my GCSEs, and I did, quite well. I actually can't think of any times that I failed at something important to me.

2. **How often does this happen to people you know?**

   I can't recall any time while I've been with this company when someone who was invited to apply didn't get the post.

3. **If someone else made this prediction, would you agree?**

   I suppose not. I'd base my prediction on the person's past performance. And mine has been pretty good.

4. **Are you assuming this will happen just because you're afraid it will, or is there a reasonable chance that it really is likely?**

   Of course, there's a small chance I won't be offered the post. But I'm making some unwarranted assumptions. After all, I've done the job successfully for a month.

5. **Do you have any experiences from your past that suggest your dire prediction is unlikely to occur?**

   I sure do! In the past month, I've managed the role pretty well. And I've never really failed at anything, come to think of it.

After filling out her answers to this quiz, Grace decides to reframe the *probability* of failure as a remote *possibility* – and act as if it is unlikely to happen. She goes for the interview, is offered the post and accepts. Grace finds she actually enjoys the new challenges. She looks back over her most negative thought and develops a restructured alternative one (see Worksheet 6-21).

Worksheet 6-21   **Grace's Restructured Alternative Thought**

While I don't 'feel' like a leader, the evidence says otherwise. I'm capable and doing it well!

Take one of your most upsetting negative thoughts and use the following strategy to devise an effective response to that thought.

1. **When you find yourself making a negative prediction about some upcoming event or situation, write down your most distressing negative thought.**

2. **Complete the Restructured Negative Prediction form in Worksheet 6-22.**

3. **Act on your recalculated risk by doing the thing you fear, if logic indicates you should do so.** (Here's where the *B* – for Behavioural – in CBT starts coming into the equation – see Chapter 9 for more information about this.)

4. **In Worksheet 6-23, write out a restructured alternative thought for your original prediction and use it in similar future situations.**

| **Worksheet 6-22** | **My Restructured Negative Prediction** |

My most negative prediction:

1. **How many times have I predicted this outcome and how many times has it actually happened to me?**

\
\
\
\

2. **How often does this happen to people I know?**

\
\
\
\

3. **If someone else made this prediction, would I agree?**

\
\
\
\

4. **Am I assuming this will happen just because I'm afraid it will, or is there a reasonable chance that it really is going to happen?**

\
\
\
\

5. **Do I have any experiences from my past that suggest my dire prediction is unlikely to occur?**

\
\
\
\

Assuming your answers tell you that the odds are in your favour, go ahead and test out your negative predictions. Experiment. Then write an alternative thought (in Worksheet 6-23) for your original negative thought.

If the odds of a negative outcome really are high, however, read the next section, 'Facing the worst', where you'll find techniques for coping with such outcomes.

Worksheet 6-23	My Restructured Alternative Thought

Facing the worst

The preceding section shows you how to recalculate risks because generally, when people are depressed or anxious, they greatly overestimate the probability of catastrophes – while usually grossly underestimating their abilities to cope.

But just in case you're starting to think otherwise, we're not trying to convince you that horrible things never happen. They do. People get sick, accidents happen and relationships end. What then? Imagining yourself facing the worst is a useful exercise – it helps you see that you can get through anything you fear. The following example shows you how facing the worst helps Joshua make a decision and develop a restructured alternative to his negative thought.

Joshua has been single for the past 20 years. Since his painful divorce, he's been footloose and fancy free, with any number of casual relationships. Between work and his frenetic social life, he's steered well clear of any serious relationship. Now at age 50, Joshua fears he's fallen in love with someone special, who feels the same way about him. He's terrified that things won't work out, and if he settles down and commits to the relationship, ultimately he'll be rejected, and he's convinced that he just couldn't bear that.

Joshua faces the worst in Worksheet 6-24, identifying and working through his greatest fear.

Worksheet 6-24	Joshua's Facing the Worst

Joshua's most negative thought: I'd rather just have casual relationships as long as I can, and perhaps even be alone in the long-term, than risk the pain of rejection again. I really don't think I could deal with that.

1. Have I ever coped with anything like this in the past?

I was rejected by my ex. It took me quite a while, but I got through it. Today, I'm actually fairly happy.

2. How much will this affect my life a year from now?

If she rejects me, I'll be hurt and alone. But I've been fine on my own – and have always managed to find someone for a fling whenever I wanted. A year from now, I suspect I may be sad, but I'm pretty sure I'll be over the worst of the rejection.

(continued)

Worksheet 6-24 *(continued)*

3. **Do I know people who coped with something like this? How did they do it?**

I have lots of friends who've lost relationships. They got through it by staying active and seeking support from others. A couple of my friends went to counselling, which they said helped.

4. **Do I know anyone I could turn to for help or support?**

Over the years, I've developed a pretty good network of friends. I know I could get support from them. My family has always been there for me, too.

5. **Can I think of a creative new possibility that could result from this challenge?**

If this relationship doesn't work, I think I'll explore the possibility of voluntary work abroad. I've always wanted to do something like that. I love travel and meeting new people. I think that experience would be very meaningful to me.

Now, Joshua's ready to devise a more realistic alternative restructured thought (see Worksheet 6-25).

Worksheet 6-25 **Joshua's Alternative Restructured Thought**

If I do get rejected, I can handle it. I think I love this woman, and I'm a lot older — my days of sowing my wild oats are behind me. Now I feel more like taking the risk, committing myself to this relationship and seeing what happens.

Take one of your most negative thoughts and face the worst in order to devise an effective response to that thought.

1. **When you find yourself thinking of a catastrophic outcome that you feel you just couldn't cope with, write down your most negative thought.**

2. **Face the worst, using Worksheet 6-26.**

3. **Restructure your negative thought with an alternative, using Worksheet 6-27.**

Worksheet 6-26 **Facing the Worst**

My most negative thought:

1. **Have I ever dealt with anything like this in the past?**

_____

_____

_____

_____

2. How much will this affect my life a year from now?

_____

_____

_____

_____

3. Do I know people who coped with something like this? How did they do it?

_____

_____

_____

_____

4. Do I know anyone I could turn to for help or support?

_____

_____

_____

_____

5. Can I think of a creative new possibility that this challenge might lead to?

_____

_____

_____

_____

Worksheet 6-27   **My Alternative Restructured Thought**

Use the techniques in this chapter to combat your negative thoughts. Take each thought and find an alternative. The more thoughts you restructure, the better you'll get – both at the restructuring process and in how you feel.

Reflecting on Chapter 6

This chapter has several exercises and ideas for overcoming anxious and depressed thinking. Work through it carefully – it isn't a timed test. Do download any extra forms you need from www.dummies.com/go/adwb. After completing the exercises and looking at your thoughts in new and different ways, take time to reflect on your new insights using the space in Worksheet 6-28.

Worksheet 6-28	My Reflections

Chapter 7

Seeing Clearly: Gaining a New Perspective

*B*efore getting out of bed every morning, most people open their eyes and look at their world. Some people then put on their glasses, others put in contact lenses, and some need neither. Looking through a correcting lens can improve vision. But many people don't realise that everyone looks at life through different lenses at different times. And some of these lenses may be distorting.

Life-lenses are strongly held beliefs or assumptions that you have about yourself, your relationships with others and your world. They powerfully influence how you respond to, interpret and feel about events, even though you may not be aware that you're looking through them.

Perhaps you know people who view the world through rose-tinted spectacles. As perpetual optimists, they see the best in everything and everyone. On the other hand, you probably know some who seem to see life primarily in shades of grey. They expect the worst, rarely seeing the positive side of things.

In this chapter, we help you understand the nature of life-lenses and how they are responsible for colouring your view of the world, people, events and even your self-image. This chapter helps you identify whether your lenses are dirty, cracked, grey, smoky, rose-coloured or clear. We enable you to identify which lenses you look through, recognise the distress they can cause and show you how to update and replace problematic life-lenses with new ones that suit you far better.

Examining Your Distorted Perceptions

Like everyone else, you go about your daily life with certain underlying assumptions that you take as givens. You probably assume day follows night, if you drop something heavy, it usually falls straight down, and if you stand in the way of a moving vehicle, you'll get run over. Not questioning these assumptions makes life more predictable – and safer!

Life-lenses are special types of unquestioned assumptions. These assumptions or beliefs influence how you feel about yourself and your experiences. For example, you may look through a *perfectionist* lens and believe that you must always be perfect. Or perhaps yours is a *vulnerability* lens, so you see the world as a dangerous place. As you explore the lenses, or *schemas*, underpinning your assumptions, you can see how they contribute to the foundation of your most distressing emotions, such as depression, anxiety, worry, irritability, apprehension and even anger.

Life-lenses are the broad themes or assumptions you live by. These themes directly influence the kinds of thoughts you have and, in turn, how you feel about what happens to you. Each life-lens can be activated by many types of events.

Susan and Diane work as sales assistants at a local department store. The manager of their department leaves, and both apply for the vacant post. Although they're both well qualified, an external applicant is appointed. Susan reacts angrily, saying, 'I deserved that job. They had no right giving it to an outsider. Don't expect me to be welcoming or cooperative.'

Diane reacts quite differently. She feels miserable and sighs, 'I'm sure they made the right decision picking someone else. I really shouldn't have got my hopes up. I know I'm not management material.'

Susan and Diane have different lenses. Susan has an *entitlement* lens. She believes that she always deserves the best, that the world owes her and whatever she wants should be hers. On the other hand, Diane has the lens of *inadequacy*. She thinks that she's not good enough and that others are more skilled and talented than her. Diane assumes she couldn't do the job even though her supervisor said she has the appropriate ability and background.

Same event. Different thoughts and feelings. Susan's entitlement life-lens makes her prone to irritability and anger when she's thwarted. Diane's inadequacy lens leads towards depression when her ability is judged.

Susan and Diane see many different events in their lives from their particular distorted perception. For example, when they're both unexpectedly stuck in traffic, they view this event through their own life-lenses and thus have different thoughts and feelings. Susan's entitlement life-lens leads her to feel rage and think, 'No one in this town knows how to drive. What idiots!' Diane, who looks through a life-lens of inadequacy, berates herself, 'I should have left earlier. Why didn't I listen to the traffic report this morning? I'm an utter idiot!'

With some understanding of life-lenses, you're ready to take a look at which lenses may be affecting you and your life. After all, changing the way you feel starts with identifying your distorted perceptions. If you aren't aware of your own life-lenses, you're powerless to do anything about them.

Worksheet 7-1 helps clarify which life-lenses may be causing you trouble. After you identify them, we tell you a little more about how they work, where they come from and most importantly, what you can do about them. Before you start seeing which lenses apply to you, bear in mind the following:

- ✔ **Answer as honestly as possible.** Sometimes, people respond how they think they 'should' rather than by being honest. Self-deception isn't useful, and there's no one else you need to try and fool.

- ✔ **Take time reflecting on various events and situations you've experienced that are relevant to each lens.** For example, in answering questions about fearing abandonment versus avoiding intimacy, think both about relationships you've had, as well as about how you feel and react to those close to you. Don't rush this task.

- ✔ **Base your answer on how you feel and react in situations that relate to each lens.** For example, if you frequently feel inadequate but know in your head that you're actually not, base your answer on how you feel when your adequacy comes into question – perhaps when you're expected to perform.

✔ **Don't worry about inconsistencies.** As you can see in Worksheet 7-1, lenses come in opposite pairs. You may well find yourself using one lens at one time and the exact opposite at another. So, if you're a perfectionist, you may also frequently feel inadequate on making a mistake. Or if you frequently feel unworthy and undeserving, you may also find yourself feeling quite angry and entitled when your needs unexpectedly go unmet. People often flip between opposite lenses, so don't let a little inconsistency bother you.

✔ **Answer on the basis of how often each lens describes you.** If only certain bits of the description apply, just underline them, rating yourself on how often they apply to you.

Use a scale of 1 to 5 to rate the frequency with which each lens describes you:

✔ **1** is almost never

✔ **2** represents occasionally

✔ **3** is for sometimes

✔ **4** means usually

✔ **5** is almost always

Worksheet 7-1	Identifying Distorted Life-Lenses
Lens	*Opposing View*
___Unworthy: I don't feel like I deserve to have good things happen to me. I feel uncomfy whenever someone does something nice for me.	___Entitled: I deserve the best of everything. I should have almost anything I want. If my needs unexpectedly go unmet, I feel threatened, sad or angry.
___Fearing abandonment: I need lots of reassurance to feel loved. I feel lost without someone in my life and worry about losing those I care about. I'm jealous and cling to my loved ones because of my fear.	___Avoiding intimacy: I don't like getting close to anyone. I'd rather steer clear of any emotional involvement. I don't really want anybody in my life.
___Inadequate: I feel as if I'm not as talented or skilful as most others. I just don't measure up. I don't like taking on things I've never done before if they look difficult.	___Perfectionist: I feel that I've got to do everything perfectly. I feel like there's a right and a wrong way, and that I want to do things right.
___Guilty: I feel like everything that goes wrong is my fault. I worry about whether I've done the wrong thing. I can't stand hurting anyone else.	___Without a conscience: I don't let stupid things like morality and conscience stop me if I want something badly enough. I never care what other people think.
___Vulnerable: Disasters frequently happen. I worry a lot about the future. I'm scared; and the world feels like a dangerous place.	___Invulnerable: I'm invincible – nothing can ever hurt me. The world treats me extremely well. I'm always very lucky, and never worry about taking precautions.
___Help-seeking: I depend heavily on others and feel better when they take care of me. I can't handle life on my own.	___Assistance-spurning: I hate asking for favours, and I hate when others try to help me.

(continued)

Worksheet 7-1 *(continued)*

Lens	*Opposing View*
___*Impulsive:* If I want to do something, I follow my impulses. It's hard for me to set limits with people, so I tend to get walked on. I'd rather express my emotions than control them.	___*Highly controlled:* Nothing's worse than losing control. I never let anyone see how I feel. I like to always have my hand on the rudder. I don't like working for someone else, and I can't stand leaving my fate to others.

Any life-lens that you rate as 3 or above probably gives you trouble occasionally. Don't worry if you find that you rate many life-lenses as 3 or above. Loads of people have a range of these problematic assumptions. Change takes time, but you can do it – one lens at a time.

Now reflect on what you discovered about any of your problematic life-lenses. In Worksheet 7-2, jot down thoughts about how your life-lenses may be causing you to have troubling emotions. Don't worry if you're not quite sure of the connections; we give you more ways of seeing the lenses' influence on your life in the next few sections of this chapter.

Worksheet 7-2 **My Reflections**

_____

_____

_____

_____

Focusing on how you see the world

You may wonder just what mischief life-lenses can get up to and why we say they're the root cause of most emotional turmoil. The examples in this section give you an idea of their tricks. After you complete this section, we bet you'll be amazed at just how much life-lenses colour your vision and your emotional life.

After you identify your life-lenses, take time to consider more examples of how the lenses lead to problematic thoughts and feelings. Notice how life-lenses consist of broad themes, while thoughts are specific to a given event.

Jim, Paul and Will are friends and neighbours. All three have teenage daughters of a similar age who also are best friends. One evening, the girls are late home. The three dads have very different reactions. See how life-lenses influence their view of this identical event and each dad's response to his daughter.

Jim has a *guilty* life-lens. He feels as though he's done something wrong, even when he isn't at fault (see Worksheet 7-3).

Worksheet 7-3	Jim's Life-Lens Perspective	
Event: My daughter is half an hour late home.		
Life-Lens	**Thoughts**	**Feelings**
Guilty. Worrying if I've done something wrong.	I must be an awful dad, otherwise she'd be here at her usual time.	Miserable and depressed.

Paul likes to be in charge and feels uncomfortable when others challenge his authority. His lens is one of *over-control* (see Worksheet 7-4).

Worksheet 7-4	Paul's Life-Lens Perspective	
Event: My daughter is half an hour late home.		
Life-Lens	**Thoughts**	**Feelings**
Over-control. I like to be in charge of everyone and everything.	How dare she be late? I'm her father! She'd better show some respect and do what she's told.	Anger.

Will's predominant life-lens is *fearing abandonment*. He worries that the people he cares about will leave him and needs frequent reassurance that he's loved (see Worksheet 7-5).

Worksheet 7-5	Will's Life-Lens Perspective	
Event: My daughter is half an hour late home.		
Life-Lens	**Thoughts**	**Feelings**
I worry about losing people I care about; I don't think I could stand it if I lost someone close to me.	Oh no, she's probably had an accident. She might be hurt. I couldn't go on if I lost her	Fear and anxiety.

These three examples show how life-lenses affect people's thoughts and feelings. And now? You guessed it! It's your turn to discover the influence of your lenses using Worksheet 7-6. Just reading about them isn't nearly as effective as actively working through them – so off you go!

1. **When events happen and you notice distressing feelings, write down the event.**

   An event can be something happening in your world or something that runs through your mind. Do be specific.

2. **In the middle column, write down the thoughts or interpretations you have about the event.**

   Describe how you perceive or think about it. If you find this tricky, Chapter 6 gives more information about events and thoughts.

3. **In the right-hand column, write down any feelings you have about the event.**

   Refer to Chapter 4's Daily Unpleasant Emotions List for suggestions.

4. **Review your distorted life-lenses in Worksheet 7-1 (you did fill it in, didn't you?).**

   In the left-hand column, note down the lens or lenses that best describe your thoughts and feelings. Briefly define the lens, based on your reflections in Worksheet 7-2. You can tailor the definition in any way, so it fits you.

5. **In Worksheet 7-7, reflect on what this exercise tells you about your problematic emotions, and where they come from.**

Worksheet 7-6   **The Influence of My Life-Lenses**

Event:

Life-Lens	*Thoughts*	*Feelings*

Event:

Life-Lens	*Thoughts*	*Feelings*

Event:

Life-Lens	*Thoughts*	*Feelings*

For more copies of this form, visit www.dummies.com/go/adwb. The more examples you do of this exercise, the better you understand the influence your life-lenses have on you.

Worksheet 7-7   **My Reflections**

Understanding the origins of your perceptions

Usually, people's perspectives, both distorted and clear, are established in childhood. You don't automatically see yourself as inadequate, undeserving, entitled or as a perfectionist. You learn these patterns through repeated experiences. Life-lenses emerge from emotionally powerful events, including abuse, abandonment, betrayal, criticism, natural disasters, loss and rejection.

Some distorted lenses even develop from over-concern, rather than neglect. Some parents who worry excessively may as a consequence overprotect their children, who subsequently feel vulnerable. Other parents overindulge their children, ostensibly through love and caring, but their kids may end up feeling entitled.

When searching to understand and change your perspectives on life, reflect on how your lenses were formed in the first place. When you understand the origins, you can let go of both the idea that you're a mess – and that you're responsible for being one! Self-forgiveness releases energy that you can use to design new lenses for clearer vision.

Sophie struggles with depression and anxiety. She fills in Worksheet 7-1 on distorted life-lenses and identifies the life-lenses of avoiding intimacy and being entitled. She also realises that she's a perfectionist, who swings to the opposite position of feeling inadequate when she makes a mistake. Sophie reflects on how her childhood has contributed to her life-lenses. She then completes the Childhood Origins of Life-Lenses exercise shown in Worksheet 7-8 and reflects on her findings in Worksheet 7-9.

Worksheet 7-8	**Sophie's Childhood Origins of Life-Lenses**
Lens	*Opposing View*
Unworthy: This life-lens doesn't apply to me.	Entitled: My mother always made me feel like our family was better than others. I have to admit she spoiled me, too.
Fearing abandonment: This life-lens doesn't really fit.	Avoiding intimacy: Although I was told I was special, I never felt anyone listened to me. Whenever I was sad or lonely, my parents told me how lucky I was to have all the toys, clothes and luxuries I did. I decided it was better to never need anyone.
Inadequate: Whenever I made a mistake, my father made me feel stupid.	Perfectionist: My family was incredibly concerned about how we looked to others. My parents were really critical, so I tried to be perfect.

Worksheet 7-9	Sophie's Reflections

When I look back on my childhood, I realise that my family was pretty cold. They expected me to be perfect, and when I wasn't, they sneered at me. No wonder I feel anxious about being perfect, and feel depressed when I'm not. There wasn't a lot of love in my family, so I've learned to keep my distance from others. I was taught that possessions and status are more important than people, so I've put practically all my energies into getting the things I want. But I feel empty and lonely.

To explore the origins of your life-lenses in the same way that Sophie did, follow these instructions and complete worksheets 7-10 and 7-11.

1. **Review each life-lens that you rated as 3 or above on your Identifying Distorted Life-Lenses questionnaire (see Worksheet 7-1).**

2. **Think back on how events in your childhood formed the basis for each life-lens.**

   Feel free to look back at Chapter 2 for help with ways of recalling past feelings and events.

3. **Jot down anything from your childhood that you believe may have contributed to each perspective.**

4. **After you complete this exercise, take some time to reflect on any new insights you discover and record them in Worksheet 7-11.**

Worksheet 7-10	Childhood Origins of Life-Lenses
Lens	*Opposing View*
Unworthy:	Entitled:
Fearing abandonment:	Avoiding intimacy
Inadequate:	Perfectionist:
Guilty:	Without a conscience:
Vulnerable:	Invulnerable:

Lens	*Opposing View*
Help-seeking:	Assistance-spurning:
Impulsive:	Highly controlled:

Worksheet 7-11	**My Reflections**

Replacing Your Distorting Lenses

After you complete the exercises in the preceding sections, you're likely to identify which lenses cause you problems. In this section, we give you three techniques for replacing any distorted lenses. It would be great if you could just chuck them out. But old habits die hard – these were forged amid the fires of childhood turmoil (see 'Understanding the origins of your perceptions'). So you need to proceed slowly but surely.

You may find replacing those old lenses is more challenging than you expected. Despite committing loads of time and energy, when you're tired or stressed, you find yourself swapping your new perspective for the old. That's to be expected – getting the hang of seeing life through your new perspective takes time. You're bound to fall back into old habits from time to time. Just aim to use the new lenses more often than the old. Eventually, you'll discover you can't even find the old ones. If the task is too difficult, do see a qualified counsellor or psychologist.

Distinguishing between 'then' and 'now'

Life-lenses develop from emotionally significant events in childhood, and they make sense when seen in context. While your world has no doubt changed considerably over the years, you probably still look through many of the same old lenses, even though they don't give you a clear vision of present-day reality.

As you can see in Worksheet 7-8, Sophie developed the life-lens of perfectionism. As a child, she was sternly criticised whenever she was less than perfect. Her lens helped her minimise that criticism and was a healthy adaptation to her life at the time. But today, as an adult this lens causes her anxiety, stress and even depression when she fails. Plus today, no one in her life is nearly as critical as her father was. So she no longer needs to be perfect to escape criticism. But her perfectionist lens distorts her vision. Sophie completes the Then and Now Exercise in Worksheet 7-12 to help her understand how her past experiences cause her to overreact to current triggers. Seeing this connection helps her to replace her life-lens.

Worksheet 7-12	Sophie's Then and Now Exercise	
Problematic Life-Lens	*Childhood Image(s)*	*Current Triggers*
Perfectionist: I feel like I must do everything perfectly, and if I don't, it's awful.	My mother would scream at me if I got my clothes dirty. My father was never satisfied with anything but straight A's. Even when I got them, he was never impressed. Both of my parents always talked about other people critically. They put people down for just about anything.	If I get snag or ladder my tights, I freak out. And a stain on my blouse drives me totally batty. I can't stand being evaluated at work. I lose sleep for days. Even just one rating that's less than 'outstanding' can trigger my depression. I constantly judge everything I do — my hair, my housecleaning, my job, and sometimes I'm over-critical of others about trivial things.

Adam comes from a warm and caring family. When he was eleven, his parents moved so he'd be in the catchment area of a good school. He was averagely bright, reasonable at sports and had many friends. You'd guess he was unlikely to develop any distorted lenses.

But on a beautiful summer's day, a highly disturbed person went on a violent rampage through the school. Adam witnessed the event and was slightly injured. He subsequently suffered from nightmares, experienced intrusive images of the event and was easily startled. Understandably, Adam developed a vulnerable life-lens.

As an adult, anxiety often overwhelms Adam. His vulnerable life-lens is activated by events only superficially similar to the original trauma. Adam completes the Then and Now Exercise in Worksheet 7-13 in order to help himself understand how his past experiences contribute to his current responses. This connection helps him start replacing his lens.

Worksheet 7-13	Adam's Then and Now Exercise	
Problematic Life-Lens	*Childhood Image(s)*	*Current Triggers*
Vulnerable: I'm scared; the world feels very dangerous.	The image of a gun suddenly pointing at me is burned deeply into my brain. I hear the screams of the kids. I see blood and feel searing pain. I thought I was going to die.	When someone cuts me up in traffic, I feel the same surge of adrenaline and fear. Crowds make me feel nervous. I find myself watching my back.

Problematic Life-Lens	Childhood Image(s)	Current Triggers
		Whenever I meet someone new, I get anxious and have issues about trust. I question the motives of even the nicest people.

Right! It's your turn! Complete the Then and Now Exercise (see Worksheet 7-14) for each problematic life-lens you identified in Worksheet 7-1 earlier in this chapter. Worksheet 7-14 is a useful way of reminding yourself that your feelings and reactions today have more to do with times long gone than with your current reality.

1. **In the left-hand column, identify any distorted lens rated as 3 or above on Worksheet 7-1.**

   Briefly describe each lens, using Worksheet 7-2. Tailor the definition to the best fit.

2. **Reflect on your childhood and, in the middle column, record any memories or images that probably had something to do with the development of that lens.**

   Look over Worksheet 7-10 for ideas.

3. **Be alert for which events trigger which lens, noting them down in the column on the right.**

Because each lens often has it's exact opposite, plus a variety of triggers, you need to fill out a separate form for each distorted lens. Whenever a lens is triggered, look over this Then and Now Exercise to remind you what your reaction's all about.

Worksheet 7-14	My Then and Now Exercise	
Problematic Life-Lens	*Childhood Image(s)*	*Current Triggers*

Check out www.dummies.com/go/adwb to download extra copies of this form.

All distorted lenses require a range of strategies to see any improvement. No single exercise is likely to be the magic solution. Do always consider professional help if your own efforts don't suffice.

After you complete the exercise, take some time to reflect on what you find out about yourself and your feelings. Record your reflections in Worksheet 7-15.

Worksheet 7-15	My Reflections

Carrying out a cost-benefit analysis of current life-lenses

Replacing lenses triggers some anxiety in most people because you believe (whether consciously or unconsciously) that your lenses protect or benefit you in some important ways. For example, with a vulnerable lens, you probably think that seeing the world as dangerous helps you avoid harm. Or looking through a dependency lens, the chances are that if you think in this way, you can find the help from others that you truly need.

But you may not have as much awareness of the costs of your lenses. They can make you pay, big time! We now reveal the hidden costs of distorted lenses. Only if you're convinced that a particular lens overall does more harm than good will you have the motivation to change it.

Karl, a 22-year-old engineering apprentice, loves a good time. He sees his world through an impulsive, minimal control lens. Karl rarely sets limits on himself or others – he doesn't think he needs to. He just says what he thinks and does what he wants. His high intelligence and easy-going personality have enabled him to get by – until recently.

Lately, Karl's drinking, which has never been under great control, has escalated. He hangs out at pubs until closing time. The resulting hangovers often mean he's late in or doesn't pitch up for training courses, and his results start falling below the pass level. Karl gets a verbal warning in the same week he is breathalysed and found to be over the limit. He staggers under this double whammy and starts getting depressed. Alarmed, his parents push him to go and see Occupational Health.

The OH consultant refers him for psychological therapy, so off he trots. After discovering that Karl believes he has the right to be impulsive, his therapist suggests that he fill out a Cost–Benefit Analysis of this perspective. And as it's tricky to spot the costs of any perspective, his therapist suggests that he first identify any advantages of this lens (see Worksheet 7-16).

Worksheet 7-16	Karl's Cost-Benefit Analysis (Part I)

Life-Lens: Impulsive. I believe it's great to just chill. I should be able to do what I feel like. It's great to express feelings and do what feels good.

Benefits	Costs
It feels good to do what I want.	
I know how to have a good time.	
I don't have to be a slave to rules and do what I'm told.	

Benefits	Costs
My friends know I speak my mind and that I'm honest.	
I like showing how I feel no matter what.	
I don't have to deny my needs.	

Karl's pretty quick to list the benefits of his distorted lens. In fact, at this point, he's not even sure it's distorted at all. However, his therapist urges him to carefully consider any negative consequences, or costs, of his impulsivity lens. Worksheet 7-17 shows Karl's completed Cost-Benefit Analysis.

Worksheet 7-17   **Karl's Cost-Benefit Analysis (Part II)**

Life-Lens: Impulsive. I believe it's great to just chill. I should be able to do what I feel like. It's great to express feelings and do what feels good.

Benefits	Costs
It feels good to do what I want.	It feels good at the time, but later I wind up hungover – which feels anything but!
I know how to have a good time.	I have a good time for a while, but is it worth risking my apprenticeship?
I don't have to be a slave to rules and do what I'm told.	When I ignored the drink/driving rules, I spent the night in the cells. I never want to do that again!
My friends know I speak my mind, and that I'm honest.	I've hurt some pretty good friends by being so blunt. I don't like doing that.
I like showing how I feel no matter what.	It's not always that clever to say everything I feel. I'm a lousy bluffer, and my uncontrolled temper gets me into trouble.
I don't have to deny my needs.	Eventually, this will all catch up with me. My life's spinning out of control this way.

As Karl completes his Cost-Benefit Analysis, a realisation dawns: 'My perspective on impulsivity is ruining my life!' He feels strongly like doing something about what he now sees as a real problem.

A Cost-Benefit Analysis helps you boost your motivation to replace problematic life-lenses. Take your time and carefully complete Worksheet 7-18.

1. **Choose one of the distorted lenses that you identified in Worksheet 7-1 and write it at the top of the worksheet.**

   Write a brief definition of it, based on your reflections in Worksheet 7-2. Tailor the definition to best fit you.

2. **Consider all the possible advantages to this perspective and record them in the left-hand column.**

   Some may spring readily to mind, while others may take considerable thought. Write down everything you come up with.

3. **In the right-hand column, note all conceivable disadvantages to seeing the world from this perspective.**

   Considering the advantages first, and then moving on to the counter-arguments is often easier. After you do this, add to the list any additional costs that you come up with.

4. **Review your Cost-Benefit Analysis carefully.**

   Make a decision about which column carries the most weight – the disadvantages (costs) or the advantages (benefits). Write down your conclusions in Worksheet 7-19.

Worksheet 7-18	My Cost-Benefit Analysis
Life-Lens:	
Benefits	*Costs*

Go to www.dummies.com/go/adwbfd to print out extra copies of this form, and fill one out for each problematic life-lens you identify.

Worksheet 7-19	My Reflections

Taking action: Modelling a new look

We designed the exercises in the previous two sections to increase your motivation and set the stage for replacing your lenses. In this section, our guidelines for developing an action plan show you how to prepare for a brand-new look. Ready . . . steady . . . go!

To tackle the next step, start by working out what effect your life-lens has had on you, your emotions and your life. For example, if you have a perfectionist perspective, you may find this leads to high levels of tension and worry as you fret over every little error.

The next step is to devise a plan that tests the assumptions behind your life-lens. For the perfectionist lens, you can test out the assumption that you must never make mistakes by trying an experiment. Deliberately make small mistakes – and then see what happens!

To help you devise your own action steps, Worksheet 7-20 contains some examples for each distorted lens. Be creative with your experiments, but don't go overboard!

Worksheet 7-20	Experiments to Test Perspectives
Distorted Perspective	*Opposing View*
Unworthy: I'll ask someone for what I want.	Entitled: I'll stop insisting that others meet my needs.
I'll repeatedly tell myself that I deserve good things.	I'll start regularly giving to charity.
Fearing abandonment: I'll resist checking on my loved ones so often.	Avoiding intimacy: I'll reveal more about myself and express my feelings to others.
I'll stop asking for reassurance that my husband loves me.	I'll join a social organisation and work on getting to know the people there.

(continued)

Worksheet 7-20 *(continued)*

Distorted Perspective	*Opposing View*
Inadequate: I'll join Toastmasters and learn to give public speeches.	**Perfectionist:** I'll wear unmatched socks and see what happens.
I'll volunteer to lead a project at work.	I'll try to make as many trivial mistakes as I can in one day (walk in through the exit, park over a line in the car park and so on).
Guilty: When I feel guilty about something, I'll ask a trusted friend if I'm being too hard on myself.	**Without a conscience:** I'll work hard to find something to apologise for at least once a week.
When I feel at fault, I'll make a list of all the possible causes of the problem.	I'll admit to making mistakes.
Vulnerable: I'll do something I'm afraid of, such as fly in an aeroplane.	**Invulnerable:** I'll undertake first aid training, and see what I learn.
I'll stop overprotecting my kids so much.	I'll always wear my seat belt when I'm in the back seat, and won't wait to be reminded.
Help-seeking: I'll complete a project entirely on my own.	**Assistance-spurning:** I'll ask someone for help with something once a week.
I'll offer help without waiting to be asked.	I'll start asking for directions when I'm lost.
Impulsivity: I'll join the AA in case I break down.	**Overcontrolled:** I'll leave more decisions up to my partner.
I'll join a gym and develop both my muscles and my self-discipline.	I'll shut up and stop giving unwanted advice to my adult son.

These sample action steps are just ideas, but if one or more look helpful, great! Your action steps do need to specifically address the ways in which your distorted perspectives affect your life. Make your steps small, doable and entirely about you and your issue. After you design your action steps, make sure you actually do them! And if you have trouble carrying out some action steps, try breaking them down into smaller steps.

Fill out Worksheet 7-21 with your Life-Lens Action Steps.

Worksheet 7-21	My Life-Lens Action Steps
Lens	*Opposing View*
Unworthy:	Entitled:
Fearing abandonment:	Avoiding intimacy:
Inadequate:	Perfectionist:
Guilty:	Without a conscience:
Vulnerable:	Invulnerable:
Help-seeking:	Assistance-spurning:
Impulsivity:	Overcontrolled:

The lenses you see through were largely formed around events in your childhood, often those over which you had little control. So you certainly don't deserve blame for seeing the world through them. However, the responsibility is yours for doing something about replacing them. It's a slow, arduous process, and takes patience, but the new, clear vision that results from your efforts is worth the wait.

Squeeze your eyes shut. Now open them up. How's your vision? Any clearer? What thoughts come to mind? Jot down a few of your thoughts and feelings in Worksheet 7-22.

Worksheet 7-22	My Reflections

Chapter 8

Maintaining Mindfulness and Achieving Acceptance

In This Chapter

▶ Taking your thoughts less seriously

▶ Embracing your feelings

▶ Staying connected to the present

Sit quietly for a few moments and pay attention to your breathing. Feel the air as it passes through your nostrils and slowly fills your lungs. Experience the sensation of your lungs deflating as you exhale. If thoughts come into your mind, notice them as an observer and allow them to float past. Re-focus on your breathing.

This breathing exercise is designed to introduce you to mindfulness. *Mindfulness* is a state of awareness of the present, in the absence of judgement, analysis and reasoning. In other words, it's awareness, without thinking about your thinking or entering into dialogue with your thoughts. To achieve mindfulness, you've got to get the hang of *acceptance,* which involves patience and tolerance as well as willingness to feel and experience 'what is' without resistance. In this chapter, we guide you through the process of accepting your thoughts and feelings, so that you can achieve mindfulness.

Appreciating the Benefits of Losing Your Mind!

You aren't the same as your mind. Sounds weird, doesn't it? But read on, and all will become clear.

Separating spectator from referee

Sit back and wait for a thought to enter your mind. There's no rush. One's bound to come along pretty soon. When it does, ask yourself this question: Who noticed that thought? The obvious answer is *you.* The you that observes, breathes and experiences – the you who isn't the same entity as your thoughts or your mind.

The following exercise helps you connect with the mindful, observant you by first demonstrating how easily you can get caught up in thoughts that come from an overly evaluative, judgemental and critical state of mind.

Have you ever sat at your desk, surrounded by stuff requiring attention, and tried looking at it all as if it belonged to someone else? (You wish!) The following are some of our critical descriptions of our workspaces that an outsider would probably totally agree with:

✔ Piles of papers are stacked everywhere. What a mess!

✔ How can anyone do any work in this place?

✔ Who could spend hour upon hour at a keyboard, chained to one spot?

✔ How many glasses and cups are going to accumulate before we run out of clean ones in the kitchen?

✔ That picture on the wall is wrinkled and warped, and hanging at an angle.

✔ The tangled mess of computer wires under the desk looks like a snake pit.

✔ How many books are on those shelves? And just look at the dust on them!

✔ Who's going to make a start on the filing? And when?

✔ With all this chaos, we'll never finish this ^*!&*%#^@ book!

Coming up with these critical, judgemental observations is surprisingly easy. You'll probably find accessing the observing, non-evaluative you much more difficult. The observing, non-evaluative you merely looks at and experiences what's around you, without those negative evaluations. Here's what we experience when we're being mindful:

> *Right now, the radio is softly playing a golden oldie in the background. The aroma of newly baked bread is mouth-wateringly delicious. A clock ticks. We see papers piled in stacks of varying heights, the flat computer screen, smooth-finished wooden desks and shelves, and the new cordless telephone. The different-coloured cables make patterns under the desk. The plastic keys of the keyboard are smooth and light grey. We are aware of the textured fabric of our chairs, white paper reflected in the quartz lamp's light and a freshly brewed hot cappuccino. We also feel our breath gently going in and out.*

The first judgemental look at our present moment leads to feelings of irritability and of being both overwhelmed and discouraged. When we simply allow ourselves to experience what's in front of us without evaluation, we actually feel quite relaxed. The tasks at hand seem less daunting. We stop all that self-criticism and soon become absorbed with writing.

Try this three-part exercise. Even if you're thinking 'This is daft', 'How can this possibly help me?' or 'I'll do this when I have more time', don't give in to those thoughts. Just work through Worksheets 8-1, 8-2 and 8-3 NOW! It only takes a few minutes, honest!

1. **Sit and look at everything around you.**

2. **Find something negative in everything you see.**

3. **Write down every critical thought that comes to mind in Worksheet 8-1.**

4. **Notice how you feel when you finish and write those feelings down.**

Worksheet 8-1	Your Critical State of Mind
Critical thoughts:	
1.	
2.	
3.	
4.	
5.	

6. _____

7. _____

8. _____

9. _____

10. _____

Feelings after writing critical thoughts: _____

_____

_____

_____

_____

1. **Take a fresh look around you, but this time don't judge or evaluate.**

   Connect with your senses. Describe what you experience as objectively as you can. Record it in Worksheet 8-2. Ignore all structure, punctuation and grammar.

2. **Notice how you feel now. Jot these feelings down in Worksheet 8-2.**

3. **Reflect on this exercise and write your conclusions in Worksheet 8-3.**

Worksheet 8-2	**Observing Your S.tate of Mind**

Observations, sensations and experiences: _____

_____

_____

_____

_____

Feelings after writing observations and experiences: _____

_____

_____

_____

_____

Worksheet 8-3	**My Reflections**

_____

_____

_____

_____

_____

Changing the frequency: Tuning in and out of your mind's chatter

Depressed and anxious minds just jabber away, usually predicting catastrophes, making critical judgements and generally seeing the world as a scary place. A part of your mind acts almost like a sports commentator, not only describing what's happening to you, but also making value judgements about you, including:

- ✔ I'm not good enough.
- ✔ I'm a terrible person.
- ✔ I'll never make it.
- ✔ I don't deserve good things.
- ✔ I'm pretty useless.
- ✔ I'll fail if I try.
- ✔ I can't do this.
- ✔ No one will like me.
- ✔ If I ask him/her out, s/he'll reject me.
- ✔ I'm bound to be unmasked as the fake I am.
- ✔ I'm going to fall apart.
- ✔ What if I get cancer?
- ✔ I might throw up.
- ✔ What if I'm reduced to tears?

Do you ever have thoughts like those in the preceding list? Tune into them using this exercise.

1. **Listen to your mind's chatter as it growls through your head.**

2. **In the left-hand column of Worksheet 8-4, write down the comments that you hear repeatedly.**

3. **Think of a good friend of yours. Change your mind chatter into a statement that applies to your friend and re-write that statement in the right-hand column.**

   For example, change 'I'm bound to be unmasked as the fake I am' to 'Richard, you're bound to be unmasked as the fake you are.' Or change 'I'm a terrible person' to 'You're a terrible person, Richard.'

4. **Imagine how you'd feel saying this rewritten statement to your friend and record your reflections in Worksheet 8-5.**

Worksheet 8-4	Re-Directed Mind Chatter
Mind Chatter	*Mind Chatter Said to a Friend*

Mind Chatter	Mind Chatter Said to a Friend

Worksheet 8-5   **My Reflections**

Would you really say the statements in Worksheet 8-4 to a friend – let alone to yourself? So how about you consider being nicer to yourself – and to your friend. Stop being so mean to both of you. When your mind chatters, remind yourself to be your own best friend, or even to be your Compassionate Mind. (See Chapter 6 for more on these approaches.)

Using mental sarcasm successfully

In Chapters 5, 6 and 7, we show you how the thoughts and beliefs running through your mind contribute to emotional distress. These thoughts are almost always both distorted and built on insubstantial foundations of flimsy evidence. Look back to those chapters for a review of how you can wage war against unhelpful thoughts and beliefs.

While one option is to challenge your unhelpful thoughts, it doesn't always work. Sometimes a warrior needs to change tactics. In this section, we ask you to put down your weapons. Instead of going to war, we show you how to disarm damaging thoughts with humour. After all, it's hard to be in turmoil when you're chuckling and being silly.

When you hear negative chatter, thank your mind for having those thoughts. Tell your mind how creative it's being. (Yes, this does involve more than a hint of sarcasm.) Look at the following example, and then have some fun taking on your own thoughts.

Joseph works in publishing and is doing a part-time evening course training to be a counsellor. He hates his job and hopes that qualifying in counselling will enable him to change careers. His schedule is gruelling, and at times he gets discouraged. He tracks his mind chatter and notices three recurring thoughts. After reading about successful sarcasm, he decides to respond playfully to his mind's chatter in Worksheet 8-6.

Worksheet 8-6	Joseph's Successful Sarcasm
Mind Chatter	*Playful Response*
I'll never be able to finish this degree.	Thanks, mind! That's really encouraging. What a useful perspective!
Even if I finish the degree, I'll make a lousy counsellor.	Wow, mind. That's sooo helpful! Thanks a lot!
I'm going to be stuck with my job for the rest of my life.	Good thinking! I really like it when you come up with such creative ways of helping me.

Try thanking your mind whenever you hear unhelpful chatter. Beware of taking such chatter seriously – it's sure to drag you under. But if you play with the thoughts, you can render them powerless. Complete the exercise in Worksheet 8-7 and then record your reflections in Worksheet 8-8.

1. **Pay attention to your negative mind chatter.**

2. **Write down upsetting thoughts that you hear repeatedly in the left-hand column in Worksheet 8-7.**

3. **Come up with a playful response in the right-hand column; consider complimenting or even thanking your mind.**

Repeat this exercise whenever your mind starts chattering. Thank it, smile and move on!

Worksheet 8-7	Successful Sarcasm
Mind Chatter	*Playful Response*

Here are some other ways to play with your mind's chatter. Try singing the negative thoughts to the tune of 'Happy Birthday' or 'Row, Row, Row Your Boat'. You can also speak the thoughts out loud in a silly-sounding voice – how about Homer Simpson or Donald Duck? When you sing your thoughts or recite them in a ridiculous voice, it's much harder to take them seriously.

Worksheet 8-8	My Reflections

When you identify negative chatter and disarm it with humour (rather than waging war on it), you then need to involve yourself in another activity. This enables you to move on from that negative thought and get absorbed in something else.

Achieving Acceptance

Have you ever had your car stuck, really stuck, in the mud? Round and round spin the wheels – with you and the car going absolutely nowhere (except perhaps deeper into a hole). The first bit of advice has to be 'when you find yourself in a hole, stop digging!' And then you have to accept where you're at to get where you want to go.

So, if you get stuck, take your foot off the accelerator and let the car rock back. Then gently accelerate again until the tyres start spinning, and again, take your foot off the accelerator. Continue rocking in this way until you're finally out of the mud.

No, this isn't an advanced driving handbook. What we're saying is that in order to move forward, you must ease up and accept where you're at for the moment. Then, when the time's right, you can gently push ahead.

Perhaps you're wondering what acceptance has to do with anxiety and depression. Well, everyone feels anxious or sad at times. Recognising and accepting all those feelings is important because if you absolutely can't stand feeling worried or low, you're going to feel even more upset when you experience these normal feelings. And when you get more upset and distressed about being distressed – well, that's clearly not very helpful.

While it's great to feel good most of the time, probably the only humans who don't feel some anxiety or sadness are, well . . . dead. Besides, if you don't know sadness, how can you know what happiness is? Without worry, you don't appreciate calm. Work on accepting a certain level of uncomfortable emotions as part of your life.

One way to accept negative feelings is to view them objectively. Imagine that you're writing a report on the experience of anxiety or depression. To accurately express the experience, you need to acquire a dispassionate understanding of the essence of your emotions. In other words, observe and accept your feelings without judgement. As you do, you'll probably find your distress lessening. If you're depressed or anxious, accepting the emotional angst dispassionately helps you handle your unpleasant feelings without becoming more upset. Read through the following example and try out the exercise when you're feeling troubled.

Michelle needs to renew her road tax, so she pops over to the Post Office in her lunch hour. Though there's only one counter open, she's pleased to see only four people ahead of her. Then, the man at the head of the queue starts getting annoyed and argues with the teller. The argument continues, and the supervisor is summoned. As they get increasingly irate, Michelle looks at her watch and starts fretting about getting back to work on time. She recalls the Accepting Angst Dispassionately exercise (see Worksheet 8-9) and runs through it in her mind.

Worksheet 8-9   Michelle's Accepting Angst Dispassionately

---

1. **Write about your current physical feelings. Is your tummy upset? Are you sweating? Is your heart pounding? Do your shoulders feel tight? Describe everything going on in your body in objective terms.**

   Humph! I'm rocking on my feet and shifting my weight from one foot to the other. I can feel the tension in my shoulders. My breathing's fast and shallow. Now my heart's racing. How interesting.

2. **Notice fluctuations in these physical feelings. Over time, feelings vary in intensity. Are the waves long or short? How high do they go at their peak and how low at their ebb?**

   Now that I'm paying attention, I can see that these feelings change every few minutes. Strange — as I'm observing them, they actually seem to be lessening.

3. **Predict how long you will have these physical feelings. An hour, a minute, a day, a year?**

   They probably won't last longer than I'm here for.

4. **Notice with dispassion the thoughts that go through your mind. Imagine those thoughts floating away on clouds. Write them down and say goodbye as they float away.**

   It's interesting to notice my thoughts. I'm thinking things like, 'I'm going to be late and that's horrible' and 'That twit! Who does he think he is anyway?' It's funny, but as I listen to these thoughts objectively, they don't seem so important.

5. **Predict how long these thoughts will last. An hour, a minute, a day, a year?**

   They're already floating away as I focus on them.

The next time you notice unpleasant feelings, work through the exercise in Worksheet 8-10. If you have this book or a blank copy of Worksheet 8-10 with you, write down your reactions immediately. If you don't have the worksheet to hand, do what you can from memory. The main goal is to adopt an objective perspective, describing your feelings and thoughts without judging.

Worksheet 8-10	Accepting Angst Dispassionately

1. Write about your current physical feelings. Is your tummy growling? Are you sweating? Is your heart pounding? Do your shoulders feel tight? Describe everything going on in your body in objective terms.

_____

_____

_____

2. Notice fluctuations in these physical feelings. Over time, feelings vary in intensity. Are the waves long or short? How high do they go at their peak and how low at their ebb?

_____

_____

_____

3. Predict how long you will have these physical feelings. An hour, a minute, a day, a year?

_____

4. Notice with dispassion the thoughts that go through your mind. Imagine those thoughts floating away on clouds. Write them down and say goodbye as they float away.

_____

_____

_____

5. Predict how long these thoughts will last. An hour, a minute, a day, a year?

_____

The point of this exercise is to accept the way you feel in the moment without evaluation or judgement. Think of yourself as a scientist interested in objective observation and description. This exercise is particularly useful when you find yourself in frustrating, unavoidable predicaments, such as:

- ✔ Being stuck in a traffic jam.
- ✔ Standing in a long slow-moving queue.
- ✔ Sitting through a boring meeting.
- ✔ Weaving through crowds.
- ✔ Suffering through travel delays.
- ✔ Waiting for someone who's late.
- ✔ Meeting a deadline.
- ✔ Being rejected.
- ✔ Receiving criticism.
- ✔ Feeling afraid.
- ✔ Doing something scary, such as giving a talk.
- ✔ Feeling sick.

Focusing on the Present Moment: Now Is the Time

Many people find their thoughts dwelling on the past or the future. This experience can make them pretty miserable, if the focus is negative, which it frequently is. If you really think about it, most of what you get unhappy or worried about concerns events that have happened or are still to come. You feel guilt for past wrongdoings and worry about future calamities.

When you spend too much time in the past or future, you're bound to ruin your present. You lose the enjoyment and pleasure you could otherwise experience. Rarely is the present as difficult as your memories or predictions.

Imagine it's a really gorgeous spring day. Warm, sunny, with blue skies and little fluffy white clouds. The daffodils are out in full bloom. You're enjoying a pleasant walk.

Sounds pretty idyllic, no? And then we add: 'To the dentist!' Changes the feel, doesn't it? The moment you move your focus from the present wonderful walk to the future 'heading for the dentist', we bet your emotions changed pretty quickly – and probably not for the better!

Worksheet 8-11 helps you focus on the present moment. Practise this exercise for four or five minutes at least once per day. You can do it almost anywhere, and you'll probably find you feel really refreshed afterwards. (Some people initially need to time themselves because judging five minutes without a watch or clock can be tricky at first. Getting the feel of how long is five minutes becomes easier as you practise routinely.)

Worksheet 8-11　　　　　　　Embracing Present Moments

---

1. Sit comfortably in a chair, on the floor or wherever you like.

2. Extend your legs and place your feet about shoulder-width apart.

3. Put your hand on your abdomen and feel your breath go in and out.

Take your time breathing and keep it low and slow.

4. **When you feel comfortable, close your eyes. Continue to think about your breathing.**

5. **When thoughts intrude, let them be. Notice them and watch them float away. Just keep breathing – low and slow.**

6. **Sit quietly.**

   When you first start this exercise, you may feel an urge to scratch some part of your body. When that sensation occurs, concentrate mentally on the itchy area and the desire is likely to pass.

7. **Remain for just five minutes of stillness.**

   If you feel a muscle tensing, send your mental effort to that area. Study the feeling, and it will pass.

Five quiet minutes is all it takes to become mindful of the present. Follow the preceding steps, and then take a few moments to reflect in Worksheet 8-12 on how you felt.

Worksheet 8-12   **My Reflections**

_____

_____

_____

_____

_____

You can carry out almost any activity mindfully, connecting only with the sensations of the activity itself without judging, evaluating or analysing. For example, eating is something you do fairly often, so you have loads of opportunities to practise it mindfully. Relatively few present moments elicit high distress, and mindfulness connects you with the present. Mindful connection with the present takes some practice, so don't rush the process or judge your success or failure. Instead, simply practise, practise and then . . . practise!

 Try this mindfulness exercise at any meal (see Worksheet 8-13). You'll find yourself slowing down and enjoying your food more than before. In fact, people who eat mindfully typically lose weight more easily (if that's what they're trying to do) because they're no longer eating to get rid of unpleasant feelings. After you work through the steps, record your reflections in Worksheet 8-14.

Worksheet 8-13   **Eating Mindfully**

---

1. **Look at what you're about to eat.**

   What colours can you see? Are they shiny or dull? What's the texture like? Is it smooth, rough or varied?

2. **Smell the food.**

   Is it sweet, garlicky, fishy, pungent or something else?

3. **Take a small piece of food and put it on your tongue.**

   What does it feel like?

4. **Gently, slowly, move the piece around your mouth.**

   Are you salivating? Does this food need to be chewed?

(continued)

Worksheet 8-13 *(continued)*

---

5. As you chew, note the different tastes and textures that are released.

6. As the food begins to break down, feel it as it gets close to the back of your throat. Swallow.

7. Start again with the next piece of food.

Worksheet 8-14   **My Reflections**

_____

_____

_____

_____

Part III
Taking Action with Behaviour Therapy

'Marjorie's decided to come to your
party after all despite her social phobia.'

In this part . . .

One approach to fighting depression and anxiety is by changing your behaviour. By changing what you do, you can change the way you feel. We guide you step by step through methods for overcoming fear and anxiety. Furthermore, we provide encouragement for engaging in healthy and pleasurable activities.

People who are emotionally upset usually find themselves unable to solve many of their everyday problems. Therefore, we conclude this part by offering a structured problem-solving skill we call C.R.I.C.K.E.T.

Chapter 9

Facing Your Fears: Avoiding Avoidance

● ●

In This Chapter

▶ Figuring out your fears

▶ Facing fear one step at a time

▶ Tackling obsessions and compulsions

● ●

*T*his chapter is all about fear and anxiety. But isn't this book about anxiety *and* depression? In that case, why focus on fear? And how is fear connected to depression? Well, the connection is pretty close, actually. When you feel anxious, you're usually responding to something you fear. Prolonged anxiety and fear frequently leads to depression. And if you're already depressed, feeling anxious and afraid can easily worsen your depression. So, fear and anxiety, here we come!

If you experience fear and anxiety, you probably avoid the things that make you feel uneasy. For example, if you're terrified of snakes, you probably don't choose jungle adventure holidays. If crowds make you feel really edgy, you give the opening day of the Sales a miss. So where's the problem?

Though avoidance makes you feel less anxious at the time, in the long run, it increases anxiety. How so? Well, when you decide to avoid something you fear, you instantly feel huge relief – and wow, does it feel good! In these cases avoidance is like a reward. Generally, you do the things that you're rewarded for more often. So next time, you're likely to avoid again. You probably increasingly avoid other, similar events.

The problem is that avoidance feeds on itself over time. If crowds make you really nervous, you may start by avoiding only huge crowds. Then because huge crowds make you feel so awful that you can't bear them, you get unused to being in large groups – and then you find smaller crowds start making you nervous, too. So you avoid smaller and smaller crowds, shopping when it is less and less busy. Your avoidance grows until you're barely able to leave your house – you don't know how many people are out there!

In this chapter, we give you a list of common anxieties and fears that many people experience, so that you can identify those causing you the most distress and choose which to confront. We show you how to reduce your fear into manageable steps, guiding you one step at a time up the Staircase of Fear. Bet you can do it! Finally, we review a form of anxiety known as *obsessive-compulsive disorder* (OCD) and explain both the similarities and differences in its treatment, compared to other types of anxiety.

To Each, Their Own: Meeting Up with Your Fears

Most people have at least a few minor worries or anxieties, and that's no big deal. A little anxiety prepares you for action. When you hear a loud noise, you jump, look up and get ready to run. This surge of anxiety means your body can respond quickly – and that's a good thing.

But when fears and worries start dominating your life, you probably want to take action. The first step in doing so involves working out exactly what makes you anxious. Go through our 50 Fears Checklist in Worksheet 9-1 and tick any items that particularly worry you.

Worksheet 9-1	50 Fears Checklist

- ❑ Germs
- ❑ Crowds
- ❑ Air travel
- ❑ Snakes
- ❑ Feeling panicky or out of control
- ❑ Leaving the house
- ❑ Heights
- ❑ Public speaking
- ❑ Rodents
- ❑ Being trapped in a small place
- ❑ Bugs
- ❑ Leaving appliances switched on
- ❑ Leaving doors and windows unlocked
- ❑ Getting a disease
- ❑ Being alone
- ❑ Thunderstorms
- ❑ Drowning
- ❑ Being buried alive
- ❑ Dogs
- ❑ Getting contaminated by chemicals, radiation and so on
- ❑ Throwing up in public or in private
- ❑ Driving on the motorway or on busy roads
- ❑ Sexual performance
- ❑ Meeting new people
- ❑ Talking on the telephone
- ❑ Rejection
- ❑ Financial problems
- ❑ Saying something embarrassing
- ❑ Making mistakes
- ❑ Needles and injections
- ❑ Having blood pressure taken
- ❑ Going to the doctor
- ❑ Going to the dentist
- ❑ Going shopping

❑ Travelling

❑ Trains

❑ Job interviews

❑ Taking medication

❑ Undergoing surgery

❑ Lifts

❑ Open spaces

❑ Being criticised

❑ Using public toilets

❑ Racing heartbeat

❑ Eating in public

❑ Looking stupid

❑ Darkness

❑ The sight of blood

❑ Confrontation and disagreement

❑ Being far from home and unable to get back

Write down your top five fears in Worksheet 9-2. If you didn't recognise any fears in the preceding list, but have fears we didn't include, write them down in Worksheet 9-2 and read on.

Worksheet 9-2	**My Big Five**
1.	
2.	
3.	
4.	
5.	

If none of your fears seriously interfere with your life, you may decide to keep them – and that's fine. For example, Elaine (co-author of this book) goes out of her way to avoid entertainment with horror themes. And guess what – she has no intention of doing anything about it! It doesn't prevent her from enjoying a wide range of alternatively themed entertainments to share with others. If Elaine had to overcome this fear, she knows how to, but she's quite happy finding horror upsetting and disturbing. So she chooses to keep this fear.

Exposure: Getting to Grips with Your Fear

What bothers you? Choose anything you'd like to overcome. (Maybe one of your Big Five in Worksheet 9-2.) The best way to do it – is to do it! Not all at once, but in graded steps.

The *exposure technique* for facing and overcoming fear involves breaking your fear down into manageable steps, then tackling each one. After you conquer one level – and even though you're still a bit scared – you climb to the next level.

You can carry out exposure in real life and in your imagination. Some scary situations are tricky to manufacture, such as thunderstorms on demand. But many are easily imagined. Typically, facing things in your imagination is less scary than experiencing them in real life, but most people find working on their fears via their imaginations also works, and is certainly a start.

Identifying your fears

The first stage in exposure involves focusing in on your fear. What provokes a specific fear? Makes it better or worse? With this information, you can construct a *staircase* enabling you to go from fear and anxiety to a better place. Your staircase is all the situations and activities that evoke your fear. Tackling your fear involves scaling this staircase, starting with the lowest, easiest level and getting progressively harder.

Your view from the top is fantastic, but the climb is challenging. (Make sure your steps aren't too far apart, in case you scare yourself off.) Remember to take your time and use the following example as a guide.

Jon is painfully shy, especially with women. He has several good male friends but quakes at the thought of asking a woman out. He tries online dating and finds that e-mail conversation's pretty easy. But he baulks at suggesting meeting face-to-face for fear of rejection. Jon vows to overcome this fear by his 30th birthday. His first step is to assemble the building blocks for his Staircase of Fear (see Worksheet 9-3).

Worksheet 9-3   **Assembling Blocks for Jon's Staircase of Fear**

---

1. **How does your anxiety or fear begin?**

   Imagining phoning to ask someone out frightens the life out of me. Just talking to a woman can trigger anxiety. Even female sales assistants scare me!

2. **What activities do you avoid?**

   Obviously, going out with women. I avoid parties and any opportunity to talk to single women. I won't speak to single women on the phone. I even avoid the staff canteen with the excuse that I've got too much to do. My shyness seems to be getting worse, and lately I'm avoiding meeting and talking to new men as well as women.

3. **What other situations or activities could your fear conceivably affect?**

   Everything about the whole relationship thing scares me. If I had a date, what should I do or say? I wouldn't know when to make an advance — that's really scary. Losing the one brief relationship I had in the sixth form really hurt. So if I did find someone else, chances are she'd just reject me, too. I just about can't even ask directions from a woman if I'm lost.

4. **Do you use anything to cope with things that scare you, such as drugs or alcohol? Do you have others do things that you find too hard? Do you distract yourself with songs, rituals or chants?**

   My GP has prescribed medication, which I may take if I know I've got to talk to a woman. I avoid groups and meetings and let colleagues cover for me.

5. **What awful things might happen if you faced your fear? What's the worst?**

If I asked someone out, I can hear my voice shaking and see me clamming up. I'd look like a prize twit — tummy churning, sweat pouring. If we went on a date, she'd probably laugh in my face, walk off or make an excuse to leave early. And if anyone was daft enough to go out with me a second time, I bet she'd end up breaking my heart.

After Jon completes the questions for assembling the blocks for his Staircase of Fear, he moves on to the next step, which helps him order the blocks according to how much fear they cause (see Worksheet 9-4). He reviews what he wrote in Worksheet 9-3 and uses that information to identify specific activities that he fears carrying out. He rates each activity on a scale of 0 (no fear) to 100 (his worst imaginable fear). Jon ensures that the items cover the full range of fear, from very little fear to overwhelming fear, and everything in between.

Worksheet 9-4	Constructing Jon's Staircase of Fear
Fearful Activity	*Fear Rating (0–100)*
Asking a woman out, face to face.	85 (terrifying)
Phoning and suggesting going out.	75 (pretty scary)
Having a conversation with a woman I don't know.	65 (tough, but probably manageable)
Eating lunch in the staff canteen and talking to colleagues.	35 (I can handle this)
Suggesting a second meeting to someone I've asked out on a date.	90 (Almost unthinkable!)
Asking for help from a female sales assistant.	25 (not very difficult, but there is some tension)
Going to a party.	70 (really difficult)
Imagining asking someone for a date and being rudely rejected.	45 (If it really happened, it would be even worse than imagining it. But just imagining it scares me.)
Going on an outing with a social club.	75 (Pretty scary just thinking about it.)
Taking on some voluntary work and talking to female volunteers there.	60 (not easy)
Taking up public speaking via Adult Education and talking to others in the class.	80 (I hate speaking to groups, but it's part of my problem, I think.)
Joining the social club at work.	55 (not my idea of fun, but getting on to the committee and arranging the meetings is something I can do.)

Jon next places the items that are least scary for him at the bottom and those that are most frightening at the top, creating a staircase for scaling his fear (see Worksheet 9-5).

Worksheet 9-5 **Jon's Staircase of Fear**

Suggesting a second meeting to someone I've asked out on a date (90)

Asking a woman out, face to face (85)

Taking up public speaking via Adult Education and talking to others in the class (80)

Phoning and suggesting going out (75)

Going on an outing with the social club (75)

Going to a party (70)

Having a conversation with a woman I don't know (65)

Taking on some volunteer work and talking with female volunteers there (60)

Joining the social club at work (55)

Imagining asking someone for a date and being rejected rudely (45)

Eating lunch in the staff canteen and talking to colleagues (35)

Asking for help from a female sales assistant (25)

In Worksheet 9-6, select the fear you identified at the beginning of this section and answer the following questions, to construct your Staircase of Fear.

Worksheet 9-6 **Assembling Blocks for My Staircase of Fear**

---

1. How does your anxiety or fear begin?

_____

_____

_____

2. What activities do you avoid?

_____

_____

_____

3. What other situations or activities could your fear conceivably affect?

_____

_____

_____

_____

4. Do you use anything to cope with things that scare you, such as drugs or alcohol? Do you have other people do things that you find too hard? Do you distract yourself with songs, rituals or chants?

_____

_____

_____

5. What awful things might happen if you faced your fear? What's the worst?

_____

_____

_____

After you examine your fear, you can move on to breaking it down into small steps, or blocks, and rating the fear associated with each activity.

1. Review your answers in Worksheet 9-6.

2. In Worksheet 9-7, list six to twenty items or activities that you fear carrying out or have difficulty even imagining.

3. Rank each item on a scale of 0 (no fear) to 100 (worst imaginable fear).

4. If you find that there are large gaps in level of difficulty, perhaps nothing from 25 and 55, try filling in the gaps – no single step should be too huge.

Worksheet 9-7	Constructing My Staircase of Fear
Fearful Activity	_Fear Rating (0–100)_

(continued)

Worksheet 9-7 *(continued)*

Fearful Activity	Fear Rating (0–100)

You can obtain extra copies of these forms at www.dummies.com/go/adwb.

Climbing other people's Staircases of Fear

People all have their own fears and worries, but they frequently see that they've got a lot in common. Seeing a selection of the various staircases we've found may be helpful to you in creating your own. The following examples can help you get started, but do appreciate that your own staircase is unique to you.

Lawrence is petrified of flying. Forced to fly for business, he's so anxious he heads for the bar and downs three drinks before boarding. On the plane, he has three more and can barely stagger off on landing. Watching the bags go round and round on the baggage carousel makes him nauseous.

The next morning, Lawrence suffers through a board meeting, his head pounding and his tummy churning. The concerned looks from colleagues convince him that he has a problem. He vows to find a better way to manage his flying phobia. Worksheet 9-8 is it!

Worksheet 9-8　　　　　　　　**Lawrence's Staircase of Fear**

Taking a three-hour flight to Germany by myself without drinking (95)

Taking a short flight to Scotland by myself without drinking (90)

Taking a short flight to Scotland with my wife without drinking (85)

Imagining myself on a flight that has lots of turbulence (70)

Making a booking for a flight (65)

Driving to the airport for my flight (60)

Packing for my flight (50)

Watching films about planes (30–55 depending on the film)

Driving to the airport imagining that I'm going to my flight (40)

Watching planes take off and land and imagining myself on one of them (30)

Visiting the airport without flying (20)

Chris suffers from panic attacks and a fear of crowds. His panic attack sensations include sweating, rapid heartbeat and a horrible tightness in his chest. When he gets an attack, Chris feels like he may be dying. Chris stays away from crowded places. He does the household shop at all-night supermarkets, when few people are around, and wherever possible, buys on the Internet to avoid shopping centres. He feels worst in places where he thinks he may have trouble escaping, like crowded cinemas. Worksheet 9-9 shows Chris's Staircase of Fear.

Worksheet 9-9   **Chris's Staircase of Fear**

Attending a popular movie on opening night (95)

Attending a premier football game (90)

Attending a local football game (85)

Going shopping on a Saturday afternoon (85)

Walking around the shops by myself on a weekend (80)

Walking around the shops with a friend on a weekend (75)

Going to the shops by myself mid-week (70)

Imagining being trapped in a big crowd (65)

Going to the shops with a friend mid-week (55)

Attending a film matinee by myself during the week (45)

Attending a film matinee with a friend during the week (40)

Imagining waiting in a queue at a crowded cinema (35)

Going to the post office by myself (30)

Going to the pharmacy by myself on the weekend (25)

Walking around the shops by myself before they open (20)

Lydia worries constantly. She frets about her family and friends, as well as her physical and financial figures. She particularly worries about travelling and her savings. When she has a trip planned, she packs weeks in advance and repeatedly reconfirms her reservation. She also denies herself minor luxuries well within her means. Furthermore, she worries about the security of her husband's love. Anxiety spoils Lydia's enjoyment of life. Worksheet 9-10 illustrates this.

Worksheet 9-10	Lydia's Staircase of Fear

Planning a trip to America for the family (90)

Allowing my son to take the trip with his school (85)

Making myself buy new bedroom furniture (80)

Going for a day without asking my husband if he loves me (70)

Going for a day without asking my husband if I look okay (60)

Putting off packing for a holiday until the day before (50)

Going for two days without calling my mother to check on her (45)

Reconfirming my travel plans once instead of my usual ten times (40)

Stopping asking my son about his homework every day (30)

Inviting my friend Rebecca to lunch (20)

Imagining having a cheque bounce (15)

Leaving the wash up in the sink overnight (10)

If your anxiety includes significant physical symptoms such as difficulty breathing and changes in heart rate, see your GP before treating the anxiety on your own or even enlisting the help of a counsellor.

Building your own Staircase of Fear

Now comes the fun part . . . well, maybe not fun, but certainly an eye-opener. Using the information you've recorded and the examples in the previous section as a guide, you can now build your very own Staircase of Fear.

1. **Review the scary steps you listed in Worksheet 9-7.**

2. **Pick the least frightening item and make it the bottom step in Worksheet 9-11.**

3. **Continue adding items to Worksheet 9-11, writing activities in their order of scariness.**

Try to make your steps reasonably evenly spaced in terms of the amount of fear involved – around five points apart – so if you rate one step a 25, make your next step around 30 to 35. If you don't have one, find it!

You may need to practise some of your steps in your imagination. For example, if you fear illness, we don't particularly advise you expose yourself to deadly viruses. But you certainly can visualise being ill and recovering, in your mind.

| Worksheet 9-11 | My Staircase of Fear |

If you find that developing or climbing your Staircase of Fear is so difficult that you just can't manage by yourself, do consult a mental health professional.

For extra copies of this form, visit www.dummies.com/go/adwb.

Conquering Everest: Scaling Your Own Staircase

After you construct your first Staircase of Fear (see the previous section), you're ready to face your fear directly. Oh, help! This could be tricky, huh? Yes, facing a fear can be tough going, but if you just focus on each step as it comes, and climb slowly, you'll succeed.

Take the steps as slowly as you need to. Remember, if you find the process too difficult, consult a mental health professional. You don't have to do this alone.

Go back up to the section 'Identifying your fears' and review Jon's story. He's afraid to go out with, or even talk to, women. After constructing his Staircase of Fear (Worksheet 9-5), Jon's ready for the first step in confronting his fear. He's going to talk to a female sales assistant. (It's at the bottom of his list, therefore it's the easiest for starters.)

Jon goes to the shopping centre and the first assistant he sees is drop-dead gorgeous. His anxiety soars, so he walks past, practising some breathing and relaxation techniques. After he feels a little calmer, Jon approaches her and asks 'Where's Customer Services?' Because he feels pretty anxious even during this brief conversation, he knows he needs to repeat this step a number of times before he's ready to climb the next step in his staircase. He also knows he'd better do this elsewhere, in order not to arouse suspicion!

Jon spends much of the afternoon in the centre going from one assistant to another, in different shops. By the end of the day, he chats easily with one assistant, feeling only a fraction of his previous anxiety. Jon knows he still needs to repeat this step, but feels ready to also begin the next one. Slowly but surely, he scales and conquers his Staircase of Fear.

Jon tracks his progress in the Scaling the Summit Exercise (Worksheet 9-12). At each step, he records the anxiety he experiences and jots down his thoughts. He repeats the activity until his anxiety decreases by at least 50 per cent, and then climbs to the next step.

Worksheet 9-12	Jon Scaling the Summit
Activity	*Anxiety Ratings: 0 (no fear) to 100 (terrified)*
Talking to a female sales assistant.	30, 30, 25, 20, 20, 15, 10, 10: This was tougher than I thought it would be at first, but it got to be almost fun.
Eating lunch in the staff canteen and talking to colleagues.	20, 20, 15: This one was a doddle.
Imagining getting refused for a date.	45, 40, 40, 40, 35, 40, 30, 35, 25, 20: I thought this exercise would be silly. I really didn't realise how upsetting it could be to imagine something like this.
Volunteering to be on the social club committee at work and going to the meetings.	65, 70, 70, 60, 30, 30: This started out a lot harder than I thought it would be, but it didn't take too long to come down.
Having a conversation with a woman I don't know.	70, 70, 65, 65, 55, 70, 55, 40, 65, 35. This is still pretty difficult. I know I need to keep on practising, but I think I can handle the next step all the same.

As you can see, the first time Jon carried out an activity, his anxiety wasn't always at the level he had expected from his Staircase of Fear (see Worksheet 9-5). As he repeated the activities, his anxiety went up and down, but generally the trend was downward.

Before you begin exposure, or what we call *scaling the staircase,* start out in a reasonably relaxed state. Practise the following brief breathing exercise; it gives you a quick way of managing anxiety when it crops up and escalates. (Find more relaxation strategies in Chapter 13.)

1. Take a slow, deep breath in through your nose.

2. Hold your breath for a few seconds.

3. Breathe out very slowly through your mouth.

4. As you breathe out, make a slight hissing sound.

5. Concentrate on all the physical sensations throughout your body.

6. Repeat ten times.

Now, the hard part – climbing your Staircase of Fear.

1. **In the left-hand column of Worksheet 9-13, write down the activities from your Staircase of Fear (see Worksheet 9-11) in order of difficulty, with the easiest first.**

2. **Tackle the first step and carefully observe how you feel.** If the item involves an imaginary scene, find a comfortable place to sit and relax. Lie back, close your eyes, and picture the feared item as though it were occurring. Stay with the image as long as it takes for your anxiety to reduce by at least 50 per cent.

3. **In the right-hand column of Worksheet 9-13, rate how anxious the activity or imagery makes you feel on a scale of 0 (no anxiety) to 100 (terrifying).** Include any interesting reactions or observations.

4. **Repeat each activity and rate each repetition until your anxiety has dropped by around 50 per cent.** If your anxiety is still high, try the breathing technique for a minute or so. If this doesn't calm you down, consider leaving the activity and breaking it down into smaller, more manageable steps.

5. **Move on to the next scariest step when your anxiety has dropped and you feel you have mastered the preceding item.**

6. **Slowly does it!** Getting to the summit can take time.

7. **When you reach the summit of your Staircase of Fear, take a few moments to reflect on the experience and what it's meant to you in Worksheet 9-14.**

Worksheet 9-13	**Scaling the Summit**
Activity	*Anxiety Ratings: 0 (no fear) to 100 (terrified)*

(continued)

Worksheet 9-13 *(continued)*

Activity	Anxiety Ratings: 0 (no fear) to 100 (terrified)

You can download as many copies of this form as you want at www.dummies.com/go/adwb.

If you find the task of climbing your staircase too daunting, have a go using the following helpful suggestions to make your climb successful.

- ✔ Consider asking a trusted friend or family member to be with you on your first attempt at a difficult activity. Just be sure you do it later by yourself.

- ✔ Don't give in to mind chatter such as, 'I can't do this', 'This is stupid', 'I'll look an idiot' or 'This exercise won't help!' Thoughts like these are merely thoughts, nothing more. Notice how interesting this mind chatter is, but don't be seduced into believing it. (See Chapter 8 for more about dealing with mind chatter.)

- ✔ Consider rewarding yourself for the successful completion of any difficult steps. Treat yourself to something special – you deserve it!

- ✔ Allow yourself to feel some discomfort. After all, this work is difficult. It's okay to feel anxious at times – that shows you're making progress. Remember, no pain, no gain.

- ✔ Keep reminding yourself that you can overcome your fears. Be positive. Beating your fears may take some time, but you can do it.

- ✔ Don't use crutches such as alcohol or excessive medication to get through steps. Crutches diminish the effectiveness of exposure. Try not to distract yourself with chants, songs or other rituals, either.

- ✔ Practise the opening scenarios in your head first. Have a couple of alternatives at the ready.

- ✔ Climb those stairs slowly. Exposure takes time, and this isn't a race!

Worksheet 9-14 **My Reflections**

_____

_____

_____

_____

_____

If you find yourself avoiding the exposure activities in this chapter, we suggest you do a back flip (not literally!) to Chapter 3, which discusses ways of identifying and overcoming what's stopping you from changing.

Exposing Obsessive-Compulsive Disorder

Obsessive-compulsive disorder (OCD) is a particular type of anxiety disorder. OCD frustrates and challenges both those with this problem, as well as their loved ones. Besides causing considerable distress, OCD can be quite a time-stealer.

Essentially, *obsessions* are unwanted images, impulses or thoughts that come into a person's mind. People can feel over-responsible for their own and others' health and safety, feeling it's entirely up to them to prevent accidents and illness. Obsessions may take the form of excessive worry about contamination by germs, chemicals, radiation or concerns about whether doors and windows are unlocked or appliances left on. Other obsessions common to OCD include a fear of being overwhelmed by an impulse to hurt someone you love, to engage in inappropriate sexual behaviours, violate your personal religious beliefs or act in socially unacceptable or strange ways.

Compulsions are repetitive undesired actions or mental strategies that people do to reduce anxiety, and are triggered by the obsessions. They often include excessive hand washing, over-cleanliness, hoarding objects, a rigid manner of arranging objects or of getting dressed, checking and rechecking things (such as locks), or counting things.

Many people have obsessional tendencies and occasionally do some of the preceding things – that's no problem. You only have problems with OCD when these behaviours begin to seriously interfere with your relationships, work or sense of freedom. For more information about this problem, look for our book *Overcoming Anxiety For Dummies* (Wiley).

Obsessive-compulsive disorder can be a serious, debilitating problem, and most people who suffer from OCD require professional help. You should only attempt the strategies that follow if your problems are fairly mild; do consider using this book in collaboration with your psychologist or counsellor.

The approach for treating OCD is similar to the treatments for anxiety and fear that we present earlier in this chapter; we cover a few minor differences in the following sections.

Overcoming obsessions

Because obsessions consist of thoughts or mental images, exposure often takes place in the imagination. This approach is valuable as many obsessions don't require acting out, such as those where you fear you'll violate religious, social or sexual boundaries.

If you do have obsessions that involve unacceptable sexual activities or physically hurting yourself or others, consult a mental health professional rather than attempt imagination-based or real-world exposure techniques.

Your Staircase of Fear (Worksheet 9-11) may indicate aspects of your obsessions, but you need to consider the questions in Worksheet 9-15 to construct and climb a staircase based on an obsession.

Worksheet 9-15	Obsessional Exposure

Write down your three most distressing obsessional thoughts or images. They may be related to one another.

_____

_____

_____

Look over Worksheet 9-15 and do the following:

1. **Next to each item, rank how upsetting each is on a scale of 0 (not upsetting) to 100 (totally disturbing).**

2. **Find a comfortable, private place to sit and work through this exercise.**

3. **In your mind, visualise the image or repeat the thought over and over and over and over and over and over and over and over and over and over and over and . . . (Got the idea?)**

4. **Continue repeating the thought or image for 20 to 30 minutes, or as long as it takes to reduce your level of upset by at least 10 to 20 points.**

5. **Re-rate the thought or image on the same scale – 0 (not upsetting) to 100 (totally disturbing).**

The act of exposing oneself to obsessional thoughts and images is quite the opposite of what people with OCD usually try to do. They often try to instantly eradicate obsessive thoughts and images that arise. The problem is that attempting to suppress thoughts only makes them surface more frequently.

For example, whatever you do, DON'T THINK ABOUT PINK ELEPHANTS! Thinking about them is ABSOLUTELY FORDIDDEN!

Telling yourself to not think about something doesn't work.

Clobbering compulsions

The first step in dealing with compulsions, just like treating other anxieties and fears, involves exposure. You assemble the blocks for a Staircase of Fear, order them and start your ascent. (See the previous section 'Exposure: Getting to Grips with Your Fear'.)

The key difference in the treatment of compulsions is one extra thing: not only do you expose yourself to what you fear, but you then stop yourself doing the compulsive behaviour. When you stop doing the compulsive behaviour, you're seeking to 'undo' the harm you fear may arise. The technical name for this procedure is *exposure and response prevention*. The following example shows you how it works in practice.

Gina has the compulsion to wash her hands a lot. She spends around three hours a day hand-washing, in fact. She does this because she's afraid of getting ill if she comes in contact with germs. However, the compulsion is ruining her life, taking up huge amounts of time and leaving her hands in an awful state.

Gina commences building her Staircase of Fear. Worksheet 9-16 illustrates a portion of her route for Scaling the Summit. Gina repeatedly exposes herself to problematic events and activities while not washing her hands. In fact, Gina makes a concerted effort not to wash for at least an hour after each exposure.

Worksheet 9-16	Gina's Scaling the Summit Exercise
Activity (Exposure without the Compulsion)	_Anxiety Ratings: 0 (no fear) to 100 (terrified)_
Handling clothes in a departmental store.	30, 20, 15, 10: This was pretty tough at first because I kept thinking about all the other people who'd touched them before me. But it got a lot easier.
Handling money with my bare hands.	35, 30, 40, 25, 25, 30, 20, 15: This was difficult because I usually wear gloves if I handle money. I feel almost sick when I think about what's been on all the hands that money went through.
Touching door handles with my bare hands.	55, 55, 60, 60, 50, 40, 30, 30, 35, 25, 25: I hated doing this. I hope I don't get ill with all those germs. I know I have to keep practising this one, but I'm ready for the next step, I think . . .
Touching the handrails on the escalator and holding it all the way up or down.	75, 75, 80, 60, 60, 55, 55, 45, 35, 35, 35: Whew, that was hard! Yuck. But I'm ready to keep climbing. I know I can do this.
Gardening without gloves.	80, 80, 75, 70, 60, 55, 45, 55, 45, 35, 35, 35: Wow, it wasn't easy to not wash those disgusting hands every few minutes, and to wait until I'd finished the gardening session. But my hand washing overall is practically normal. I'm getting somewhere, and my garden looks great.

In addition to climbing your Staircase of Fear, while resisting the compulsive behaviour, consider:

- ✔ **Delaying your urges by 30 minutes each time you have them.** Later, you can delay for 45 minutes.
- ✔ **Changing your compulsion in various ways.** You may use different soap, arrange things a little differently or make a slight change in your routine.

Now, take a few minutes to ponder what progress you've made after dealing with your OCD problems. In Worksheet 9-17, record your thoughts and insights.

Worksheet 9-17	My Reflections

Chapter 10

Lifting Your Spirits through Exercise

●●

In This Chapter

▶ Working out how much physical activity you need

▶ Giving yourself reasons to exercise

▶ Designing your exercise strategy

▶ Manufacturing motivation to carry out your programme

●●

*W*hy devote a whole chapter to exercise in a book that deals with anxiety and depression? Well, because physical activity generally increases the production and release of naturally occurring feel-good endorphins. (*Endorphin* is actually a shortened form of 'endogenous morphine', which literally means 'morphine produced naturally in the body'.) When your brain releases endorphins, you get a sense of well-being and pleasure. And when this happens, you're far less likely to feel depressed or anxious.

In this chapter, we tell you how much exercise you need to stimulate the production of those endorphins, and we describe the myriad benefits of exercise. You get to pick your top ten reasons for either beginning or sticking to an exercise programme, and you then devise an exercise plan that works for your lifestyle. We also offer some tips for finding the motivation to keep your exercise programme alive, so you feel even more so.

Figuring Out How Much Is Enough

The best time to get into the exercise habit is when you're young because exercise helps keep you healthy throughout your life. However, it's never too late to start, even for the two-thirds of men and three-quarters of women who confess to doing less than the recommended amount, so if this includes you, don't despair. The biggest health improvements come if you've never exercised but then start doing so regularly.

If you're in good health, you can start your own exercise programme. But for men over 40, women over 50 and anyone with a chronic disease or other health concerns, check with your doctor before beginning a vigorous exercise regimen. Build up your programme gradually instead of starting with something overly challenging and suffering painful after-effects.

The UK government offers recommended guidelines for physical activity. So, take a deep breath, relax . . . here they come:

✔ Children and teenagers should be physically active about an hour a day on most days. Activities can include vigorous play, dance or organised sports.

✔ Healthy adults should be moderately physically active for at least half an hour a day, five days a week.

✔ To prevent the gradual weight gain associated with normal aging, you need to do an hour's vigorous activity per day, most days of the week.

✔ To lose weight, you should exercise between 60 and 90 minutes on most days.

✔ Most pregnant women should be exercising half an hour per day. (Check with your doctor to make sure this recommendation is right for you.)

Work out from the above how many minutes a day you should be exercising and write it here: _____

Exercise improves both physical and psychological well-being, increasing your level of fitness. Fitness includes the following improvements in:

✔ **Cardiorespiratory endurance:** Your body's ability to pump blood and circulate oxygen. To do this, you elevate your heart rate, safely, for increasing periods of time.

✔ **Body composition:** Your body's ratio of fat and lean mass. All types of exercise can help improve your body's composition.

✔ **Flexibility:** Your body's ability to move fluidly and with good range. Stretching and activities such as swimming are great.

✔ **Muscular strength:** Your body's ability to lift and push. For this, weight training is helpful.

✔ **Muscular endurance:** Your body's ability to sustain effort without getting tired. Again, a variety of exercise helps.

Appreciating the Benefits of Exercise: Why Should I?

We believe that exercise has so many benefits that – even if you aren't already doing it – you can see a change for the better if you just get going and keep at it. This section covers the many good things that can happen – plus the bad things that you can prevent – when you exercise. Some of them may surprise you, but they're all real.

Now come off it! Surely you didn't think you'd get away with just reading our list of reasons for exercising? This is a *work*book, remember? So here's how to identify *your* ten top reasons why you should be exercising.

1. **Read Worksheet 10-1 and tick any items that you're concerned about.** Some may be relevant to practically everyone; others may be particularly important to you. So if you have a family history of diabetes or colon cancer, those items may be especially important, and make it on your top ten list.

2. **After you identify the salient items, take some time to decide which are the most important and relevant to you.**

3. **Pick your top ten reasons for exercising and record them in ranked order of importance on Worksheet 10-2.**

Worksheet 10-1	Reasons for Exercising

❑ Feels fun

❑ Improves energy

❑ Decreases risk of heart disease and strokes

❑ Relieves stress, tension and anxiety

❑ Improves immune system

❑ Decreases depression

❑ Decreases blood pressure

❑ Boosts self-confidence

❑ Decreases risk of diabetes

❑ Decreases risk of breast cancer

❑ Improves lung capacity

❑ Improves ratio of bad to good cholesterol

❑ Sporting activities provide enjoyable social interaction

❑ Helps in losing weight

❑ Decreases risk of obesity

❑ Decreases risk of colon cancer

❑ Improves appearance

❑ Decreases risk of falls in the elderly

❑ Improves flexibility

❑ Improves strength

❑ Decreases risk of osteoporosis

❑ Improves sleep

❑ Increases mental sharpness and concentration

❑ Improves balance

❑ Improves quality of life

❑ Relieves symptoms of PMS

❑ Improves complexion

❑ Reduces visits to the doctor

❑ Reduces varicose veins

❑ Reduces addictive cravings

❑ Aids digestion

❑ Decreases back pain

❑ Makes you taller and more intelligent. What? Well, okay, exercise helps you stand straighter and feel brighter!

Worksheet 10-2	My Top Ten Reasons for Exercising
1.	
2.	
3.	
4.	
5.	
6.	
7.	
8.	
9.	
10.	

Fitting In Fitness

Despite uncovering some pretty convincing reasons for exercising in the preceding section, you may be wondering where on earth you can find 30 to 90 minutes a day. You're probably way too busy as it is. We agree – sort of. But remember what to do if something's too big a mouthful to chew and swallow all at once? You cut it into smaller pieces.

The first step is appreciating that you don't have to find one big chunk of exercise time. The government guidelines state that doing several 10- to 15-minute segments is just as effective as one big session. The total per day is what counts. And guess what? Exercise means just about any type of activity that occurs at a moderate level of intensity. *Moderate intensity* means you're increasing your breathing and heart rate, which you can do by mowing the lawn, dancing, swimming, bike-riding, jogging or even walking briskly. In fact, if your job is physically demanding, you may already be getting sufficient exercise every day. But religiously taking the dog out for a leisurely walk, even for 45 minutes a day, probably won't do the trick – only brisk walks count.

Everyone is different. We all have different schedules, habits, preferences and lifestyles. So an exercise programme that works for one person may not suit another. Worksheet 10-3 helps you choose exercise that you can work into your life.

1. **In Worksheet 10-3, tick all the exercise ideas that could conceivably become part of your routine.**

2. **Add a few ideas of your own to the list.**

3. **Try each and every activity you select at least a couple of times.**

4. **Make a note of your feelings and reactions in Worksheet 10-4.** Include comments on how you think you can fit these activities into your daily life.

Worksheet 10-3	Exercise Checklist

❑ Get up 15 minutes earlier each day and go for a brisk walk – with or without a dog!

❑ Set off earlier for work and either get off public transport one stop before your usual one or park some distance away, so you get a brisk 20-minute walk to work.

❑ Take the stairs rather than the lift.

❑ Take a walk at lunchtime.

❑ Exercise during work breaks.

❑ Join a gym and go three to four times a week.

❑ Find an active sport you like, such as tennis, table tennis, badminton, football, swimming and so on.

❑ Go for a jog when you get home from work.

❑ Walk around the shopping centre four or five times per week.

❑ Get a personal trainer to design a home exercise programme.

❑ Join (and go to!) a dance class or club.

❑ Ride the bike that's been gathering cobwebs in your garage to work and for fun at weekends.

❑ Buy an exercise video/DVD and work out at home regularly.

❑ Go to a yoga or a Pilates class.

❑ Take other active classes such as spinning, kickboxing or step aerobics.

❑ Buy any of the range of home fitness machines, including a treadmill, rower, stationary bike, elliptical trainer, or riding/surfboarding simulators. (Try them out first to ensure you want to make the investment.)

❑ Exercise while watching television. (You can use many of the preceding machines in front of the television.)

❑ Wear leg weights when walking – but take them off before going into the office!

❑ Watch sports on TV. Nope! Sorry, that one doesn't count!

❑

❑

❑

❑

Worksheet 10-4	My Reflections

_____

_____

_____

_____

Waking Up Your Willpower

Working through the preceding section gives you some pretty good reasons for exercising (ten, in fact!). Hopefully you find a few types of exercise that fit into your life, and you try them out. But though your intentions may be good, what happens when your initial enthusiasm and commitment to do something positive for yourself fade? Or, how do you get started if you haven't even found that initial enthusiasm?

Defeating defeatism

The problem with finding and maintaining motivation to exercise lies in distorted, demotivating thinking (see Chapters 5, 6 and 7 for more on distorted thinking). Demotivating thinking keeps you from taking action and puts you in a defeatist frame of mind, where you're doomed to fail. When your thinking is distorted, your mind's full of the reasons why you can't possibly exercise. It's hard to get moving when defeatist thoughts dominate. But we have a strategy. The following example gives you an idea of how you can deliver the knockout punch in your fight to defeat defeatism.

Janine, a busy mother of two, works as a travel agent. Every morning she dashes off to drop her kids at nursery, squeaks into work almost on time and then tries to do the urgent shopping in her lunch hour. She hurries home to cook for the family, and after supper, she's usually shattered. It's no wonder Janine suffers from mild depression. When her doctor suggests she begin exercising to improve her mood and health, Janine laughs mirthlessly, saying, 'You've got to be kidding! I don't have a spare second in my day – let alone around an hour.'

But fortunately, Janine has a copy of the *Anxiety & Depression Workbook For Dummies*. She completes the Defeating Defeatism Exercise. Worksheet 10-5 shows what she comes up with, and Worksheet 10-6 has her reflections on the exercise.

Worksheet 10-5	Janine's Defeating Defeatism Exercise
Demotivating Thoughts	*Motivating Thoughts*
I don't have time to exercise.	I could watch a half hour less TV, or get up a little earlier, or even exercise while I'm in front of the TV.
I can't afford baby sitters or childcare, so I can't get to exercise classes.	I could get a video or DVD to follow at home. I could even do something energetic with the children; they'd love a long walk or a bike ride.
I feel so shattered – I just haven't got the energy.	I must admit, they say exercise increases your energy level!
I'm too depressed to exercise.	Okay. So people say exercise can help to lift depression. Just because I don't feel like exercising, that doesn't mean I can't.

Worksheet 10-6	Janine's Reflections

I suppose I see how my thinking is bogging me down on this exercise thing. Part of the reason I feel so down is because I haven't been able to lose the extra weight I gained after my last pregnancy. What I need to do is stop listening to all these thoughts and just do it. I think I'll get the kids and we'll all hop on our bikes and head for the library, where I'll choose a DVD of a home exercise programme.

Most people who struggle to find space for exercise in their lives have thoughts like Janine's. But just because you think something doesn't make it true. Therefore, paying attention to the dialogue about exercise that runs through your head is important because then you can argue with these thoughts and in turn increase your willingness and motivation to exercise.

To complete your own Defeating Defeatism Exercise:

1. **Read the demotivating thoughts in the left-hand column of Worksheet 10-7 and circle those that are relevant to you.** These thoughts are the most common ones people have that get in the way of exercise.

   If you have thoughts that aren't on the list, feel free to add them in the extra spaces provided.

2. **For each thought that you circle or that you add, develop a motivating thought that's a counterargument, which refutes and debunks the demotivating one.** As you develop your counterarguments, ask yourself:

   • Is the demotivating thought exaggerated or illogical in any way?

   • Is the thought just an excuse not to exercise?

   • Is there a better way to think about this demotivating thought?

   • If a friend of mine said something similar, would I think it was completely legitimate – or would it sound like an excuse?

   • Is the thought helping me in any way?

   • What would happen if I simply tried acting as though the thought weren't true?

   If you struggle to come up with motivating thoughts, head back to Chapters 5, 6 and 7 for loads of ways to defeat such thinking.

3. **Jot down your reactions to this exercise in Worksheet 10-8.**

Worksheet 10-7	My Defeating Defeatism Exercise
Demotivating Thoughts	*Motivating Thoughts*
I don't feel like exercising now. I'll start doing it when it feels right.	
I just don't do exercise. It's not who I am.	

(continued)

Worksheet 10-7 *(continued)*

Demotivating Thoughts	Motivating Thoughts
It's not worth the trouble to exercise.	
Exercise is a silly waste of time.	
I don't have the time to exercise.	
I'm too tired to exercise.	
I'm too old to exercise.	
I hate exercise.	
I'm too depressed or anxious to exercise; I'll do it when I feel better.	
I'm too out of shape to exercise.	
I'm in too much pain to exercise.	
Gyms and equipment cost too much; I just don't have that kind of money.	
Exercise just isn't worth the effort.	

Worksheet 10-8 **My Reflections**

Charting your progress

An effective way to boost motivation is to keep a record of your exercise. Make a note of the physical activity you do everyday and write down your reactions to the activity. When you commit yourself to writing something down, you tend to pay more attention to what you do. That's just part of human nature. The following is a brief example of an exercise record; read it through before starting your own.

Boris works in publishing. He feels like his life is out of control: he can't save enough money to replace his temperamental old car, his social life is flat and frankly boring, and his mood is low. He's aware that both his stomach and waistband are expanding, and he feels pretty hopeless. Boris talks to a friend who urges him to join a gym to get active again. Feeling he has nothing to lose, Boris does just that and begins recording his daily physical activity, both in and out of the gym (see Worksheet 10-9).

Worksheet 10-9	Boris's Physical Activities	
Day	*What I Did*	*How I Felt*
Monday	I used the stairs rather than the lift at work.	I was really panting. But each step was one in the right direction!
Tuesday	I made it to my exercise class.	Didn't keep up with all of it and felt a bit silly, but I did feel better afterwards.
Wednesday	Absolutely zero. I was a total couch potato.	Mea Culpa! I completely wimped out!
Thursday	Took the kids out for football in the park.	Felt really close to them. It was fun, and they were much better behaved that night.
Friday	Second session this week at the gym — not bad going!	Hopefully I'm getting into the habit already. And the class was pretty friendly, overall.
Saturday	Tried out the new dry ski slope with friends.	One person was even worse than me! No bones broken, and it was kind of fun. Winter holiday sorted!
Sunday	Nothing at all. One big fat zero!	Hey, it's okay to have a day off. Why not re-frame it and say I chose to have a lovely, relaxing day?

Use Worksheet 10-10 to track your exercise progress. You'll be surprised at how writing everything down really does keep you focused on your goal.

Worksheet 10-10	My Physical Activities	
Day	*What I Did*	*How I Felt*
Monday		
Tuesday		
Wednesday		
Thursday		
Friday		
Saturday		
Sunday		

You can get copies of this form at www.dummies.com/go/adwb. Download as many as you need for your own use.

Beating yourself up when you don't succeed at any task doesn't help you get or stay on track. Just acknowledge that you didn't do what you wanted to – THEN. Your past actions (or inactions) don't mean you won't succeed this time. So get into gear, and off you go!

Chapter 11

Taking Pleasure from Leisure

• •

In This Chapter

▶ Introducing pleasure back into your life

▶ Staying out of trouble

▶ Overcoming obstacles to pleasure

• •

*I*t's difficult to be anxious or depressed when you're having fun. Laughter, enjoyment and pleasure wreak havoc with feelings of sadness or worry because they stimulate your body to release *endorphins,* brain chemicals that increase your sense of well-being. Unfortunately, when you suffer from anxiety or depression, you tend to cut down on, or even totally cut out, pleasurable activities. The fewer pleasurable things you do, the fewer endorphins your body produces, and the worse you feel. So it's high time you bring pleasure back into your life, as part of your healing process.

In this chapter, we help you choose from a variety of healthy pleasures centring around activities, people and events that can do you good and enable you to combat anxiety and depression.

Pinpointing Your Pleasures

Emotional distress interferes with clear thinking. If you're sad or worried, you may have difficulty identifying any activities that sound pleasurable. Not to worry. We've created a Pool of Pleasurable Activities in Worksheet 11-1. As you can see, it's not full of mega-wonderful or enormously intense pleasures. Instead, the list contains a wide range of simple pleasures because research shows that more frequent, simple pleasures actually provide greater enjoyment than occasional spectacular ones.

You may need to look closely at your life to spot and pay attention to the simple pleasures that you may have been missing, or merely taking for granted.

1. **Peer into the Pool of Pleasurable Activities in Worksheet 11-1.**

2. **Tick any activities that sound appealing to you now or that you enjoyed in the past.** Add an option or two of your own.

3. **Choose different coloured pens to highlight the following three categories of activities:** those that: a) you used to do, but do no longer, b) you've never tried, and c) you're still doing, but possibly very infrequently, and perhaps you're barely aware of doing them.

4. **In Worksheet 11-2, identify ten pleasures that you believe you can begin to establish, or re-establish, in your life.**

Worksheet 11-1	My Pool of Pleasurable Activities

❑ Amateur dramatics or performance

❑ Creating art

❑ Travelling near or far

❑ Shopping

❑ Listening to music

❑ Drinking tea

❑ Playing a sport

❑ Camping

❑ Eating out with friends

❑ Eating chocolate (in small quantities!)

❑ Taking a hot bath

❑ Gardening

❑ Exercising

❑ Going to the countryside or seaside

❑ Reading a good book

❑ Finishing a small task

❑ Going to a live sporting event

❑ Dancing

❑ Going out for a meal

❑ Getting a massage

❑ Visiting a friend

❑ Drinking a glass of wine, fruit juice or whatever pleases your palate.

❑ Making love

❑ Going to a bookshop or library

❑ Smiling and greeting someone (for example, saying 'good morning')

❑ Spending time with family

❑ Sitting in the sunshine

❑ Cooking something special

❑ Walking through an interesting area

❑ Playing with your pets

❑ Taking a walk – with or without your pets

❑ Playing cards or games

❑ Smelling fresh flowers

❑ Surfing the Internet

❑ Taking up a hobby

❑ Going to a museum

❑ Taking a nap

❏ Swapping work clothes for others more comfortable to lounge about in

❏ Going to a film

❏ Going to a concert or play

❏ Going to a comedy club

❏ Taking a yoga class

❏ Flying a kite

❏ Meditating

❏ Taking pictures

❏ Sleeping in

❏ People-watching

❏ Taking a scenic drive

❏ Going to a coffee shop and having a cappuccino

❏ Learning how to spell cappuccino! Or learning anything new!

Worksheet 11-2	Top Ten Pleasures That May Work for Me
1.	
2.	
3.	
4.	
5.	
6.	
7.	
8.	
9.	
10.	

If our Pool doesn't provide intriguing possibilities, you may be really struggling to make space for pleasure in your life. We help you deal with that problem in the section 'Overcoming Joy Destroyers' later in this chapter.

After you create your own list of pleasurable activities, it's time to schedule them into your life. Here's how:

1. **In Worksheet 11-3, for each day of the week, write down one or more pleasurable activities that you plan to engage in.** Select a range of activities across the week, ideally choosing some you haven't done in a while – or ever.

2. **After you complete the pleasurable activity, circle it to record your achievement.**

3. **Notice how you feel at the end of a week during which you've increased your simple pleasures.**

4. **Jot down your observations under My Reflections in Worksheet 11-4.**

Worksheet 11-3	My Simple Pleasures
Day	**Pleasurable Activities**
Monday	
Tuesday	
Wednesday	
Thursday	
Friday	
Saturday	
Sunday	

Overcoming depression and anxiety demands more than just adding pleasure to your life, important though that is. Chapter 12 has information on doing more of other types of important activities to give you a sense of mastery or accomplishment.

Worksheet 11-4	My Reflections

_____

_____

_____

_____

Getting Too Much of a Good Thing

We don't want you taking this pleasure idea too far. Pleasures are great, of course, but taken to excess some may land you in mildly hot water or even be downright harmful. Do bear in mind the possible dangers, and watch out for:

✔ Drug abuse and substance misuse, including excesses involving prescription medicines

✔ Sexual promiscuity: uncharacteristically lowered inhibition or risk-taking that you may later regret

✔ Alcohol to excess: more than 21 units of alcohol (men) or 14 units (women) per week

✔ Hanging out with people you know cause or get into trouble

✔ Sleeping to excess

✔ Becoming a television, Internet or social-networking site addict

✔ Overeating

✔ Excessive caffeine consumption

✔ Exercising to extremes

✔ Shopping beyond your budget

✔ Reckless driving

✔ Gambling

✔ Thrill-seeking through risky behaviours

✔ Shoplifting

Even healthy activities like exercising or dieting, when taken to extremes or overdone, can become a problem, making it far harder for you to overcome anxiety and depression. If any of the preceding ring true for you, please first remember that you are using this workbook to give you a fresh perspective. Recognising a potential problem is the first step towards a solution. You may feel able to try solving your problem on your own, but if not, do consider seeking professional help.

Overcoming Joy Destroyers

Ideally, you've chosen ten potentially pleasurable activities, either from our Pool (see Worksheet 11-1) or other ones that you've come up with yourself, and have made space for them in your daily life without too much trouble. However, we do know that many people don't find this task all that easy.

Emotional distress and especially depression cause distorted thinking (see chapters 5, 6 and 7). In this section, we focus on the thoughts that are most likely to interfere with your efforts to increase pleasure in your life. Three types of distortions typically get in the way: thoughts of being undeserving and unworthy, thoughts that pleasure is a silly waste of time and thoughts that tell you this strategy hasn't a snowball in hell's chance of working!

Deserving delight

Depression and anxiety affect your self-esteem – and not for the better. When you're sad or anxious, you probably don't think too highly of yourself. And along with low self-esteem come thoughts such as:

✔ I don't deserve happiness or pleasure.

✔ I'm not good enough.

✔ I'm useless – or a burden.

✔ I'm not doing enough as it is, so I certainly don't have time for pleasure.

✔ If anything, I deserve punishment, not pleasure.

✔ I've let everyone down. How can I justify having fun?

As you'd predict, such thoughts don't exactly result in a strong desire to go on a pleasure hunt. They also increase emotional distress in general. Clearly, you must restructure these thoughts. Here's an example of how to restructure those joy-destroying thoughts.

Tessa suffers from depression. Her counsellor suggests that she increase the pleasurable activities in her life. Tessa notices that she's resisting the idea, so she and her counsellor explore the reasons behind her reluctance. They discover two joy-destroying thoughts standing in the way: 'I don't deserve pleasure' and 'I'm insufficiently productive as it is'.

Tessa and her counsellor work together to rethink her joy-destroying negative thoughts. Worksheet 11-5 shows what they come up with.

Worksheet 11-5	Tessa's Rethinking Joy-Destroying Thoughts
Negative Thought	*Restructured Thought*
I don't deserve pleasure.	No one has to earn pleasure. Putting pleasure back in my life is part of how I can get over my depression.
I'm not productive enough as it is.	Part of the reason I'm not getting enough done is because I'm so depressed. If I decrease my depression, I'll be more productive.

If you find that you're resisting doing things that bring pleasure into your life, it's likely you're under the influence of one or more joy-destroying thoughts. Here's how you identify such thoughts and develop more adaptive ones:

1. **Read through the negative, joy-destroying thoughts in Worksheet 11-6.** These are people's most common thoughts that prevent them from getting fun out of life. Circle all that apply to you.

2. **Add any thoughts that aren't on the list in the extra spaces provided.**

3. **For each thought that you've circled or added, develop an alternative restructured one to refute it.** Ask yourself the following questions:

   • Is this negative thought actually exaggerated or illogical in some way?

   • Is there a better way to think about this negative thought?

   • If a friend of mine said that, would I think it was totally legitimate – or would it sound somewhat self-defeating to me?

   • Is this thought helping me?

If you're struggling to come up with restructured thoughts, see Chapter 3 for how to defeat the distorted thinking that's standing in your way.

Worksheet 11-6	Rethinking Joy-Destroying Thoughts
Negative Thought	**Restructured Thought**
I don't deserve happiness or pleasure.	
I'm insufficiently productive as it is, so I certainly don't have time for pleasure.	
I'm not good enough.	
I deserve punishment, not pleasure.	
I've let everyone down. How can I justify having fun?	

Taking fun seriously

Common thoughts among the pleasure-challenged people of the world are: 'Having fun's really a waste of time' and 'Fun is just silly'. These people usually think that work and accomplishments are quite okay, but fun, entertainment or even relaxation are most definitely not. Their leisure activities typically expand their knowledge, improve skills or consist of things they think are 'good for them'.

Certainly, expanding your horizons is no bad thing. However, you also need space for rubbishy novels, silly films, a walk in the park and light-hearted entertainment. These can make all the difference.

'What difference?' you may well ask. Well, research shows that pleasure is part of the underlying foundation for a healthy life. Pleasure decreases anxiety and depression because it makes the body release endorphins, chemicals that make you feel grrrreat. But pleasure has other important physical and emotional benefits such as:

- ✔ Improved immune function
- ✔ Decreased experience of chronic pain
- ✔ Decreased risk of heart attack
- ✔ Decreased stress
- ✔ Prolonged life expectancy
- ✔ Enhanced sense of well-being
- ✔ Improved overall health
- ✔ Increased productivity

Did you notice that last item, 'increased productivity'? Many people think that non-work related activities aren't justifiable and are merely time-wasting. Actually, the opposite is true: putting pleasure into your life actually makes you *more* productive when you are working. You have more enthusiasm and energy both for your work and play! So you're very likely to do more, rather than less, if you take the occasional break.

If you fall into the 'fun is frivolous' mind trap, take some time to seriously consider the benefits of pleasure. Think about what pleasure and its benefits can mean to you and your life. Jot down your conclusions under My Reflections in Worksheet 11-7.

Worksheet 11-7	My Reflections

_____

_____

_____

_____

_____

Shattering self-fulfilling prophesies

Minds burdened by depression and anxiety do a curious thing: they make predictions about how much you're likely to enjoy various activities. And with amazing consistency, these predictions are invariably negative. Recognise any of the following?

- ✔ I know I won't enjoy myself alone one bit.

- ✔ That sounds so boring.

- ✔ I'll just look stupid.

- ✔ I'm just feeling too miserable or anxious to get any kick out of that.

- ✔ I'm too anxious to go to, let alone enjoy, that party.

Sound familiar? Research shows that, especially when you're depressed or anxious, such predictions are worse than merely occasionally unreliable – they're actually reliably wrong! In other words, when you push yourself to engage in a potentially pleasurable activity, you're highly likely to discover that you enjoy it more than you think you will.

But if you believe what your mind tells you and take its negative predictions as reality, you'll head down the wrong road repeatedly. You'll avoid pursuing pleasure and looking for fun alternatives. Perhaps you encountered road-works and lengthy delays on your normal route. So you find a long-winding alternative. One year later, you completely forget that road-works do normally end and assume they're still in your way. So you ignore other options for ages longer, meaning unnecessary hours of driving. Just because something wasn't fun once doesn't mean it can never be so again. Go on! Give it a try!

To help you overcome your mind's negative predictions, try defeating your Joy Destroyers with restructured thinking:

1. **From Worksheet 11-1, choose five potentially pleasurable activities that you're willing to try.**

2. **List those activities in the left-hand column of Worksheet 11-8.**

3. **Predict the amount of enjoyment or pleasure each activity may give from 0 (no fun at all) to 10 (maximum pleasure).** Note it in the middle column.

4. **Do the pleasurable activity.**

5. **Rate how much enjoyment you actually experienced from doing each activity, using the same scale of 0 (no fun at all) to 10 (maximum pleasure).**

6. **Write about your observations and conclusions under My Reflections in Worksheet 11-9.**

Worksheet 11-8	Defeating the Joy Destroyers	
Activity	*Predicted Fun (0–10)*	*Experienced Fun (0–10)*

Can you see any trends in Worksheet 11-8? Do you experience more pleasure than you'd expect for most of your activities? If you don't see this, keep going a while longer – repeating some of the activities, but also trying others. If nothing gives any fun or pleasure, please do get professional help – it can make all the difference to your world.

Though progress may feel very slow, the pleasure you feel will probably increase gradually over time. Repeat this exercise whenever you choose, particularly after doing more work on your depression and anxiety.

Worksheet 11-9	**My Reflections**

Chapter 12

Tackling Life's Problems: Just Do It!

• •

In This Chapter

▶ Manufacturing your own motivation

▶ Pulling apart your problems

▶ Creating a step-by-step problem-solving game plan

• •

Depression and anxiety drain energy, hope and motivation. When your mind is full of negative emotions, it's hard to get moving. Everyday tasks seem overwhelming – simple problems appear complex, while mere molehills magnify into mountains. A vicious cycle begins. Not getting things done and not solving problems then makes you more depressed and anxious, and with ever decreasing energy, the mountain looms still larger.

In this chapter, you discover how to get going again. We warn you about the trap of waiting for motivation to come and find you and give you a plan of action, enabling *you* to do the finding, rather than vice versa! We also provide a comprehensive step-by-step game plan for untangling your problems and applying solutions.

Awaiting Mr Motivation

Especially if you're depressed, you may find yourself spending a lot of time free-wheeling and even back-pedalling. You're not accomplishing what you want, and you aren't even able to take the first step toward reversing inactivity. You're probably saying to yourself, 'I'll get round to all that when I feel like it.' Aha! Gotcha! You've fallen headlong into the Awaiting Motivation Trap. You're buying into the common myth that if you only wait long enough, Mr. Motivation himself will knock on your door and galvanise you into action. The stark reality is that action creates motivation; initially, it doesn't happen the other way around. After you get started and you do more, the more you want to do. The following example highlights the relationship between action and motivation.

It's Saturday morning and this weekend is the next deadline for writing five more chapters. But the Muse isn't here – no inspiration beckons, and the computer appears to glower menacingly from the desk in the study. Truth be told, about 101 activities seem more preferable today. Merely thinking about anxiety and depression, let alone writing about it, is more than enough to depress anyone, particularly on this beautiful sunny morning with its cloudless blue sky. And the thought of settling down to write is becoming more unappetising by the minute. So why not just put it off until we're more motivated?

That plan has two little problems: not only will we probably miss the publication deadline, but there's no guarantee that however long we wait, Mr Motivation is ever going to come along. Taken to the extreme, we never finish the book, you never read it and our publisher is really most displeased. The short-lived relief at the prospect of not writing on this beautiful Saturday morning will be followed by a whole load of grief.

Then what's the alternative? To just do it, irrespective of motivation or Muse. And then guess what – something almost miraculous happens: the whole mood changes. It's fun writing about writing being the action that's creating motivation, instead of the other way around. And what's even better – we can say, practising what we preach – it really works!

One way to jump-start action is by creating an *activity log,* as in the following example. You can see that an activity log is an action plan that plots out at least one small activity to accomplish each day and includes space to record how the task went and how it feels to complete it. Keeping track of the activities and small tasks you accomplish can give you sufficient incentive to keep going. Your motivation slowly but surely increases, and you find yourself doing even more than you expected.

Jean looks around her house, feeling overwhelmed and thoroughly ashamed of herself. She sees dishes piled everywhere, out-of-date magazines and newspapers covering the surfaces, and unopened letters, including what are obviously bills, lying higgledy-piggledy all over the place. She hasn't vacuumed or dusted for over a month, and the task of tackling the bomb site her home has become feels just too huge. Jean just hasn't a clue where to begin.

Jean manages to drag herself to her women's support group that meets on Wednesday evenings. She confesses her difficulty in tackling basic daily chores and describes the state of her home. One of the group suggests that Jean fill out an activity log. Worksheet 12-1 shows Jean's result.

Worksheet 12-1	Jean's Activity Log	
Day	*Activity*	*Outcome*
Monday	Wash just the few dishes lying in the sink and leave the rest.	After I got started, I ended up doing the lot. It actually felt great!
Tuesday	Pay a few of the most urgent bills.	It took me all day to get around to it, but I did it. Didn't make me feel much better – probably as I'd procrastinated so long.
Wednesday	Check through my bank and credit card statements.	Just couldn't face it! Felt too discouraged and overwhelmed.
Thursday	Pop into the garage mini-market on my way home.	I've been having cereal and long-life milk for too long. The fresh fruit and veggies made a difference, and the pre-prepared meal was easy and tasty!
Friday	Vacuum the house.	Not my favourite activity, but I did feel I'd done something useful. The spiders weren't best pleased!

Day	Activity	Outcome
Saturday	Clean the kitchen.	Really went to town on that one. The kitchen's smiling, and I must admit I'm starting to feel just a little better.
Sunday	Took my car to the supermarket carwash and had it washed while I did a week's shopping.	This really perked me up. The poor thing hasn't had a bath in over five months!

Jean notices that after she starts doing an activity, she usually feels better. She realises that facing finances – paying her bills and checking statements – is a particularly problematic area. She decides to ask her cousin, a book-keeper, to come over and help her get started straightening out her finances and setting up a user-friendly system. Overall, Jean finds that the activity log really does help her get going again.

If you've been feeling stuck lately and overwhelmed by all you need to do, we recommend you create your own activity log to get back on track.

1. **Think about the various tasks you're putting off.**

2. **Choose one activity for each day of the week and list it in the middle column of Worksheet 12-2.**

   Start with small tasks and break big ones into smaller bits. For example, don't plan on clearing the whole shed in one day. Instead, tackle one messy shelf at a time. Make sure each task you include is do-able.

3. **On each day, complete the corresponding task and, in the right-hand column, write down how it went and how it made you feel to do it.** If you don't complete a given task, don't beat yourself up; just move on to the next.

4. **After you finish a week's worth of tasks, jot down your observations of what you learn under My Reflections (see Worksheet 12-3).**

If you find this exercise useful, continue it for several weeks. After you start feeling motivation returning, you probably don't need to continue with it. But feel free to restart it whenever motivation starts slinking out the door.

Worksheet 12-2		My Activity Log
Day	*Activity*	*Outcome*
Monday		
Tuesday		
Wednesday		

(continued)

Worksheet 12-2 *(continued)*

Day	Activity	Outcome
Thursday		
Friday		
Saturday		
Sunday		

You can download more copies of this form at www.dummies.com/go/adwb.

Worksheet 12-3   **My Reflections**

_____

_____

_____

_____

Playing the Problem-Solving Game: C.R.I.C.K.E.T

When people are emotionally distressed, many situations seem overwhelmingly difficult. Anxiety and depression make even small problems appear insurmountable because emotional pain interferes with clear thinking.

When you feel overwhelmed, you tend to avoid problems and procrastinate for as long as possible. This avoidance is unfortunate because unaddressed problems have a nasty tendency towards growing rather than shrinking. But if avoidance isn't the answer, what is? We've devised a way to break problems down and for you to work out what to do with them. We call the plan C.R.I.C.K.E.T – which seems fair enough! Here's what C.R.I.C.K.E.T stands for:

✔ **C:** Seeing the *central core* of your problem. You describe the problem and its causes, plus your beliefs and feelings about the problem.

✔ **R:** Running through the routes. You identify possible options to address the problem.

✔ **I:** Investigating outcomes. You consider the most likely results for each option.

✔ **C:** Committing to a choice.

✔ **K:** Keeping it up.

✔ **E:** Easing your emotions. Deal with the distress associated with the solution you choose.

✔ **T:** Testing it out. You try out your plan in a *test match* and make appropriate adjustments.

In the following sections, we review the C.R.I.C.K.E.T game plan. To give you a picture of how this process works, you follow Donald as he solves a work-related problem. You see how he completes each component of C.R.I.C.K.E.T's problem-solving process, and then we tell you how to apply this to yourself.

C.R.I.C.K.E.T is a successful game plan for life, irrespective of whether you're feeling emotional distress. Even if you're feeling great, you can still employ it in tackling any of life's frustrating issues, which are bound to crop up at some time.

Seeing the central core (C)

Instead of acting like an ostrich, burying your head in the sand, take a good hard look at your problem. Get information about it. Think through the causes and the relative importance of the problem to your life. Guess what? You're neither the first nor last to experience a particular problem. Collect information through talking to others, reading books and articles or by searching the Internet. Finally, reflect on what feelings this problem stirs up in you.

Donald feels frustrated in his work as a mechanical engineer. He hasn't been given the level of responsibility he believes he's capable of, nor has he had the rewards or recognition he's expected. His frustration grows as he ruminates sleeplessly in the early hours. He realises that the situation is contributing to his mounting depression. Donald goes online and researches comparable jobs; he also reads some books about career advancement. He takes the first step in tackling his problem, defining the *central core* (see Worksheet 12-4).

Worksheet 12-4	Donald's Central Core: C.

I'm unhappy with my job. I want more responsibility, a better salary and the accompanying recognition. I've been here for a whole six years, and I'm still doing the same things as when I started. I don't think the problem is a lack of skills; I'm pretty sure of my abilities. One of the books I've read suggests that maybe I haven't been assertive enough and made myself known around here. The problem's been disturbing my sleep, so it's clearly important.

After describing his problem in great detail, Donald's ready to go on to the next step, *running through the routes* (see the following section) to explore his options.

Using Donald's scenario as a guide, complete Worksheet 12-5:

1. **Describe the central core of your problem.**

2. **Consider reading books and articles or searching the Internet for helpful suggestions.** Record any relevant information you find.

3. **Include information about possible causes of your problem.**

4. **Include your emotional responses to the problem.** Do you feel depressed, frustrated, anxious or perhaps something else? (We cover ways to identify your emotions in Chapter 4.)

5. **Indicate how important the problem is to you, perhaps with a number out of 100.**

Worksheet 12-5	My Problem's Central Core: C.

Running through the routes (R)

After you illuminate the central core of your problem, you're ready to get cracking and be a bright spark! This step asks you to brainstorm all the possible ways of tackling your problem – the possible *routes* you can take. Include everything you come up with, irrespective of how silly some ideas may sound. Muzzle your internal critic – let your imagination run wild.

If you're stuck coming up with solutions, consider reading some books – your local librarian or bookseller probably has some ideas of relevant ones. Ask people close to you or trusted people who have gone through similar problems for recommendations.

Donald researches the job market, reading up about career advancement in his field. He talks with friends and colleagues to brainstorm his routes and options. After a lot of research and thought, he lists his ideas (see Worksheet 12-6).

Worksheet 12-6	Donald's Core and Routes: C.R.

Core: I'm unhappy with my job. I want more responsibility, a better salary and the accompanying recognition. I've been here for a whole for six years, and I'm still doing the same things as when I started. I don't think the problem is a lack of skills; I'm pretty confident about my abilities. One of the books I've read suggests that maybe I haven't been assertive enough and made myself known around here. The problem's been disturbing my sleep, so it's clearly important.

Routes

I can look for another job.

I can work on my assertiveness skills, do training through work, maybe take an evening class or even go to Toastmasters.

I can ask for a meeting with my supervisor and discuss my concerns.

I can ignore the work situation, and instead try to find fun and satisfaction through outside pursuits.

I could resign and go self-employed.

I could tell the boss where to get off.

I could sign up for further training. If I show them how much I do know, and how good I am, it might just impress my superiors.

I could network a bit, and even start going to all those stupid work social events (heaven forbid!).

Donald feels he's explored all his possible routes for solving his problem. He's now ready for the next step in C.R.I.C.K.E.T's problem-solving process, committing to a choice.

Identify your routes by following these instructions:

1. **In Worksheet 12-7, note the situation you describe in Worksheet 12-5.**

2. **Gather data from books, the Internet, friends – basically anywhere.**

3. **Run through a range of routes to deal with your problem and write them down in the space provided.** Include the routes of going nowhere, doing nothing different, staying just where you are and keeping the status quo.

Don't censor your ideas. Include anything with the remotest chance of helping.

Worksheet 12-7   **My Core and Routes: C.R.**

Core:

_____

_____

_____

_____

Routes:

_____

_____

_____

_____

Investigating outcomes (1)

After you list all the possible routes for solving your problem, you need to consider the most likely outcomes for each of those. We're not asking you to be a fortune teller. Obviously, you can't know for absolute certain how each route will turn out, but you can make educated guesses. So have a go. Evaluate what you think is most likely to happen. Worksheet 12-8 describes Donald's core problem again, then covers what he comes up with.

Worksheet 12-8   **Donald's Core, Routes and Investigation: C.R.I.**

Core: I'm unhappy with my job. I want more responsibility, a better salary and the accompanying recognition. I've been here for a whole for six years, and I'm still doing the same things as when I started. I don't think the problem is a lack of skills; I'm pretty confident about my abilities. One of the books I've read suggests that maybe I haven't been assertive enough and made myself known around here. The problem's been disturbing my sleep, so it's clearly important.

Routes	*Investigating Outcomes*
I can look for another job.	I could, but fat chance of that in this recession! Actually, this a pretty good firm, and if I left now, I'd lose my seniority, and I'm not sure I'd find anything much better.
I can work on my assertiveness skills, do training through work, maybe take an evening class or even go to Toastmasters.	It's taken a while to see it, but the colleagues who have made the most progress are the sociable ones, who speak up for themselves and aren't afraid to answer back. Maybe skills training is the answer.
I can ask for a meeting with my supervisor and discuss my concerns.	Tried it before, and it didn't help. But perhaps I can do it differently this time — and even put into practice some of that assertiveness training stuff.
I can ignore the work situation, and instead try to find fun and satisfaction through outside pursuits.	But I'm committed to my work — no way do I want to be a straight nine to five type. I think the work problem needs sorting, not ignoring and avoiding.
I could resign and go self-employed.	Not the best economic climate for that. Better not risk my mortgage right now. Perhaps keep this one for a later date.
I could tell the boss where to get off.	Pretty tempting, that! But it might just backfire, and now's not the time to be handed my P45 and a month's salary in lieu of notice.

Routes	Investigating Outcomes
I could sign up for further training. If I show them how much I do know, and how good I am, it might just impress my superiors.	What courses do I want or need? I've got my City and Guilds, and promotion doesn't seem linked to higher qualifications when I look at colleagues.
I could network a bit, and even start (heaven forbid!) going to all those stupid work social events.	That fits with the assertiveness and sociability ideas. It could just do the trick. And even though I don't feel like it — who knows, some people seem to get a kick out of mixing — perhaps I could too . . . eventually!

Fill out your own description of your core, routes and investigation of outcomes.

1. **Write down your problematic situation in Worksheet 12-9.** This time, feel free to abbreviate your situation – you're probably pretty familiar with it by now.

2. **Briefly list your routes from Worksheet 12-7 in the left-hand column.**

3. **Investigate the outcomes for each option and write them in the right-hand column.**
   All you're looking for is the most obvious, likely ones because you never know for sure what will happen until you actually have a go.

Worksheet 12-9 **My Core, Routes and Investigations: C.R.I.**

Situation: _____

_____

Routes	Investigating Outcomes

(continued)

Worksheet 12-9 *(continued)*

Routes	Investigating Outcomes

Committing to a choice (C)

To choose how best to handle your problem, you first need to go through the previous steps – carefully considering each route and investigating its most likely outcome (see Worksheet 12-9). Reflect on how each would make you feel – if you actually chose it. Some routes may seem pretty difficult, while you're sure to have some that you obviously would never select.

When you make your selection, commit to it, even if it seems very difficult. You may want to tell others what you plan to do – doing so often makes the commitment feel more binding and makes you think twice before back-tracking and reneging on it.

Though it may not seem the case, deciding to make no choice is really making a choice. Doing nothing is an action of sorts – you're choosing to keep still – and has its own set of likely outcomes.

Donald weighs up his options and their potential consequences, and decides to work on his communication, assertiveness and networking skills. He decides to sign up for some courses, read books and start going to work dos.

To make your choices, do the following, using Donald's example as a guide.

1. **Review your C.R.I. form (see Worksheet 12-9).**

2. **Choose the option or options that seem to make the most sense to you – the ones most likely to get you what, and to where, you want.**

3. **Jot down your selection in Worksheet 12-10.**

Worksheet 12-10   **My Choice: C.**

Keeping it up (K)

This C.R.I.C.K.E.T step is for the faint-hearted. If you find you're flagging – don't lose heart now. You're nearly there . . . just a bit further, and then you can reap the wonderful harvest you've painstakingly sown and nurtured! Go on! Only for a little longer! Set aside a small reward for yourself every time you investigate an outcome.

Easing your emotions (E)

Many people make decisions to do something but then procrastinate agonisingly when it comes to carrying out those decisions. Why? Because many actions arouse anxiety, fear or distress (see Chapter 9). If your choice of options makes you tremble, consider the following tips:

✔ **Role-play and rehearsal:** Using your imagination, see yourself practising your solution. Imagine the process going well, and if you want, imagine how you'll deal with problems that may come up, seeing the process through to a good ending. Or even better, rehearse your solution aloud, by yourself or with a trusted friend. The more you rehearse, the more you're likely to feel prepared and calm in the real-life situation.

✔ **Self-talk:** Think of some positive statements that you can repeat to yourself as you carry out your plan. Consider writing them on a card to carry with you as a reminder. Positive statements may include:

- This is the right thing to do.
- I can put up with the discomfort; it won't last long.
- I worked hard to consider other alternatives; this is my best shot.
- I have the absolute right to carry this out.

✔ **Brief relaxation strategy:** Not only is this technique quick and simple, but it helps calm acute anxiety. (See Chapter 13 for more information and practice with relaxation techniques.)

1. Take a slow, deep breath in through your nose.
2. Hold your breath for a few seconds.
3. Breathe out through your mouth very slowly.
4. As you breathe out, make a slight hissing sound.
5. Repeat ten times.

After you work through these recommendations, write down your personal plan for easing your emotions in Worksheet 12-11.

Worksheet 12-11   **Ways to Ease My Emotions: E.**

_____

_____

_____

_____

_____

Testing it out: The test match (T)

Running through your solution and reviewing its effectiveness are crucial to your success. At this point, you've gone through the problem-solving process and are ready to put all that theory into practice in a test match. Decide when would be a good time to execute your plan, and then do it! Afterwards, evaluate how your plan worked.

Donald decides to improve his communication and social skills, so he completes the actions he selected earlier in the process. Worksheet 12-12 shows Donald's reflections on how his solution worked out.

Worksheet 12-12	Donald's Test Match: T.

I think some of these strategies are working for me. Just last week, I was asked to take the lead on a project. That's a first. And I've noticed that others are coming to me for advice. My presentation last week actually went okay; and I didn't faint, throw up or even embarrass myself — or my department! But I think now's the time to improve my skills by signing up for some of that IT training. Hey! It could even be exciting. It feels like a good start.

As you can see, Donald's plan and his test match work out pretty well. Yours may or may not. If your plan isn't an instant success, be sure to include in your test match reflection any ideas for continuing what you're doing or making alterations to your game plan. You can even run through C.R.I.C.K.E.T's whole game plan again and discover additional routes and possibilities.

Use Worksheet 12-13 to record your reflections on your test match, in which you put into practice your problem's solutions. You may find it helpful to keep a copy with you – in your bag, wallet or pocket – so you can add to it as situations arise. The worksheet can serve as a useful reminder of what's working well . . . and what isn't.

Worksheet 12-13	My Test Match: T.

You may find it helpful to put the whole C.R.I.C.K.E.T problem-solving process on one form, as in Worksheet 12-14, making whatever notes you like. You can use this condensed form after you go through the preceding steps of committing to a choice.

Worksheet 12-14	My C.R.I.C.K.E.T Game Plan	
Step	*Notes*	
Core		
Routes		
Investigated Outcomes		

Step	Notes
Choice	
Keeping It Up	
Easing Emotions	
Testing It Out: The Test Match	

Part IV
Feeling It Where It Hurts: Healing the Body

'Took ages to persuade Darren to come
sky diving. He was always anxious about
whether his parachute would open or not.'

In this part . . .

Depression and anxiety have an important physical, or biological, component. Emotional problems may be due to chemical imbalances, illnesses or chronic stress, while many health problems can be underpinned or exacerbated by emotional factors.

In this part, we show you how to relax your body through breathing, exercise, muscle relaxation and improved sleep. Then we help you decide whether or not medication is a useful part of your treatment. If you do decide to take medication, we give you tips on talking to your doctor, plus ways to identify and record any side effects.

Chapter 13

Taking the Relaxation Route

. . . .

. . . .

*W*here are the blasted car keys? Got 'em! Scrape the frost off the windscreen, roar down the motorway. Your mobile rings and you fumble to answer it – hands free, of course. Brake lights loom ahead, and you, plus the car behind, barely stop in time. Shaking to the core and pouring with sweat, you eventually inch forward, as the jam tortuously unsnarls. And that's just the start of Monday morning!

Modern life produces an ongoing series of triggers that rev up your entire nervous system. Your body prepares you to react to perceived dangers and stressors by orchestrating a complex *fight-or-flight response*:

✔ Your brain sends messages to your nervous system to go into high gear.

✔ The pupil in the centre of your eye expands to let in more light.

✔ Your heart beats faster.

✔ Your digestion slows, meaning more energy's available for the large muscles, which gear up for action.

✔ Blood flow increases to the arms and legs so that you can run or fight.

✔ Sweating increases, and as the water evaporates, you cool down.

All these responses are pretty handy if you need to physically defend yourself or run away. But typically, most people in morning traffic jams don't jump out of their cars and beat up other drivers – or abandon their cars and race off to work. Well, okay, maybe in some places, but surely not here!

The consequences of chronically revving up your body's fight-or-flight response can include experiencing high blood pressure, chronic muscle spasms, tension headaches, suppressed immune system, irritable bowel syndrome, ulcers and many other physical effects. Quite a high cost for responses you rarely actually utilise when dealing with most situations. So what's the alternative?

In this chapter, we look at the benefits of relaxation. We give you some quick, effective strategies for teaching your body to chill out, even when you find yourself in stressful situations. Finally, we show you how to enhance the quality of your sleep, which further increases your ability to cope with stress.

Appreciating Relaxation: What's in It for Me?

Your life's probably sufficiently hectic and stressed as it is. You're quite likely already over-committed, and the last thing you think you need is for some bright spark to suggest taking on yet more! We agree: time for many people is a pretty scarce, highly precious commodity. And developing the ability to relax does take some time. So why on earth bother spending time on getting the hang of this particular skill? Well, relaxation can:

- ✔ Reduce your blood pressure
- ✔ Improve your immune response
- ✔ Increase your sense of well-being
- ✔ Help you feel less angry and irritable
- ✔ Encourage better sleep
- ✔ Decrease your risk of heart and other chronic diseases
- ✔ Reduce pain
- ✔ Decrease anxiety
- ✔ Improve your mood
- ✔ Improve your ability to cope
- ✔ Improve your productivity

Not bad at all? Relax for a few minutes of each day, and chances are you'll improve your health and sense of well-being. Not only that, but you're likely to more than make up for the time lost through relaxing, as you become more efficient and productive.

How do you know if you're a pretty calm person who doesn't need to improve your relaxation skills? Do the following exercise to help you decide whether spending a little time relaxing is a good idea for you.

1. **Think about how you've felt over the past week.**

2. **In Worksheet 13-1, write down all situations and times when you felt truly calm and relaxed.**

3. **Write down all the situations and times you recall feeling tense and stressed.**

4. **Look at the balance, take stock of your life and reflect on whether you need to do something about your approach to relaxation.**

Worksheet 13-1	Personal Relaxation Review
Times I Felt Relaxed this Week	*Times I Felt Tense this Week*

Times I Felt Relaxed this Week	Times I Felt Tense this Week

Very rarely, some people report that relaxation actually induces feelings of panic and loss of control. If that starts to happen to you as you work through activities in this chapter, stop immediately and consult a mental health professional.

Breathing Out the Tension

You may not realise it, but the way you breathe can increase or decrease your tension. Many people breathe in a way that's counterproductive to relaxation: they breathe too shallowly, restricting their breathing to the upper chest area, or they breathe too fast. Sometimes, people under stress find themselves holding their breath, which further heightens their body's arousal.

Filling your lower tummy: Abdominal breathing

Your breathing isn't nearly as effective when you take air primarily into your upper chest. Such shallow breathing fails to fill your lungs properly, and it can lead to stress and hyper-ventilation. This type of breathing isn't how you naturally breathe when you're at rest. Watch a baby breathing and you'll see how the tummy rises and falls more than the chest area. Often, as people grow older, they somehow leave behind this early style of breathing. Perhaps that's because you're trying too hard to stand up straight, hold that tummy in and generally be in control of everything, including your breathing, instead of trusting your body to get on with it and regulate your breathing all by itself!

The following exercise shows you what it's like to breathe like a baby.

1. **Lie down on your back on a soft carpet, a mat or a bed with your head on a thin book or pillow.**

2. **Bend your knees slightly so your entire back is flat and you feel comfortable.**

3. **Place one hand on your tummy.**

4. **Place one hand on your chest.**

5. **Breathe in a way so that the hand on your tummy rises and falls higher and lower than the one on your chest.**

6. **Breathe this way for several minutes.**

7. **Notice how you feel and write your observations in Worksheet 13-2.**

Worksheet 13-2	My Reflections

_____

_____

_____

_____

You can practise abdominal breathing practically anywhere, anytime. For example, take three minutes at work to concentrate on breathing deeply. You don't even have to lie down (just make sure you won't be disturbed!). Sit quietly and breathe, letting your stomach rise more than your chest, so that you completely fill your lungs. You'll probably be amazed by how much just three minutes of abdominal breathing refreshes you. With practice, this may even become your new normal breathing style.

Telling your body to hold it: Anti-panic breathing

If you ever feel intense anxiety or panic, your breathing no doubt quickens and becomes shallower. These changes may increase your heart rate and blood pressure, you may feel dizzy and your thinking may get a bit confused.

The breathing technique that follows can short-circuit the effects of panic on your breathing. Practise it now, and from time to time when you're not in a state of panic, so that you know how to do it when you need to most.

1. **Inhale slowly and deeply through your nose.**

2. **Hold your breath and count to six.**

3. **Slowly breathe out through your mouth while making a very slight hissing noise.**
   This noise helps you slow your rate of breathing. The noise should be subtle; only you need to hear it. Hissing snake-sounds may just get others worried!

4. **Repeat this five to ten times, until you feel that you've calmed down a bit.**

5. **In Worksheet 13-3, write your observations on how this exercise makes you feel.**

Worksheet 13-3	My Reflections

_____

_____

_____

_____

Going with the flow: Gentle breathing

It really doesn't get any simpler than this breathing technique, and it doesn't take much time either. Give it a go!

1. **Find a comfortable place and sit down.**

2. **Simply pay attention to your breathing.** Become aware of the air as it flows through your nose and into your lungs. Notice how your muscles pull and then push the air gently in and out.

3. **Allow your breathing to develop a slow, even flow – in . . . and out.**

4. **Imagine bringing a delicate flower with dainty petals up to your nostrils. Soften your breath so that the petals remain still as you breathe in and out.**

5. **Continue to be aware of the air as it goes through your nose and lungs.**

6. **Note how focusing on your breathing gradually relaxes and calms you.**

7. **Feel how refreshing the air is.**

8. **Continue gentle breathing while focusing on the feel of the passing air.**

9. **In Worksheet 13-4, write your observations on how this exercise makes you feel.**

Consider practising gentle breathing for five minutes every day for ten days or so. You may discover that you want to continue one or more of the breathing strategies in this section for the rest of your life. Relaxed breathing is a simple yet powerful way of teaching your whole body to relax. Gradually, you'll find yourself able to employ such breathing to reduce stress whenever you encounter it.

Worksheet 13-4 **My Reflections**

_____

_____

_____

_____

_____

Letting It Go: Reducing Your Muscular Tension

According to extensive research, one of the best methods for teaching your body to relax is called *progressive muscle relaxation*. It may sound scary and complicated, but you can find easy-to-follow instructions for this type of muscle relaxation in a variety of books, CDs and on the Internet. The evidence shows that muscle relaxation really does work. So here we give you one of our favourite muscle relaxation strategies. Initially, this technique takes about 15 or 20 minutes. With practice, you'll be able to become relaxed in less and less time. After a while, some people are able to relax their bodies within just two or three minutes!

To get the most out of this relaxation exercise, find a quiet place where you're unlikely to be disturbed. Switch off your mobile, remove your shoes and loosen any tight belt or clothing.

You may find relaxing easier if you record the following instructions in advance. Responding to verbal instructions is probably more relaxing than reading each step, and then doing it. If you decide to make a recording, be sure to speak slowly and calmly.

The following relaxation procedure is an extract from our book, *Overcoming Anxiety For Dummies* (Wiley). Practise it often, until you can do it without having to hear or read the instructions. This technique involves systematically tensing various muscle groups and holding that tension for a few moments – perhaps five or ten seconds. Then you release the tension and allow relaxation to take over. The procedure starts with your hands and arms, moves through the neck, back, and face, and progresses down the legs and feet.

1. **Take a deep breath, drawing the air into your abdomen.** Hold it there for 3–4 seconds. Concentrate on the feelings, and then slowly exhale and let the tension go. Imagine your whole body as a balloon that loses air as you exhale, releasing the tension as the air goes out. Take three more such breaths and allow your entire body to go increasingly loose, limp and floppy with each breath.

2. **Squeeze your fingers into a fist.** Feel the tension. Hold it while you slowly count up to 6–10 seconds. Then release the tension, let it flow away, and feel your hands go limp as you relax. Repeat two or three more times.

3. **Raise your arms to shoulder height.** Tighten all your arm muscles, both inside and outside the lower arms. Use your hands to check the tension's really tight. Hold that tension a few seconds, and then imagine a string that suspended your arms is cut. Let your arms fall suddenly downwards with a thump and then relax. Repeat two or three more times.

4. **Lift your shoulders as though you were a turtle trying to draw your head back into your shell.** Hold the tension, and then let your shoulders drop. Feel the relaxation deepen for 10 to 15 seconds.

5. **Pull your shoulders back, bringing your shoulder blades closer together.** Hold that tension a little while, and then let it go.

6. **Scrunch up your entire face.** Squeeze your forehead down, screw up your eyes and furrow your eyebrows. Clench your jaw, contract your tongue and lips. Let the tension grow and hold it – then let go and relax.

7. **Gently let your head tip back, but stop before it becomes painful.** Feel the muscles tighten in the back of your neck. Notice that tension and hold it, and then let go and relax. Feel the relaxation deepening.

8. **Gently lower your chin toward your chest.** Tighten your neck muscles, let the tension increase, hold it and then relax. Feel the tension melting away like candle wax.

9. **Tighten the muscles in your stomach and chest and maintain the tension.** Really tight! Like you're expecting a punch to the stomach. Hold it for a few seconds, and then let it go.

10. **Arch your back, for example by pressing your shoulders against a chair.** Hold that contraction, and then relax. Repeat several times.

    Be careful not to over-arch your back and cause pain. Skip this step if you've had back pain in the past.

11. **Contract your buttocks to gently lift yourself up.** Hold the tension, and then relax and feel the tension melt away as the relaxation deepens.

12. **Squeeze and relax your thigh muscles.**

13. **Contract and relax your calves by keeping your heels on the floor and curling your toes back towards your face.** If you get muscle cramps, don't overdo this exercise. Only curl your feet as far as is comfortable. Hold the tension . . . then let go, allowing the tension to drain into the floor.

14. **Gently curl your toes downwards, maintain the tension and then relax.** Repeat several times, feeling the relaxation deepen with each repetition.

15. **Take a little time to scan your entire body.** If you find any areas of tension, allow the relaxed areas around them to come in and replace the tension with relaxation. If that doesn't work, repeat the tense-and-relax procedure specifically for the tense area.

16. **Spend a few minutes enjoying the relaxed feelings.** Let relaxation spread and penetrate every muscle fibre in your body. Notice any feelings you have. You may feel warmth, or even a floating sensation. Perhaps you feel a sense of sinking down. Whatever it is, allow it to happen. When you feel ready, you can open your eyes, carry on with your day, perhaps feeling like you're just back from a short holiday.

Although we recommend you initially spend 15 or 20 minutes a day on the muscle relaxation exercises, later you can shorten the time considerably. With practice, you can tense up several muscles groups at once. For example, you may tense hands and arms at the same time. Eventually, you may tense all the muscles in your lower body at once, followed by all the muscles in your upper body. If you tend to carry most of your tension in your neck, shoulders or back, try tensing and relaxing just those muscles. Repeat the tense-and-relax cycle once or twice on any especially tight muscles.

Use Worksheet 13-5 to track your thoughts and observations about using progressive muscle relaxation.

Worksheet 13-5	**My Reflections**

To Sleep, Perchance to Dream

Depression and anxiety disrupt sleep. Some people have trouble falling asleep, while others wake up in the early morning hours and can't get back to sleep. Some people suffer from both problems. The opposite is also possible – a few people with anxiety or depression sleep far too much, and don't even feel refreshed.

Trouble sleeping probably adds to your emotional distress. And as your emotional distress increases due to sleep deprivation, no doubt your sleep problems worsen, resulting in a vicious cycle.

Serious, chronic sleep disturbances may be a symptom of a major depressive disorder or an undiagnosed physical problem. Consult your doctor if you have major, serious, ongoing sleep problems.

In this section, we help you develop good sleep habits. First, answer the questions in Worksheet 13-6, describing your sleep habits.

Worksheet 13-6	**Seven Sleep Situations**

1. What do you normally eat or drink in the few hours prior to going to bed?

(continued)

Worksheet 13-6 *(continued)*

2. What are you normally doing a few hours before bedtime?

_____

_____

_____

3. Describe the room you sleep in, including the temperature, lighting, noise level, the bed and the furnishings.

_____

_____

_____

4. About how long does it take you to get to sleep? How many hours of sleep do you get on an average night?

_____

_____

_____

5. How many times a week, and how many times per night, do you wake up in the middle of the night? And too early in the morning? Does it take you long to get back to sleep?

_____

_____

_____

6. Do you worry a lot about not getting enough sleep?

_____

_____

_____

7. Do you have nightmares? What are they like? Do they disturb you?

_____

_____

_____

Your answers to these questions give you a good picture of your sleep patterns. To make it still clearer, consider asking your partner's views on questions 1–3. You may be surprised to find a different view from the one you hold about yourself and your patterns. If, however, you conclude that you don't have a sleep problem, feel free to skip the rest of this chapter! But if you clearly struggle with sleep, read on. The following sections tell you what you need to know about the seven key sleep-related issues that each question in Worksheet 13-6 poses.

1: Watching what you eat and drink

You probably know that caffeine is a stimulant and, therefore, keeps many people awake. Some people don't seem to experience much effect from caffeine, while others can lie awake for hours after a single cup. Coffee isn't the only culprit though; other sources of caffeine include tea, many soft drinks, chocolate and some pain relievers. Read the labels of what you're consuming or you may be wide awake all night!

You may think that alcohol is a depressant, and therefore the effect will be the opposite of caffeine. So it should do the trick and put you straight to sleep, right? Well, not exactly. Some people find a glass or two of wine relaxing and helpful in falling asleep. However, too much alcohol interferes with restful sleep. So while you may indeed fall asleep quite quickly, chances are you wake in the middle of the night and have great difficulty getting back to sleep. And for that matter, too much of anything, including rich foods or especially late mealtimes can disrupt your sleep.

When it comes to eating and drinking before bed, if you just have to have something, try herbal tea without caffeine, such as chamomile or valerian. Or have a small glass of milk, hot malted milk drink or a light snack. And we probably don't have to tell you not to drink gallons of fluids before you go to bed or you'll be up all night for different reasons!

2: Doing what's right for you

One key to restful sleep is going to bed in a reasonably relaxed state. Strenuous or aerobic activities tend to stimulate the body, so steer clear of these for at least an hour before heading for bed, though lovemaking does seem to be an exception! Arguments are another no-no, so try to steer clear of them, particularly around bedtimes.

Develop a regular winding-down routine that you go through prior to bed. A warm bath (not overly hot, which can be stimulating for some), quiet music, a good book (probably not a horror one) or a little light-hearted television can all help you wind down.

Experiment with what works for you – and what doesn't – before bedtime. For some, the drama of the evening news doesn't have any stressful effects. Others find a murder mystery quite calming. Still others actually find aerobic exercise is just perfect for tiring them out and ensuring log-like sleep.

3: Setting the scene for sleep

The environment you sleep in plays a major part in determining the quality of your sleep. For most people, sleep comes more easily when it's dark. But what if you work on a night shift and need to sleep during the day? Consider getting heavy blackout-type curtains or wearing a sleep mask, as darkness normally tells your brain it's time to sleep.

How about that mattress you've had for the past 20 years? Is it really still comfortable? For some, the floor or couch works better, if sleep proves elusive in bed. For most people, however, a really good mattress is worth every penny. Consider the quality of your sheets, in order to make your sleep setting even more inviting. Satin-style can be surprisingly inexpensive – and fun! If you have health problems, such as severe arthritis, you may find that an electric bed that allows you to adjust your posture is a great help. Do make sure you get medical advice though, as this option is usually costly.

When it comes to your sleep setting, noise levels can make a big difference. Explore how to make your environment relatively silent. Alternatively, try masking noises with more palatable sounds from a fan, a softly playing radio or CD, or even a sound machine.

Finally, temperature matters. For most, cooler is better, and if it's too chilly, you can always snuggle down under extra blankets, or get a warmer quilt. Sleep researchers have found that core body temperature tends to decrease during good quality sleep.

4: Getting neither too much nor too little

How long does it take you to fall asleep? If you lie restless in bed for more than about half an hour, we recommend that you get up. What? Get up when all you really want is to sleep? This advice may sound counterproductive, but your brain needs to associate your bed with sleep. So if you lie in bed too long without actually sleeping, your brain tends to get mixed up.

Choose not very pleasant or even boring activities to do when you get out of bed during the night. Your brain then starts associating this with getting up during the night-time, and you'll probably find you're in no hurry to get out of bed. Do make sure you don't do anything stimulating when you get up, as this will decrease your chances of going back to sleep. However, if you do decide to pay your accounts in the middle of the night, ensure you check your addition in the morning.

How many hours of sleep do you get per average night? Although people differ in their sleep needs, most function pretty well on six to eight hours per night. Generally, if you feel rested, you're probably getting enough sleep, while if you don't, perhaps you're getting too much or too little. And when you don't actually feel like getting out of bed, remember the reply to the old question 'How much sleep does the average person need?' The answer is: Five minutes more!

One possibility, if you don't feel rested after six to eight hours of sleep, is that you're suffering from *sleep apnoea,* in which you repeatedly stop breathing for a brief time during the night. You awaken briefly to gasp for air, and then you fall back asleep, only to have your breathing cease yet again. You may or may not be aware that you stop breathing and wake up, so ask your partner. Sleep apnoea results in very poor quality sleep and frequently leads to nodding off in the daytime. Snoring can be a sign of sleep apnoea, but that's not always the case. If you think you may have sleep apnoea, your doctor can refer you for specialist diagnosis and treatment.

5: Mending broken sleep

Waking up once or twice a night is pretty common, and nothing to be concerned about. However, waking frequently, or being unable to get back to sleep after waking can be a problem. Check with your doctor, as waking up frequently may indicate:

- Prostate problems for men.
- Hormonal problems, more commonly in women.
- Restless leg syndrome, in which you experience discomfort in your legs or feet and have the urge to keep moving them.
- Medication issues.
- A major depressive disorder (for which this workbook can help, but you need professional assistance as well).
- A variety of physical conditions.
- Other serious emotional disorders (again, this workbook can help, but you should still seek help from a mental health professional).

If you eliminate the preceding possible problems and continue to wake frequently or are unable to get back to sleep, follow the advice in this chapter. In particular, don't lie awake in bed for more than half an hour. If you can't drop off within that time, get up, do something else and try again a bit later.

Even with a decent dose of nightly sleep, some people *feel* they're not sleeping for as many hours as they really are. If you feel rested during the day, chances are you really are getting enough sleep. If you don't feel rested, something is likely amiss.

6: Worrying yourself awake

Sleep's very important, right? It's so important that if you don't get enough, your day will be utterly ruined. If you don't sleep enough, you may make terrible mistakes and even become ill! You MUST get enough sleep!

Well, hang on a second. These types of catastrophic thoughts are bound to keep you awake at night and make the next day pretty miserable to boot. When you find yourself thinking such thoughts, turn to Worksheet 13-7 for some more reasonable ways of restructuring your situation. Add your own sleep-sabotaging thoughts and effective responses to them in the blank boxes. (Chapters 5, 6 and 7 give you strategies for dealing with flawed thinking.)

Worksheet 13-7	Sleep-Sabotaging Versus Sleep-Promoting Thoughts
Sleep-Sabotaging Thoughts	*Sleep-Promoting Thoughts*
If I don't get enough sleep, I'll be wrecked, and my day will be utterly ruined.	I've survived dozens of days after insufficient sleep. I don't like it, but actually some of those days were absolutely fine.
It's horrible when I don't fall asleep right away.	I don't like not sleeping, but it's not the absolute worst thing that's ever happened to me. Maybe I can use my relaxation skills and at least rest a little better. This isn't the end of the world.
Not enough sleep is bad for me — and even dangerous.	I suppose it's a bit dangerous to drive when I'm very tired, but I can monitor my fatigue and stop for a break, or even the night, if I have to. People don't generally die from insufficient sleep.
I can't stand not sleeping.	I'm just catastrophising here. I simply don't like not sleeping, and there are many worse things. Worrying about it will only make it a whole lot worse. I just need to accept whatever happens, or read Chapter 8 of the *Anxiety & Depression Workbook For Dummies* if I have trouble accepting it.

Worries about things other than sleep can also interfere with you getting a good night's sleep. If you're a worrier in general, we recommend you read and carefully work through the exercises in Chapters 5, 6 and 7.

7: Harnessing nightmares

 Do nightmares come galloping into your dreams on a regular basis? Everyone has the occasional nightmare, but if they routinely disturb your nights, leaving you feeling upset and/or unable to get back to sleep, try the strategy in Worksheet 13-8, which was developed by sleep specialists Drs Krakow and Neidhardt.

Worksheet 13-8 **Taming Nightmares**

---

1. **Write down a description of your nightmare immediately after you experience it.** Dreams tend to fade quickly from memory, so keep a pen and paper ready at your bedside.

_____

_____

_____

2. **Write down your thoughts and feelings about your nightmare.**

_____

_____

_____

3. **Rewrite your nightmare with a happier, better outcome.**

_____

_____

_____

4. **Rehearse your new dream in your mind several times before you go to bed the next night. Record how your night goes.**

_____

_____

_____

Navigating to the Land of Nod

Review the seven key sleep issues we cover earlier in this chapter. Think about which recommendations may improve your sleep. In Worksheet 13-9, write out a personal sleep plan of changes to make to your sleep behaviour. Record your observations as you carry out the new plan.

Worksheet 13-9	My Personal Sleep Plan

Chapter 14

Making Up Your Mind about Medication

In This Chapter

▶ Deciding whether medication makes sense for you

▶ Talking through your treatment options with a medical professional

▶ Keeping track of side effects

*T*oday, we know more about the brain and its relationship to emotional problems than ever before; and that chemical imbalances in the brain accompany both anxiety and depression. Because of this growing knowledge, one view is that all you need to do to target depression is to correct the chemical imbalance and hey presto – problem solved!

Were it only that simple, we'd be recommending medication for all emotional disturbances. And we probably wouldn't be writing this book because there'd be no need for it.

For most people, medication alone doesn't eliminate emotional distress, and medication is rarely the sole strategy to employ in the process of treating anxiety and depression. But medication can play an important role in feeling better, so in this chapter, we assist you in reaching productive conclusions when considering medication options. We also explore the discussion that you and your GP need to have. Many experts believe that medication can help symptoms, while psychological therapy can help you understand the causes and reason for anxiety and depression and find ways of managing them.

If you and your doctor do decide that medication is right for you, we also help you keep track of any side effects, so that you can keep your doctor accurately informed about your condition.

Because this is a workbook and space is limited, we don't review the vast array of medications available for the treatment of anxiety and depression. If you want more information on specific medications, look at our companion books, *Overcoming Anxiety For Dummies* and *Overcoming Depression For Dummies* (Wiley). And of course, discuss the issue with your doctor.

You must make your decision about whether you can benefit from medication as a tool to help deal with your emotional distress in collaboration with your doctor. One purpose of this chapter is to make you an informed consumer. The decision rests with your doctor to determine if your difficulties are likely to respond to medication. And ultimately, it's your choice whether to consent to take the medication. So the more information you and your doctor have, the better informed your decision can be.

Asking a Tough Question: To Take or Not to Take?

One frequently asked question is, 'What's best – medication or psychological therapy?' And the answer? Both have their place. For mild depression, research suggests that these two options are roughly equally effective. Medication is probably important for severe forms of depression. But for some types of anxiety, cognitive behavioural therapy (CBT) techniques like those we describe in this book may have the edge. Some people find the best results are via a combination of medication plus psychological therapy. Using medication can help you build up the energy to take part in therapy, so medication can facilitate therapy. Whatever your decision about medication, discuss the issue with an appropriately qualified professional before finally making up your mind.

Studies show that CBT helps prevent relapse, so we strongly recommend you don't rely solely on medication. This workbook is primarily based upon the principles of CBT, therefore using it *alongside* – rather than instead of medication – can work very well. For more information about CBT, check out *Cognitive Behavioural Therapy For Dummies* by Rob Willson and Rhena Branch (Wiley).

How do you make the medication decision? First, you need to understand that certain situations point strongly towards taking medication. Worksheet 14-1 lists the key ones. Tick the ones that apply. If any describe you, do see a professional. Each additional statement you tick increases the likelihood that medication needs to be part of your treatment plan.

Worksheet 14-1 **Medication Indications**

❑ I seriously think about or plan to hurt myself or others.

❑ I feel out of touch with reality. I hear or see things that aren't there.

❑ I have severe mood swings in just one direction, or from high to low.

❑ I feel totally hopeless about things ever improving.

❑ My thoughts are constantly racing and feel out of control.

❑ I've experienced a severely traumatic event.

❑ My emotional distress is severely disrupting my life.

❑ I've tried various therapies for six months or more without improvement.

❑ My doctor says that medical conditions are primarily causing my depression.

❑ I've been depressed or seriously anxious most of my life.

❑ I just can't stand the thought of talking with someone about my problems.

❑ I feel totally overwhelmed by my emotional problems.

❑ I have a problem with alcohol/drug use in addition to depression or anxiety.

❑ I feel highly suspicious, or even paranoid.

❑ Lately, I've made really terrible outrageous decisions.

❑ I sleep poorly, and wake up really early feeling bad.

❑ My family has a history of depression.

Now use Worksheet 14-2 to reflect on the items you've ticked. Elaborate on the statements that apply to you. Use specifics to describe how these problems manifest themselves. Include your thoughts, feelings and observations.

Worksheet 14-2	My Summary of Medication Indications

_____

_____

_____

_____

_____

Most arguments have at least two sides. Worksheet 14-1 considers possible reasons in favour of medication, while other reasons exist for why you may not want to take that route. Here are some reasons people give for their decision to refuse medications:

✔ **Side effect concerns:** Medication can have side effects, especially in the first few days of taking them, before wearing off. However, modern medications generally have few side effects, which usually wear off quite quickly. We review these in detail in 'Monitoring Side Effects' later in this chapter. Symptoms can include dry mouth, gastro-intestinal problems, sexual difficulties, weight gain and headaches. Some people are more prone to side effects than others. Your doctor can suggest ways around side effects.

✔ **Worries about long-term effects:** Most medication for emotional problems appears to have relatively little short-term risk. However, some medications are comparatively new, so problems may eventually become apparent after years of use. And because some medication needs to be taken life long, the potential for long-term effects is a concern, although low when compared with an untreated depression.

✔ **Addiction:** Some medication for anxiety, such as benzodiazepines, can be potentially addictive. So, if you're on some medications for more than a few months, you may become dependent and experience withdrawal symptoms if and when you decide to stop. You can feel reassured that most antidepressants don't appear to be addictive, and also that you have a choice of many effective ways to manage withdrawal.

✔ **Pregnancy and breastfeeding:** Under careful medical supervision, certain medication for emotional distress appears relatively safe for pregnant or breastfeeding mothers. However, the data isn't comprehensive, and controversy exists around their use in such cases.

Postpartum depression, depression following giving birth, is relatively common. It can be serious if left untreated. If you experience symptoms of depression following the birth of a baby, do get professional help.

✔ **Personal preference:** Because of religious, philosophical or strong personal reasons, some people prefer not to take medication. If this is the case for you, please get treatment for your problems through self-help exercises or alternatively, make sure you see a qualified mental health professional.

Although some valid reasons exist for choosing to not take medications for anxiety or depression, if your distress is extremely severe or involves serious suicidal or homicidal thoughts, medication can be very important. If you were deciding against it, please reconsider your treatment decision and see your doctor.

To help make your decision about whether to include medication as part of your treatment:

1. **Review your reasons for and against taking medication.**

2. **Consider talking about your concerns with close friends, family, your doctor and/or a mental health professional.**

3. **Make a decision about how you want medication to fit with your overall treatment.**
   Explain your reasoning in Worksheet 14-3, noting your thoughts, concerns, feelings and observations.

Worksheet 14-3	My Medication Decision

Many people take herbs and supplements for minor emotional distress, and your doctor can also discuss options for especially severe depression. If you're interested in using herbs rather than prescription medications to help cope with anxiety and depression, consult a proper medical herbalist who is fully trained in herbal and medical contra-indications. These professionals can recommend herbs and dosages that are appropriate for you and your symptoms. Visit the National Institute of Medical Herbalists (www.nimh.org.uk) for more information.

Discussing Your Symptoms with a Doctor

If you decide to take medication (hopefully you're planning to do so in conjunction with therapy or self-help), you need to give your doctor detailed information to enable an accurate recommendation for your treatment. Forgetting what you want to say to the doctor is pretty common, as consultations are often time-pressured.

Worksheet 14-4 is a handy questionnaire for you to fill out before you visit your doctor. You may even want to give your doctor a copy of your completed worksheet as a reference. Though your doctor may need additional information, the questions in the worksheet are a good way to begin identifying some details of your condition.

Worksheet 14-4	Important Information for My Doctor

1. Describe your emotional symptoms. (See Chapter 1 for ideas.)

_____

_____

_____

2. About how long have you had these symptoms? How frequently do they appear? Have you ever had them before, and if so, where and when?

_____

_____

_____

3. **Describe how severe your symptoms have been and how they have impacted your life (see Chapter 2 for ideas).** Be sure to mention if you've had thoughts about harming yourself or others.

_____

_____

_____

4. **Describe any significant changes that have recently occurred in your life.** Include deaths, job changes, divorces, injuries, retirement or financial upheaval.

_____

_____

_____

5. **Describe any physical symptoms you've been experiencing (see Chapter 1 for ideas).** Include their frequency and severity, and how long you've been having them.

_____

_____

_____

6. **List any illnesses you've had recently and any medication (and the dosages) that you're currently taking.** Include any chronic conditions you're being treated for, such as high blood pressure, diabetes, kidney or liver disease, or asthma. Don't forget to mention birth control pills and any non-prescribed, complementary or over-the-counter remedies.

_____

_____

_____

7. **Describe the current state of your primary relationship (for example, with your spouse or partner).** If he or she is depressed or anxious, or there are difficulties in the relationship, this can affect your mood.

_____

_____

_____

8. **Do you have a family history of significant emotional problems?** Include mental health information about any close relatives.

_____

_____

_____

(continued)

Worksheet 14-4 *(continued)*

---

9. **List any herbs, supplements, vitamins or over-the-counter medications that you take.**

_____

_____

_____

_____

10. **Write down your current and past use of cigarettes, alcohol and drugs. Include frequency and quantity.** (However, whatever you tell your doctor may go into your medical records, so you may want to ask your doctor not to write everything down in your notes.)

_____

_____

_____

_____

11. **List any allergies. Have you ever had any bad reactions to any medication, herbs or foods in the past?**

_____

_____

_____

_____

12. **Are you pregnant, planning to get pregnant or breastfeeding?**

_____

_____

_____

To make life easier – and keep this book intact – you can download extra copies of this form at www.dummies.com/go/adwb.

Ever-increasing research indicates that nutrient intake from food has a significant effect on emotional and mental health and has the ability to reduce symptoms associated with poor mental health. Consult a professionally trained nutritional therapist to find out how nutrition can support your health and well-being. Find a reputable local practitioner through the Institute for Optimum Nutrition (www.ion.org.uk) or the British Association for Nutritional Therapists (www.bant.org.uk).

Monitoring Side Effects

Around half the people who take medication for anxiety or depression stop because of unpleasant, unwanted side effects and/or because they don't feel they're benefiting from the drug. They may not be aware that:

✔ Many medications can take a number of weeks to kick in and start working.

✔ Side effects very often decrease, or even disappear altogether, after a few days.

✔ The prescriber may be able to start you off on a lower dose or offer you alternatives with fewer side effects.

✔ Another medication may be added to reduce side effects.

Stopping any medication, whether for emotional or other difficulties, needs to be carefully supervised. Even medications that are not addictive in the usual sense can be problematic if stopped abruptly. Please don't discontinue prescribed medication without consulting your doctor. If you're having problems with medication, any decision whether to continue, try an alternative or add another drug to reduce side effects is best made – you guessed it – with your doctor. So do communicate with your prescriber on a regular basis about any side effects you're experiencing.

Because it's so important for your doctor to know about any side effects, complete the Side Effects Tracking Form, Worksheet 14-5. Complete this form for a month after you start any new medication for depression or anxiety. Take it along to your follow-up appointments. (You can download additional copies of the worksheet at www.dummies.com/go/adwb.)

1. **Add the date to each day of the week, and write down each symptom you noticeably experience. Write down any physical symptoms you experience such as a dry mouth, headaches or nausea, and also emotional changes such as restlessness or an increase in anxiety.**

2. **Next to the symptom, rate the intensity from 1 (minimal) to 10 (maximum).**

Of course, keep a note of improvements too.

You can combat symptoms associated with depression and anxiety as well as the side effects of some medications by consuming certain foods and nutrients. Talk with your doctor or a nutritionist about diet changes you can make to relieve dry mouth, constipation, diarrhoea, insomnia, headaches and nausea.

Worksheet 14-5

My Side Effects Tracking Form

Symptom	Monday	Tuesday	Wednesday	Thursday	Friday	Saturday	Sunday

Part V
Revitalising Relationships

'And when did you first notice your wife
was feeling depressed, Mr Pinchwort?'

In this part . . .

Your relationship often suffers when you experience substantial anxiety or depression. And when your relationships suffer, you no doubt feel more anxious or depressed. It's a vicious cycle.

In this part, we give you techniques to enhance relationships and improve communication. We also help you deal with loss and with conflict.

Chapter 15

Working on Relationships

Supportive relationships provide a buffer against all types of emotional distress. Numerous studies indicate that good relationships and social support improve both mental and physical health. Humans are social animals, biologically programmed to function better when in supportive relationships; people thrive in close-knit colonies. Improving your relationships can boost your mood, increase your ability to handle stress and enhance your sense of well-being.

The opposite also holds true – distressing emotions can confound your attempts to improve your relationships, may damage friendships, intimate relationships and relationships with both colleagues and even relative strangers. So, improving your relationships is yet another weapon in your armoury to enhance your mood and defeat anxiety and depression.

In this chapter, we review strategies to grow and strengthen practically all relationships. However, we emphasise intimate relationships because disruptions in these are most damaging and because repairing them is enormously beneficial to your mental, physical and spiritual health. Though intimate relationships are prioritised, you're likely to find that the tips work well when used with a wide variety of people. In addition, we help you cope with the loss of a relationship, which can be quite traumatic and trigger intense feelings of both anxiety and despair.

Moody Blues: Linking Emotions to Relationships

Irrespective of whether you like it, when you're anxious or depressed, you become more self-absorbed. We don't mean selfish – rather that your attention becomes focused on your problems and concerns. Although the shift in focus is quite understandable, your relationships are likely to suffer when your problems claim a disproportionate share of your energy. And then, because you're mentally and emotionally drained, you don't pay much attention to nurturing your relationships – and like all growing things, relationships need nurturing.

In addition, when you're anxious and depressed, those who care about you are likely to try to cheer you up or help in other ways. When they don't succeed, they often feel frustrated and helpless. Eventually, exhausted, they may start withdrawing from you. Their actions are understandable because being around someone who's feeling really low much of the time is hard going.

The following example shows you how depression can affect a good relationship.

Johann's mood changes with the seasons. When daylight diminishes in winter, it frequently triggers another bout of depression. (See our book *Overcoming Depression For Dummies* for more about Seasonal Affective Disorder.) Johann meets Gina in early summer, and following a whirlwind romance, they're both convinced they've found the partner of their dreams, and they marry that autumn. Johann has never been happier.

Johann warns Gina about his 'winter blues'. However, both hope that their love and her presence in his life will be sufficient for him to escape depression during the dark months. Unfortunately, depression begins to affect Johann as the days shorten. He withdraws from Gina, who tries to understand but becomes hurt and frustrated with her inability and perceived failure to cheer him up. Johann feels guilty that he's hurting his wife, but he also feels powerless to do anything about his mood swing. The relationship suffers.

In Worksheet 15-1, answer the questions about an important relationship in your life to see if depression or anxiety has been affecting it.

Worksheet 15-1   **The Relationship Impact Questionnaire**

---

1. Have you withdrawn or pulled back from your relationship? If so, in what ways?

_____

_____

_____

_____

2. Are you less affectionate than you used to be? If so, in what ways?

_____

_____

_____

_____

3. Are you more irritable or critical than you used to be? If so, in what ways?

_____

_____

_____

_____

4. Are you being less caring, giving fewer compliments or being less empathetic? If so, in what ways?

_____

_____

_____

_____

Although depression and anxiety can lead to problems in relationships, they're not the only culprits. Good relationships may deteriorate in the presence of severe emotional problems, while others may be unhealthy to begin with, and therefore naturally will worsen with time. If you wonder why your relationship isn't thriving, or perhaps if you suspect you're being abused, do see a mental health professional who specialises in working with couples.

Giving Flowers Now and Again (and Again and Again)

Have you ever received or given flowers at the start of a relationship? Ideally, relationships continue to supply 'flowers' of many varieties to both parties – compliments, companionship, good times, caring, affection, laughter and more. Most good relationships start out with enthusiasm and whole bouquets of good feelings. But too often, complacency sets in, life (something that happens while you're busy making other plans) takes over and after a while, you can easily forget about giving flowers.

When you stop cultivating a garden, weeds grow, choking the flowers. The same is true for relationships. They wither without attention. But you can water and fertilise your relationship by increasing:

- ✔ Positive talk
- ✔ Positive actions

Whether your relationship is really struggling or is doing pretty well but still isn't quite what you'd like, the strategies in this section can help you make it a whole lot better.

Communication forms the foundation of all good relationships. Everyone benefits from having trustworthy people to whom they can safely express thoughts and feelings. You can create the right environment for positive communication to grow and flourish. Try the following two exercises: the Daily Digest and the Delightful Dozen Appreciated Aspects of My Partner.

If your communication with your partner is fraught with conflict, see Chapter 16 for ideas of how to change that. And if the following exercises don't work particularly well, we recommend you see a counsellor for couples counselling.

News of the day

The Daily Digest is a way of making sure that you and your partner spend time talking – and even more importantly *listening* – to each other. The purpose of this exercise is to enhance intimacy. Do give this exercise a high priority and frequency.

1. **With your partner, agree a time when you can sit down together and talk about the day's events for around 20 minutes.** You can make your plans for the same time every day, or you may want to vary it. As to frequency, daily is best (that's why we call it the *Daily* Digest, but you can still see benefits from this exercise if you do it just three to four times a week.

2. **Agree your regular times and write them down.** Your commitments during weekdays and weekends may differ, but both still require scheduling into your timetables.

3. **When you sit down for a Daily Digest, let your partner begin and speak for around ten minutes.**

4. **Show interest in what your partner is saying by:**

    • **Asking a few questions for greater understanding**

    • **Nodding your head**

    • **Making brief comments**

    • **Expressing empathy or understanding for how your partner feels**

    Don't give advice or try to solve your partner's problem at this time. And steer clear of criticism and stirring up conflict!

5. **After your partner shares the events of his or her day, try to summarise what he or she said in a positive manner.**

6. **Ask your partner if your understanding of what he or she said is basically correct. If not, ask for clarification.**

7. **Take your turn, talking about your day and asking your partner to follow the same rules. Make any notes you want to in Worksheet 15-2.**

Worksheet 15-2   **The Daily Digest**

\
\
\
\
\
\

After you work through the Daily Digest a few times, reflect and record your thoughts in Worksheet 15-3. How did you feel before and after the exercise? Do you know any more about your partner now? Does your partner know more about you? Do you feel closer?

Worksheet 15-3   **My Reflections**

\
\
\
\

With compliments

Compliments, meant sincerely, enhance communication and increase mutually positive feelings. When you feel anxious or depressed, you may find you don't really stop and think about all the things you appreciate about your partner, let alone say them out loud. But when you don't express such thoughts, your partner may well feel unappreciated.

Work through the following exercise, the Delightful Dozen Appreciated Aspects of My Partner, to get back on the track of complimenting your partner.

1. **In Worksheet 15-4, write down all the things you appreciate, value, admire and cherish about your partner.** Include attributes such as intelligence, caring, warmth, attractiveness, talents, help with daily life (such as cooking, cleaning, finances and so on), sense of humour and anything else you can think of. Only include items you honestly feel.

Be specific in your assessment of your partner. For example, instead of saying something global like 'You're the best person in the whole world,' try going for some detail such as 'I just love the way you play with the baby.' Beware of 'buts' – they put a sting in the tail of any compliment. So, don't say, 'I really like X, *but* you could do it better by . . .'

2. **Compliment your partner at least once a day, using something from the Delightful Dozen or finding something new or spontaneous.**

3. **Create a strategy for remembering to make these compliments.** Perhaps make a note in your diary, electronic or otherwise, or set an occasional alarm!

Develop the habit of giving genuine compliments to everyone, not just your partner. Doing so is likely to make other people's days – and yours!

Worksheet 15-4	The Delightful Dozen Appreciated Aspects of My Partner
1.	
2.	
3.	
4.	
5.	
6.	
7.	
8.	
9.	
10.	
11.	
12.	

Some people dismiss compliments saying, 'You can't really mean that' or 'That's not so.' If your partner responds like this, point it out, suggest they try saying 'thank you' instead, and above all, don't give up on giving compliments. People are often dismissive not because they disagree or don't want to hear nice things about themselves, but because they may have trouble receiving and accepting compliments.

After you work on including more compliments in your conversation for a few weeks, reflect on any changes in your relationship (see Worksheet 15-5). Do you notice any increased warmth, affection or improved communication? Are you or your partner (or both!) in a better mood?

Worksheet 15-5	My Reflections

If you can't think of anything that you genuinely appreciate about your partner, your relationship is in serious trouble. Seek help from a professional trained in couples counselling, or consider whether it's time to develop a new relationship.

Rewarding Reciprocity

If communication is the foundation of a good relationship (see the 'Talking back' section earlier), sharing pleasurable activities is the structure that rests on the foundation. In this section, we show you an important technique for increasing the number of positive experiences you have with your partner. It's called Reciprocal Rewards.

Reciprocal Rewards provide an easy way for you and your partner to demonstrate your mutual affection. You make a list of small, caring actions that you both can do frequently for each other. Then you each keep track of the nice things that the other has done. These are the Reciprocal Rewards. It's important to review this strategy with your partner, and for you both to participate. Although this technique may look simplistic, research shows that it works and builds surprisingly positive feelings. Before starting on your own Reciprocal Rewards worksheet, take a look at an example.

Pat and Michelle decide to try Reciprocal Rewards because they've noticed that their relationship has been stagnating. They explore what they can do to increase the pleasure they get from one another. Michelle asks Pat to stop complaining about their finances, but in talking, they realise that this request is both negative and focused on something they frequently argue about. So, they settle on something else. Pat asks Michelle to 'be nicer' to Pat's mum. They then realise on reflection, that even this request's too vague. So they settle on Michelle agreeing to come to the phone for a few minutes' chat when Pat's mother calls.

Worksheet 15-6 illustrates a list of positive activities Pat and Michelle came up with, as the reciprocal rewards for the change in Michelle's behaviour. It also shows how they did performing these actions in their first week.

Worksheet 15-6	Pat and Michelle's Reciprocal Rewards for July
Desired Actions	*Dates Carried Out*
Michelle goes out to buy the Sunday paper.	16/7, 20/7, 21/7
Pat rubs Michelle's back.	16/7
Michelle rubs Pat's back.	16/7
The first one home puts the dinner on.	17/7, 18/7, 21/7, 22/7
Michelle buys Pat a small gift.	22/7
Pat phones Michelle at work for a brief chat.	16/7, 18/7, 19/7
Michelle talks to Pat's mother when she rings.	21/7
Pat supervises homework while Michelle watches the news.	16/7, 20/7
Pat fills up Michelle's car – with petrol!	22/7
Pat mows the lawn	18/7
Michelle brings Pat morning coffee in bed.	16/7, 17/7, 19/7, 20/7, 22/7
Pat pays the monthly accounts – then puts them onto direct debit!	20/7

Pat and Michelle discover that, to their surprise, this strategy actually leads them to feel closer and warmer towards each other. They aren't arguing as much. They enjoy the results so much that the following week they add several more items to their list. Both notice an increased desire to please the other, plus they enjoy the feeling of knowing they are appreciated. And even talking to Pat's mum is no longer such an ordeal!

1. **Work out with your partner a list of small actions that each of you interpret as an indication of caring or affection.** Each action must be:

   - Stated positively

   - Clear and specific (so you know for sure if it happens)

   - Easily executed

   - Able to be frequently carried out

   - Not something contentious that you've been arguing about

2. **List these actions in the left-hand column of Worksheet 15-7.**

3. **Each day, in the right-hand column, you both record the date when you notice your partner doing any of the agreed actions.**

4. **At the end of each day, briefly discuss the progress of your exercise with your partner.**

5. **Promise yourself that you'll do at least three of these actions daily, whether or not your partner does**. Vary your chosen actions.

Consider putting this list up somewhere – on the fridge, bedroom/bathroom mirror or some other obvious place in the house – so you both can easily keep track of each other's actions and also see the progress you're making.

Worksheet 15-7	Reciprocal Rewards
Desired Actions	*Dates Carried Out*

You can download as many copies of this form as you need at www.dummies.com/go/adwb.

You'll both inevitably slip up occasionally and forget all about the agreed rewards. Simply start doing the rewarding things again each time that happens, resisting the temptation to be critical of yourself or your partner.

After a week of Reciprocal Rewards, reflect on any effects on your relationship, and record your thoughts in Worksheet 15-8.

Worksheet 15-8	My Reflections

Dealing with Relationship Loss

Wouldn't it be nice if people lived forever, and relationships came with a lifetime guarantee that you'll 'live happily ever after'. But life's no fairy tale. Relationships break up, marriages dissolve, circumstances cause prolonged separations and people die. Loss, whatever the cause, does often mean great distress.

Depression can follow loss. When you lose someone, grieving and feeling sad are quite natural. However, grief and depression do differ. While depression often includes feelings of inadequacy and low self-esteem, grief centres on feelings of loss and loneliness. Most people find that while grief naturally decreases with time, this is less so for depression. Loss or fear of loss can also create anxiety. You may think you can't handle life without your loved one; you may feel dependent and overwhelmed at the prospect.

If you've lost someone close, first and foremost, take care of yourself. Be sure to eat healthily, avoid abusing drugs and alcohol and exercise regularly, regardless of whether you're in the mood. Just taking half an hour's brisk walk daily will do. Ensure you get enough sleep. Grieving takes a physical and mental toll, and you need all your resources.

In addition, you may want to turn to other sources of support. Don't be afraid to ask for help! Sources can include:

- ✔ Religious or spiritual support
- ✔ Bereavement support groups
- ✔ Friends and family
- ✔ Mental health professionals

If you lose someone and feel like you can't go on, or if you have thoughts of hopelessness or suicide, please seek professional help promptly.

Changing with the times

When you're grieving, it's natural to feel like staying in bed and pulling the quilt over your head. You may have a tendency to try and avoid thinking about the lost person or relationship. Some people even turn to drugs or alcohol, trying to dull or even obliterate the pain. But such strategies merely tend to make things worse.

A better approach is to explore your thoughts and feelings about the lost person. Spend some active time reviewing and reconstructing the relationship, examining what the person meant to you. This process really can facilitate moving on.

To get the most out of the following Grief Exploration Questionnaire (see Worksheet 15-9), allocate at least an hour to answer the questions. Don't rush. And do expect to feel some intense sadness or grief as you work through the questions. You may well cry, and that's expected and natural. But if you feel overwhelmed or feel that you can't handle this exercise, please seek professional help.

Worksheet 15-9	Grief Exploration Questionnaire

1. What was your life like when you were with this person?

_____

_____

_____

_____

2. What did you value about this person?

_____

_____

_____

_____

3. What was difficult about this person?

_____

_____

_____

_____

4. What lessons did you learn from this relationship, both positive and negative?

_____

_____

_____

_____

5. What is different about your life now?

_____

_____

_____

_____

6. What are you most angry or resentful about?

_____

_____

_____

_____

7. What aspects of this relationship are you most grateful for?

_____

_____

_____

_____

8. **What did you enjoy about this relationship?**

_____

_____

_____

_____

9. **Write a letter to the person you've lost.**

Doing this can help provide you with closure. Review questions 1–7 for ideas you may want to include in your letter. Feel free to be emotional. Express anything that's on your mind. This isn't a letter to be sent – it's an exercise that enables you the opportunity to feel, explore and express your emotions about the loss. Don't leave the letter around for others to see later when you may regret it.

_____

_____

_____

_____

_____

_____

_____

_____

_____

_____

Creating action strategies

You'll never identically replace anyone you've lost. People and relationships are all unique and, in a sense, irreplaceable. Nonetheless, you can pick up the pieces, move on and start to fill your life with other meaningful relationships and activities. After you begin to recover, consider the following:

✔ **Volunteer work:** A great way to regain a sense of meaning in your life is to help others. Such work can also lead to friendships and a new social circle.

✔ **Pleasurable activities:** Even if you feel sad and unmotivated, restoring pleasure to your life is possible (see Chapter 11 for more about healthy pleasures). You probably won't feel like you 'should' indulge in pleasure, but after you start to recover from your loss, allowing yourself to enjoy things can accelerate your healing.

✔ **Socialising:** Whether visiting with friends and family or going out on a date again, being with other people helps you get through tough times. Sometimes starting new relationships can initially feel scary. However, you need to learn to love again and establish new connections. Foraying forth into the world is key to the healing process.

Chapter 16

Smoothing Out Conflict

· ·

In This Chapter

▶ Defeating defensiveness

▶ Reinterpreting other people's behaviour

▶ Communicating despite disagreement

· ·

Conflict with someone you care about hurts, and when you're depressed or anxious, you're often more irritable, resulting in greater conflict. Like so many other problems related to depression and anxiety, a vicious circle ensues.

In this chapter, we help you break the negative downward spiral of conflict. We explain how negative automatic assumptions lead to defensiveness and counter-attacks. Then we show you how to stop picking these negative assumptions and override the accompanying defensiveness, which otherwise may damage your relationships. You see how identifying and understanding yours and your partner's 'hot buttons' can assist you in re-evaluating what you previously thought of as criticism. Finally, we provide tips for dealing with conflict constructively. While the focus of the chapter is working on conflicts within close relationships, such as your partner or spouse, you're likely to find that you can adapt most of the techniques in this chapter to deal with conflicts that arise with colleagues, as well as those relating to friends and relatives.

Dealing with Defensiveness

When people feel emotionally vulnerable, whether from depression, anxiety or as a result of conflict in a relationship, they all too easily jump to negative conclusions in response to loads of things their partners say or do. These *negative automatic assumptions,* so common when you're depressed or anxious, are about how you automatically interpret communications or actions in the most negative, critical ways possible. Frequently, negative automatic assumptions lead you to grossly misinterpret the true meaning of a message.

Here's a common, concrete example of a negative automatic assumption: imagine driving along the motorway, when someone cuts you up. You can interpret the driver's motive in several ways, including careless inattention or deliberately aggressive behaviour aimed at you personally. The latter interpretation may well mean you choose to respond in kind – with anything but a kind response! Escalation may follow, perhaps even leading to an episode of road rage.

Defensiveness often follows after negative assumptions point you in the direction of seeing communication or behaviour as an attack. Your defence response is often to protest your innocence – or alternatively, you may counter-attack. Saying that something's not your fault can imply that therefore it must be your partner's fault or that your partner was being deliberately hostile. Sadly, defensiveness and counter-attacks only serve to escalate conflicts. Both reactions therefore provide fuel to stoke a fiery argument.

Sarcasm usually indicates defensiveness. Pay particular attention when you hear yourself being sarcastic, and try to then rephrase your response in more reasonable terms.

Worksheet 16-1 illustrates the insidious process of how someone else's words or actions lead on to negative assumptions or defensiveness.

Worksheet 16-1	Negative Assumptions and Defensive Responses	
Initial Communication or Action	*Negative Assumption*	*Defensive Response*
'You look tired today.'	She's saying I look awful.	'You're not looking so great yourself!'
'Where are the car keys?'	He's complaining I haven't put them back where we agreed.	'How on earth would I know? You drove last!'
'Do we need petrol?'	She's referring to how I wait until the tank is practically empty before filling up.	'Why don't **you** fill the car up for a change instead of always expecting me to?'
Your partner forgets your anniversary.	Obviously our relationship's not important any more – and neither am I!	'Just you wait until something's important for you. I'll make a point of not noticing it.'
Your partner suggests some changes in something you're writing together.	She thinks I'm an idiot!	'Since when have you become the next Shakespeare?'
'The house is a bit untidy.'	He's complaining that I'm not doing my bit.	'I'm not the cleaner, you know! Do it yourself if it's not up to your exacting standards!'

Observe how in Worksheet 16-1 all the initial communications and actions contain some ambiguity. So you can't tell with any certainty if the person had hostile intentions. And even when a message or behaviour is clearly hostile, it still doesn't do much good to respond defensively – unless you really are spoiling for a fight!

Identifying your defensive behaviours

Before you can stop making negative assumptions and following them with defensive responses, you need to recognise these behaviours. We suggest you track events in which these behaviours crop up, using the following guidance. (After you identify your own defensive behaviours, we give you alternatives in the following sections – plus we explain how to deal with genuinely hostile criticism in a potentially productive way.)

1. **When your partner says or does something that you feel may have been intended as hostile, write it down in the left-hand column of Worksheet 16-2 as soon as you have the opportunity.**

2. **In the middle column, write down how you interpret what happened.** Try to be honest; don't sanitise your reaction or your language! Record how you really feel about what your partner said or did.

3. **In the right-hand column, note how you respond and assess if your response is defensive in any way.** Did you try to absolve yourself of blame or counter-attack in some way?

Worksheet 16-2	My Negative Assumptions and Defensive Responses	
Initial Communication or Action	*Negative Assumption*	*Defensive Response*

Over a period of a few weeks, review your negative assumptions and defensive responses at the end of each week. In Worksheet 16-3, reflect on how they may be causing problems in your relationship.

Worksheet 16-3	My Reflections

Checking it out

Hopefully the exercise in the preceding section has made you more aware of when you get defensive. But what's the alternative when your partner's actions or words seem hostile or negative? Our suggestion is that you try *checking it out*. This process involves first catching the urge to be defensive and stopping yourself from acting on it. Then, after you identify what you really want to say, you make a gentle inquiry about your partner's true intentions.

Mark arranges to collect Shona at 6.30 p.m. to catch the early show at the cinema, and then carry on out for dinner. He arrives breathless at 7.15 p.m. saying, 'I'm so sorry! The traffic was awful.' Shona immediately makes a negative assumption, believing Mark doesn't really care and their date is not important to him. The fact that he's late, in her view, proves he's losing interest in her. She almost says, 'That's precisely what you said last time. You're so unreliable!' Instead, because she's just finished reading Chapter 16 of the *Anxiety & Depression Workbook For Dummies,* she decides to stop, reconsider and check it out. Taking a deep breath or two, calming down just a bit, Shona replies, 'Mark, I'm a little worried that you're losing interest in me. Is that the case?' Mark's astonished at the question, replying, 'No way! Honestly, I'm really sorry if that's how it came across. There really was a terrible accident. Actually, I'm dead keen on you and really enjoy our time together.'

When you find yourself identifying what looks like a hostile situation, have a go at checking it out like Shona did. The steps are as follows:

1. **The moment you feel attacked or criticised, firmly close your mouth!**

2. **Take a slow, deep breath in and exhale very slowly. Repeat this once or twice, until you feel a little calmer.**

   While you're breathing, remind yourself that if you respond while you're really upset, the chances of saying something useful or productive have been precisely calculated at 1 in 5.86 billion.

3. **When you feel calmer, inquire about your partner's actual intentions.** Gently explain what your worry or concern is about, without accusing or attacking.

4. **Make a mental note of how the conversation goes, so you can go back and work through it later when you're feeling less stirred up.** In Worksheet 16-4:

   • Record the initial communication or action in the left-hand column.

   • Write down your negative assumption in the middle column.

   • Note how you checked out your assumption in the right-hand column.

Worksheet 16-4	My Negative Assumptions and How I Checked It Out	
Initial Communication or Action	*Negative Assumption*	*Checking It Out*

Initial Communication or Action	Negative Assumption	Checking It Out

Daring to defuse

Another alternative to defensiveness or counter-attacking is defusing. You'll find this technique particularly valuable when your partner (or anyone, really) is unmistakably criticising you.

Basically, defusing requires you to respond downright counter-intuitively. What you do is find one tiny sliver of truth in your partner's statement. Acknowledging part (or sometimes all) of your partner's concerns means you keep the dialogue going and remove the emotional charge from the interaction. There's no harm in accepting some responsibility and apologising.

However, we're certainly not suggesting that you completely capitulate or that you lie to your partner. Instead, have a real go at seeing your partner's perspective on the problem. Usually, you and your partner can find at least something to agree upon.

This technique doesn't work for dealing with direct verbal abuse. In that situation, you need to get help. Determining if you're being emotionally abused can be difficult at times. So, if you're unsure, do speak to a mental health professional.

Worksheet 16-5 illustrates some defusing options to criticism. In each defusing response, the bit in bold in the right-hand column identifies the valid part of the criticism, which the person being criticised acknowledges. In the final three examples, come up with your own ideas for effective defusing responses.

Worksheet 16-5	Defusing Criticism
Criticism	*Defusing Response*
You spend too much money.	**I know I have sometimes in the past**, but I'm not sure what you're referring to at the moment. Can you please explain what you mean?
You're always shouting at the children.	**I guess I do quite often.** I'll try and be more aware and see what else I can do when they annoy me.
The house is a mess. You never clean it.	**I can see why you can feel that.** Probably it's not as important to me as it is to you. Can we work out something that'll keep us both happy? Maybe get a cleaner?
You're always telling me what I should and shouldn't do. I'm fed up with you trying to control me.	**OK! I do like having things my way.** But we also do what you want quite a lot. What particularly are you referring to?
I feel we're spending far too much time with your relatives.	
You're behaving like a doormat, letting your boss walk over you like that.	
You need to lose some weight.	

Defuse whenever you can. It's not something that comes naturally for most people, but you may well be surprised and delighted at how much more smoothly all your relationships go after you get the hang of it.

After putting into practice the techniques of checking it out and defusing within your relationships, reflect on how these alternatives to defensiveness and counter-attacking are working for you. Did checking it out show that your partner indeed was being hostile? Or did you discover that your partner wasn't intending to be hurtful or critical? Did checking it out prevent things from escalating like they used to? When you defused your partner's comments, was a potential conflict averted? Record your reflections in Worksheet 16-6.

Worksheet 16-6	My Reflections

Redistributing Responsibility

When someone you care about is angry or distraught, you may think you're the cause in some way. This assumption is pretty common, but it isn't always accurate. When you inappropriately take responsibility for your partner's emotions, you're likely to feel distressed, and you may also become defensive, or counter-attack (see 'Dealing with Defensiveness' earlier for more on those reactions).

Often when people get upset, their responses actually have very little to do with you – even if they say otherwise! Huh? How come? Well, most of the time, we experience disproportionately intense emotions about events when one or more of our personal 'hot buttons' are pushed. These hot buttons or sensitive areas are what we call *problematic life-lenses* (see Chapter 7 for a full explanation). They're the core beliefs we have about ourselves and the world, and they trigger strong emotions.

If you can identify your partner's hot buttons, you can then understand and anticipate what triggers anger and other heightened emotions. Identifying and understanding other people's hot buttons also helps you know that their distress probably is more about their own issues than anything you're doing. Above all, understanding problematic life-lenses allows you to stop taking things personally, which in turn enables you to feel more empathetic rather than defensive.

If you haven't done so already, we recommend that you go to Chapter 7 and begin to understand your own problematic life-lenses. If you've already worked through Chapter 7, go back and review it. Understanding both your own and your partner's issues are equally important.

Here's how to work out which of the problematic life-lenses listed in Worksheet 16-7 apply to your partner.

1. **Read over the problematic life-lenses in Worksheet 16-7.**

2. **Think about the way your partner reacts to life events.**

3. **Rate each lens on how well it describes your partner's behaviour and reactions to life events.** Use a scale of 1 to 5 to rate the frequency, where 1 is almost never, 2 is occasionally, 3 is sometimes, 4 means usually and 5 represents almost always.

   You may discover that your partner uses apparently contradictory life-lenses, such as perfectionist at some times and inadequate at others. Worry not; the use of an opposite viewpoint is fairly common.

Worksheet 16-7	My Partner's Problematic Life-Lenses Questionnaire
Lens	*Opposite View*
__**Unworthy.** I don't feel I deserve good things to happen to me. I feel uncomfy if anyone does anything nice for me.	__**Entitled.** I deserve the best of everything, and should be able to have practically whatever I want. If my needs are unexpectedly unmet, I feel threatened, sad or furious.
__**Fearing abandonment.** I need loads of reassurance to feel loved. I'm lost without someone special in my life and worry about losing those I care about. I feel jealous and am clingy because of my fear.	__**Avoiding intimacy.** I'm uncomfy getting close to anyone. I'd really rather stay away from any emotional involvement. I don't really want anyone in my life.

(continued)

Worksheet 16-7 *(continued)*

Lens	Opposite View
__**Inadequate.** I'm not as talented or skilled as others. I don't measure up. I don't like taking on new things that look tricky.	__**Perfectionist.** I feel I must do everything perfectly. There's a right and wrong way for everything, and I've got to do it right.
__**Guilty.** Everything that goes wrong feels like it's my fault. I'm always worrying about whether I've done the wrong thing and can't stand the thought of hurting others, even inadvertently.	__**Without conscience.** I couldn't care less about such nonsense as ethics and morality and never let them stand in my way if I really want something. I don't give a damn for what others think.
__**Vulnerable.** The world is a dangerous place where nasty things happen. I worry a lot about the future.	__**Invulnerable.** I'm invincible. Nothing can hurt me. The world always treats me very well. I'm one of those lucky people and never need to worry about taking precautions.
__**Help-seeking.** I depend on others a great deal and feel I can't handle life alone. I feel better when others take care of me.	__**Assistance-spurning.** I hate asking for favours and don't like accepting offered assistance.
__**Impulsive.** If I want to do something, I just do it. I find it hard to set limits on others, so they frequently take advantage of me. I'd rather just say what I think and feel, than control my emotions.	__**Highly-controlled.** I must never, ever lose control – that's the worst thing imaginable! I always conceal my feelings. I always want to be part of everything. I'd hate to work for anyone and couldn't stand my fate being controlled by others.

If you scored your partner as 3 or above on any of the problematic life-lenses in Worksheet 16-7, you've found a hot button. Events linked to these life-lenses are likely to produce strong emotions – and the intensity of those emotions probably has more to do with your partner's life-lens than with you. Noting when your partner becomes upset and working out which problematic life-lens is involved is always a good move. While understanding the link may not make you feel good about your partner's turmoil, at least you can understand what's going on and perhaps let go of things more easily.

Isabella has a nasty temper. She gets angry about almost anything that goes wrong, and even small stuff gets her really worked up. Isabella's partner, Lisa, blames herself when Isabella goes off on one of her tirades. Lisa completes the problematic life-lenses questionnaire, Worksheet 16-7, considering things from Isabella's perspective. She discovers that Isabella appears to see the world through perfectionist, assistance-spurning and vulnerable life-lenses. No wonder Isabella gets upset so easily! Armed with that information, Lisa now scores the strength of Isabella's life-lenses across a range of life events (see Worksheet 16-8) and reflects on her findings (see Worksheet 16-9).

Worksheet 16-8	Isabella's Life-Lens Tracking Sheet	
Event	*Emotion and Reaction*	*Life-Lens*
I missed the due date for a bill.	Isabella was furious and yelled at me for being so stupid and careless. She said she should never have relied on me in the first place.	Perfectionist, assistance-spurning

Event	Emotion and Reaction	Life-Lens
I forgot to double-lock the front door.	Isabella was shaking with fury. She said we were really lucky that we weren't burgled.	Vulnerable
I had the window frames painted while Isabella was away on business.	She was angry with me for squandering money. She said she could easily have done the job herself. She doesn't realise that while maybe she could, she really hasn't got the time.	Assistance-spurning
Isabella left the milk out of the fridge, and it was sour by morning.	She swore furiously and thumped the wall. I somehow felt it was my fault — I should have somehow noticed and put it away … even though I'd already gone to bed!	Perfectionist

---

Worksheet 16-9   **Lisa's Reflections**

I really see now that I've been beating up myself for things that are really Isabella's issues. It's obvious to see she gets really pissed off when she's afraid and then blames me — and I go along with it. Her perfectionism drives her crazy if the slightest thing goes wrong. And she hates asking for help with anything. I'm not impressed with her temper tantrums, but at least I needn't take them so personally. I now understand that her anger isn't all about me. I don't deserve to be treated like this. I'm going to work up the courage to tell her she needs some help with all this, and I may even suggest we go together for couples counselling.

Here's how you can begin to identify and understand your partner's hot buttons – and how you can stop taking things personally.

1. **After you work out your partner's problematic life-lenses using Worksheet 16-7, observe your partner over the next few weeks.**

2. **When you notice your partner expressing strong negative emotions, record the event that appeared to trigger the reaction in the left-hand column of Worksheet 16-10.**

3. **In the middle column, record your partner's emotions and overall reactions.**

4. **In the right-hand column, identify the problematic life-lens relating to the particular emotions and reactions to each event.**

5. **Use Worksheet 16-11 to reflect on your observations.** Try to avoid taking things personally. After you start doing this, you'll find that some of your own distress subsides.

Worksheet 16-10	My Partner's Life-Lens Tracking Sheet	
Event	*Emotion and Reaction*	*Life-Lens*

Worksheet 16-11	My Reflections

Talking Tough

As we explain in Chapter 15, communication is the bedrock of any good relationship. In that chapter, we give you tools for sharing experiences and positive feelings. Here, we tell you how to tackle the more tricky issues, like concerns, disagreements and dissatisfaction. Everyone needs to discuss this stuff from time to time, but unfortunately, most people aren't very good at it. We cover two helpful strategies – *taking ownership* and *softening your message* – in the following sections. See our book *Overcoming Depression For Dummies* (Wiley) for more detail on these ideas.

Taking ownership

When communicating concerns or dissatisfaction, the language you use makes a huge difference to how heated your communication becomes. If you're critical or blaming, you're likely to get a defensive reply or even a counter-attack. *Taking ownership* means you state your concerns in terms of how they affect you, and you don't blame or accuse your partner of anything. To use this technique, you clearly state how you feel about an issue. You can ensure you're taking ownership when you start your sentences with 'I' rather than 'you'.

Don't expect to get the hang of this technique quickly or easily. Most people's usual, almost instinctive, response to strong criticism or blame is to lash out. Taking ownership takes loads of practice, but it can be well worth the effort.

Worksheet 16-12 shows several examples of blaming, with alternatives where the person takes ownership. After going through the first four examples, devise your own alternatives for the final four.

Worksheet 16-12	Taking Ownership
Blaming Message	*Owning Message*
You don't love me anymore.	I'm feeling a bit insecure. I could really use a hug and some affection.
You never wash the car unless I nag you to death.	I hate feeling I have to nag. I'd be really grateful if you can tell me a regular time you'll commit to.
You're always moaning and groaning.	I find myself worrying you aren't happy when I hear you complaining.
You really hack me off.	I'm feeling a bit cross with you.
You put far too much on the joint credit card.	
You never put your dishes in the dishwasher.	
You're always late.	
You just don't appreciate all the things I do around here.	

Of course, even when you take ownership, you may still get a negative response from your partner. This technique isn't a cast-iron guarantee, but it does better your chances of positive results.

Taking ownership can be even more effective if you not only express what you feel, but also gently state your concern.

Making your message palatable

When you need to talk about things you aren't happy with, you have basically two choices: you can try and shove the unpleasantness down using force or sweeten the bitter taste, making it more palatable and easier to swallow. Guess which works best?

The key to successfully sharing unsavoury information is to sugar-coat your message, adding a phrase acknowledging that what you're saying may not be entirely accurate or that you may be overreacting and going just a bit OTT. Chances are, you don't really believe that your sweetened message is the case, and you may feel 200 per cent justified (otherwise you wouldn't have had that reaction in the first place!). Nonetheless, sweetening can't make the situation any worse in the long run – even if you're totally in the right, it still can only help.

Look at the sweetened and unsweetened versions of various relationship concerns in Worksheet 16-13 and decide for yourself which is more likely to lead to a productive exchange, one in which you facilitate the possibility of a productive conversation and conclude with a mutually acceptable compromise. After you read through some examples, try your own version of sugar-coating the rest.

Combining sweetening with taking ownership (which we discuss in the preceding section) can convey your point even more effectively. The examples in Worksheet 16-13 show the two techniques at work together.

Worksheet 16-13	The Sweetening Strategy
Unsweetened Concerns	**Sweetened Concerns**
You're pruning the whole garden far too severely.	I may be overreacting, but it looks like you're cutting some things back harder than what's needed.
You were downright rude when you spoke to our neighbour yesterday.	I may have got this wrong, but I thought you were a bit abrupt with our neighbour yesterday.
I saw you flirting with that woman at the work Christmas party.	Perhaps I'm being oversensitive, but it did seem like you were responding to that woman's advances at the party last night, and I did feel a bit hurt.
You're spending far too much time at work and being really selfish. Your priorities are way out.	It seems like you're very often late home. Please tell me more about the projects you're involved with at work, so I can understand their importance. I do miss you when you're not here.
You're spending far too much on clothes and shoes.	
You're always shouting at the children. Can't you see they're getting scared of you and avoiding you?	
You're totally spoiling the grandchildren and turning them into ungrateful brats.	
You're always agreeing to give others a hand. But you're never around for me when we need to get things done.	

Part VI
Life Beyond Anxiety and Depression

'A friend told me that a pet helps with anxiety
so today I bought myself a puppy.'

In this part . . .

*W*e take you beyond merely getting better, and also help you prepare for possible difficulties in the road ahead. Relapses in anxiety or depression are common, but you don't have to sit back and let it happen. We tell you what you can do to minimise both your chances of relapse, and its severity and duration.

Finally, we turn our focus to what makes people happy. After all, we don't want you to just get over your emotional distress; we want you to feel true joy from your life. That's why we provide exercises that focus your efforts on finding meaning, purpose and fulfilment.

Chapter 17

Reducing Your Risk of Relapse

· ·

In This Chapter

▶ Evaluating your likelihood of relapse

▶ Watching out for relapse signs

▶ Taking steps to catch and deal with relapse early on

· ·

*T*he good news about anxiety and depression is that they're both highly treatable. Typically, you can expect that working on these problems, on your own or with professional help, will improve your mood considerably. Although relapse is common, be aware that you can do loads of things to minimise the likelihood of relapse and speed your recovery should it occur.

If you've made substantial improvement in dealing with and minimising your anxiety or depression, and you want to maintain your improvement, then this is the chapter for you. Here, we help you see if you're at risk of relapsing. Early detection of relapse signs allows you to nip problems in the bud before they become full-blown and overwhelm you. We also give you strategies to lessen the likelihood of relapse in the first place.

If you've really worked hard through the earlier chapters of this book but find that you're still feeling anxious or depressed, then this is *not* the chapter for you. You probably need professional help if you haven't improved, or if you're finding things really hard going. However, if you've improved but aren't doing quite as well as you'd like, do keep at it – doing more of what is working for you.

Assessing Your Risk of Relapse

If your main problem is depression, your risk of relapse is particularly high. In fact, if you treat your depression only with medication, you have more than a 50 per cent chance of relapsing over the next few years. Anxiety problems have a somewhat lower relapse risk.

Studies indicate that *cognitive behavioural therapies* work. These psychological techniques – which make up the core of this book – focus on changes in your thinking and behaviour, and are what most of this book is based upon. Not only do these therapies work, they also appear to significantly reduce relapse risk. So the bottom line is that if all you've tried is medication, we recommend you embrace the skills we give you throughout this book and/or see a counsellor trained in cognitive behavioural therapy.

If you have made improvements, you're probably wondering how great your relapse risk is. To calculate this, tick the items in Worksheet 17-1 that apply to you.

Worksheet 17-1	Relapse Risk Questionnaire

❏ I'm completely over my anxiety and/or depression. I have no fear it will return.

❏ I have been previously depressed more than once.

❏ I have had bouts of anxiety at times for many years.

❏ The only treatment I've tried is medication.

❏ I suffer from a long-term illness.

❏ I have had big financial problems lately.

❏ I recently lost someone I care deeply about through a relationship break-up or death.

❏ I recently experienced a traumatic event.

❏ I lost my job not long ago.

❏ I've just retired.

❏ I've been experiencing an increase in family conflict lately.

❏ Recently, I finished full-time education.

❏ When I get depressed or anxious, I know it's entirely my fault.

❏ I can't control my moods at all.

❏ I need people to like me in order to be happy.

You may think that ticking the first statement indicates a lowered risk of relapse. Surprisingly, studies show that overconfidence is also a risk factor for increasing the likelihood of relapse. While a degree of optimism is a good thing, temper it with realism. Knowing that you still have some risk of relapse is vital in helping you deal with early signs.

Ticking one of the statements above indicates you have an increased risk of experiencing a recurrence of emotional distress, while more than two means you have a high risk.

Continue putting into practice your psychological therapy for anxiety and depression until symptoms almost completely subside. Keep it up for at least six or eight weeks after you experience a return to full energy, appetite, sleep and pleasure levels. Continue medication even longer – six to twelve months after full remission of symptoms.

If you work through the exercises in this chapter and a relapse still occurs, don't catastrophise. You're not back to square one. You have already gained some effective new skills, which you can reapply. Or you can try any exercise that you haven't yet attempted. If you can't dig yourself out of the hole alone, you can always get professional help. We believe you really don't have to suffer and feel so awful. Please do something about it, and chances are you'll see improvement.

Being Forewarned – and Forearmed

With relapse, you may not notice subtle signs until suddenly you discover that all your problems have returned, possibly even worse than before.

Relapse needn't overwhelm you. After you recover from anxiety or depression, stay on top of things by undertaking a weekly review of your emotions and feelings. Over time, you can reduce the frequency of these reviews to once every month or so, as your risk of relapse lessens.

Complete the Early Warning Signs Relapse Review in Worksheet 17-2 to gauge the likelihood of a relapse. Think through each question carefully and record if it applies you.

Worksheet 17-2	**Early Warning Signs Relapse Review**

1. Have you started avoiding people lately? If so, who, when, where and why?

_____

_____

_____

_____

2. Have your thoughts been pessimistic? If so, what particular thoughts have you been having, how frequently and how intense are they?

_____

_____

_____

_____

3. Have you noticed any changes in your appetite? If so, how long has it been going on for, and have you lost or gained any weight?

_____

_____

_____

_____

4. Have you been avoiding activities or places lately? If so, what, where, when, how and why?

_____

_____

_____

_____

5. Have you noticed any changes in your sleeping patterns? If yes, what changes and how frequent are they?

_____

_____

_____

_____

6. Have you been more irritable than usual? If so, when and under what circumstances?

_____

_____

_____

_____

7. Has someone close to you said that you've been acting unusually in any way? If so, what was said, by whom and when?

_____

_____

_____

_____

8. Have you noticed changes in your memory, concentration or energy? If so, what are these changes?

_____

_____

_____

_____

9. Have you been feeling excessively guilty or have you been having a go at yourself about anything? If so, what's that been about?

_____

_____

_____

_____

10. Have you been sad or worried about anything recently? If so, what, where, when and why?

_____

_____

_____

_____

Visit www.dummies.com/go/adwb to download and print as many of these forms as you need for your own use.

If you routinely complete your Early Warning Signs Relapse Review, relapse is unlikely to sneak up on you. The moment you spot any significant signs of it (as described in Worksheet 17-2), please read and work through the next two sections of this chapter. In addition, we recommend that you go back and do more of whatever it was that successfully reduced your emotional distress previously.

Changes in energy, appetite or sleep may be due to a physical problem. If you're experiencing changes of this nature, talk the situation over with your GP.

Being Prepared

A fire can break out without warning, and at that point, it's a bit late to start devising plans to deal with it. Fire drills and prevention plans make sure that you're ready and know what to do in the event of a fire. The result is effective damage limitation. See our companion book *Overcoming Depression For Dummies* (Wiley) for more detail on how a relapse prevention plan can be similarly effective to having a fire prevention plan.

Worksheet 17-2 shows the early warning signs you should look out for. In Worksheet 17-3, we list some common events that can trigger emotional distress. Read through the list, thinking about which events you're worried may cause you trouble at some future time. For each item, jot down the specifics of your concern – who, what, where and when. At the end of the list, add any future events you think are likely and which you worry about experiencing.

Worksheet 17-3	**Fuelling the Fire**

1. Losing someone important.

_____

_____

_____

2. Being rejected.

_____

_____

_____

3. Getting sick or being hurt.

_____

_____

_____

4. Experiencing financial difficulties.

_____

_____

_____

5. Enduring major political and/or economic changes.

_____

_____

_____

6. **Suffering humiliation, shame or embarrassment.**

_____

_____

_____

7. **Additional concerns.**

_____

_____

_____

So, are we trying to get you to worry about all the bad things that may happen to you? What about our advice in Chapter 8 about the value of staying centred and concentrating on living in the present? If you've been wondering about an apparent contradiction, actually, there really isn't one. While living in the 'now' is certainly a good idea, so is being reasonably prepared for the future.

To be prepared, we suggest you design your own Relapse Prevention Plan. Take each event from Worksheet 17-3 that you think may be a problem for you and work out how you can cope if it occurs. Here's David's Relapse Prevention Plan.

 David recovered from a bout of both anxiety and depression about two months ago. He's preparing to stop seeing his professional counsellor, who's been helping him for the past six months. Before ending their sessions, David's counsellor suggests that David prepare a Coping Strategy as part of his Relapse Prevention Plan. The counsellor has David fill out Worksheet 17-4 for one of David's biggest worries. David's father and uncle both died of colon cancer in their 50s, and David's now 51, so the fear of developing colon cancer is very real for him.

Worksheet 17-4   **David's Coping Strategy**

Situation: Fear of colon cancer

1. **How would someone else cope with this situation?**

   I can't deny that it would be incredibly tough. However, my father used the last years of his life to get his affairs in order and to spend quality time with his family. He also was very helpful to many people in his cancer support group. I could do something similar, if I did develop colon cancer. On the other hand, I remember my uncle being very angry and railing against fate. He seemed to suffer a lot more. I think I'd rather be more like my father.

2. **Have you dealt with something like this in the past? How did you do it?**

   When I was in secondary school, I had meningitis. I was really ill, and everyone was very worried. I don't remember being terrified, though. I guess in the actual situation, I was able to accept and deal with the illness. So perhaps I'd be able to do that again, when and if I have any other life-threatening illness.

3. **How much will this event affect your life a year after it occurs?**

Actually, given that I'm having regular check-ups, it's quite likely that it won't be affecting me much a year after diagnosis. It would be caught at an early stage, when effective treatment's available. So I just may be catastrophising about this issue.

4. **Is this event as awful and as likely as you're making it out to be?**

Obviously not. There have been so many advances both in terms of early diagnosis as well as treatment that I think I'd be okay. As for the slim chance that I'd die, I suppose I'd work out a way of dealing with that, too. Let's face it, there'd be no other option, so I'd have to. And finally, my brother, who's just turned 64, shows no signs of inheriting cancer. It's quite possible I won't develop it at all.

5. **Are there any intriguing, creative ways of dealing with this challenge?**

I've been meaning to participate in the cancer fund-raising walk. I'll enter my name for this year's event. If I do get colon cancer, or any other terminal diagnosis for that matter, I'll join a similar support group to the one my dad did. He seemed to really benefit, as well as help others at the same time.

After completing this exercise, David realises that he can cope with even his worst fears. Seeing the benefit of the exercise, he also fills out a Coping Strategy for several other possible problems that could otherwise herald the return of anxiety and depression.

Using Worksheet 17-5, complete your own Coping Strategy. List your concern and answer the questions that follow. Fill out a worksheet for each worry you identity in Worksheet 17-3.

Worksheet 17-5	**My Coping Strategy**

Situation: _____

1. How would someone else cope with this situation?

_____

_____

_____

_____

2. Have you dealt with something like this in the past? If so, how?

_____

_____

_____

_____

3. How much will this event affect your life a year after it occurs?

_____

_____

_____

_____

4. Is this event as awful and as likely to happen as you're making it out to be?

_____

_____

_____

_____

5. Are there any intriguing, creative ways of dealing with this challenge?

_____

_____

_____

_____

Visit www.dummies.com/go/adwb to download as many copies of this form as you need for your personal use.

How did you feel before you filled out your Coping Strategy? Did answering the questions reveal anything about your fear? Take a few moments to reflect on what you've learned about preparing for future difficulties. Record your thoughts in Worksheet 17-6.

Worksheet 17-6	My Reflections

_____

_____

_____

_____

Keeping Up the Good Work

If you work hard and conquer your depression or anxiety, that's great! But you're likely to experience a few wobbles, those ups and downs when your mood goes down and your anxiety goes up! Some people seem to predominantly focus on the wobbles. They don't really notice the longish periods in between, when it's all smooth sailing. Are you one of those? Do you mainly notice changes for the worse – or do you pay attention to activities that increase your feelings of satisfaction and well-being?

Hitting record achievements

The technique we explain in this section, the Satisfaction Tracker, is designed to enable you to identify satisfying activities. This means you can highlight, focus on and maximise what's going right in your life. Increasing the focus on your well-being improves your chances of preventing relapse.

Mandy has had a tough few years. She's had problems at work, her lover ended their affair and to top it all off, she was diagnosed with breast cancer. Her physical recovery was excellent and comparatively pretty fast. However, as is common with breast cancer survivors, she suffered from depression off and on during her ordeal. Now two years on, her depression seems a thing of the past. Mandy tracks her satisfying activities as a way of consolidating her progress and reducing risk of relapse (see Worksheet 17-7).

Worksheet 17-7	Mandy's Satisfaction Tracker	
Situation	*Satisfying Thoughts*	*Satisfaction Intensity (0–100)*
A friend asked me to do her wedding photography. She paid me and says they're delighted with my work.	My hobby's becoming a second career – something I've always dreamt of.	80
I got a post teaching adult evening classes in digital photography.	Teaching adults who want to learn is great! It's worth all the hassle of getting qualified through that part-time teaching course.	70
I went on my first singles holiday and met a surprising number of kindred spirits whose experiences match mine.	It felt great to spoil myself, instead of always spending my earnings on others.	85
I went for my first long bike ride in the countryside.	I appreciate my health, strength and the beauty of nature more than I ever did before.	60
I finally got through that last pile of filing, demolishing the mountain that's built up over the last two years.	Sorting it into smaller piles and doing one a day worked! It felt great zapping the last one. I'll make sure I keep up with it from now on.	75
I wore my first strapless evening dress since my surgery.	It was a bit daunting, but I got several compliments about how good I looked.	65

Using Mandy's Satisfaction Tracker as a guide, complete your own in Worksheet 17-8 to enable you to keep track of the good things in your life. Remember to include major as well as minor events.

1. Note a particular event in the left-hand column.

2. In the middle column, write down your thoughts and feelings about the event.

3. In the right-hand column, rate the sense of satisfaction you experienced from that event. Use a scale of 0 (no satisfaction) to 100 (absolute bliss!).

4. Following the exercise, use Worksheet 17-9 to reflect on what you discover about your recovery and current well-being.

Worksheet 17-8	My Satisfaction Tracker	
Situation	*Satisfying Thoughts*	*Satisfaction Intensity (0–100)*

At www.dummies.com/go/adwb, you can download as many copies of this form as you need.

Worksheet 17-9	My Reflections

_____

_____

_____

_____

Overriding pessimistic predictions

Sometimes, activities that you anticipate being wonderful turn out to be fine, just about okay or occasionally downright disappointing. Pessimistic predictions may well be the culprits. Here's how they work their mischief.

Daniel loves golf and looks forward to playing in the club tournament. The day dawns, crisp and clear. The course is beautiful. Daniel's easily the best player in his foursome. He expects to have a really enjoyable time. But as he plays, he finds himself beset by pessimistic predictions, which take the shine off the experience. Having already read this chapter, Daniel's acutely aware of the damage such thoughts can do if they're left to roam free. So after he finishes his round of golf, he fills out his Pessimistic Predictions (see Worksheet 17-10) to get a better understanding of what his thoughts have been trying to do to him. Daniel becomes aware that he'd better do something about these thoughts, and he therefore records them, as Worksheet 17-11 shows.

Worksheet 17-10	**Daniel's Pessimistic Predictions**	
Event	*Positive Initial Thought*	*Pessimistic Prediction*
On the first tee, I drove the ball straight down the middle of the fairway.	Nice start. At this rate, I'm on form to win the tournament. of it by the end.	Wait a second. The last time I started so well, look at the mess I made
Andy commented that I'm in good form today.	He's right! I sure am!	Maybe he's trying to make me overconfident. What if I now start letting things slide?
I'm leading at the end of that round.	Maybe I'll represent my club after all.	Whenever I get such positive thoughts, I can just hear my mum warning me not to get too cocky. And she was always right!

Notice how Daniel's initial positive thoughts were tarnished by his pessimistic predictions. While these pessimistic predictions didn't go as far as making Daniel feel depressed (like the thoughts we discuss in chapters 5, 6 and 7), they do take the shine off his enjoyment. And when your enjoyment is consistently sabotaged, the likelihood of relapse increases.

So what can you do about it? Worksheet 17-11 shows Daniel's strategy for dealing with and defeating one of his pessimistic predictions.

Worksheet 17-11	**Daniel's Defence**

Pessimistic Prediction: Whenever I get such positive thoughts, I can just hear my mum warning me not to get too cocky. And she was always right!

1. **What's the evidence that either supports or refutes your pessimistic prediction?**

   I'm doing just fine. My golf's not bad, I feel secure in my employment and my family life's pretty good. Actually, Mum's been wrong about so many things in my life that it's almost funny.

2. **If a friend of yours told you that he or she had this thought, would you think it sounded reasonable – or see it as self-defeating?**

   I've had friends who are good golfers, and I've encouraged them to compete. If my friend told me that he felt like a failure because of something his mum always said, I'd ask him why on earth he feels he has to listen to her.

3. **Do you have experiences in your life that refute this thought?**

   I've won several local golf tournaments. Clearly, I'm not a total loser. And while perhaps I'll never be a Tiger Woods, I don't have to be in order to make a success of my life. Anyway, at club level, I'm actually pretty good.

4. **Is this pessimistic prediction really just one of those distorted negative thoughts? And if so, what counter-arguments can you come up with to restructure it? (See Chapter 6 for more information on negative thoughts.)**

   It's patently obvious that giving credibility to my mum's view is buying into a reality that's pretty distorted. I'm overgeneralising and dismissing evidence that shows I'm doing just fine. I can restructure my pessimistic prediction by reminding myself how well my game's developed. I don't need to heed my mother's voice any longer.

After Daniel provides counter-arguments to his pessimistic predictions, he realises that up until now, he's has been allowing distorted thinking and negative thoughts to spoil his fun.

Now that you see how it's done, work on your own Pessimistic Predictions, using Worksheet 17-12.

1. **In the left-hand column, briefly describe anything you'd expect to have been a positive experience.**

2. **If you initially had positive thoughts about it, note them in the middle column.** If you didn't have such thoughts, leave this column blank.

3. **Record your pessimistic predictions in the right-hand column.** Remember, these are any thoughts that somehow tarnished the pleasure you may have otherwise felt.

Some people almost automatically sabotage their satisfaction with such negative global views as, 'Fun is frivolous', 'I don't deserve to have a good time' or 'I should be working.' These thoughts can really get in the way of enjoying anything and everything. Watch out for such beliefs in your own thinking, and read more about them in chapters 7 and 11.

Worksheet 17-12	Pessimistic Predictions	
Event	*Positive Initial Thought*	*Pessimistic Prediction*

Download as many of these forms as you need at www.dummies.com/go/adwb.

Work through the thoughts you identify in Worksheet 7-12 and subject them to the restructuring process in Worksheet 17-13.

1. **Choose one of your Pessimistic Predictions and write it in the space provided at the top of the worksheet.**

2. **Answer each of the questions that follow in relation to that thought.** If you have trouble answering these questions, review chapters 5 and 6.

3. **In Worksheet 17-14, think through what these exercises have shown you.** Can you see how your pessimistic predictions get in the way of having fun and experiencing pleasure? Can you see the difference in how restructuring such thoughts makes you feel?

Worksheet 17-13   **My Defence Plan**

Pessimistic Prediction: _____

1. **What evidence do you have that either supports or refutes your pessimistic prediction?**

   _____

   _____

   _____

   _____

2. **If a friend of yours told you that he or she had this thought, would you think it sounded reasonable or see it as self-defeating?**

   _____

   _____

   _____

   _____

3. **Do you have experiences in your life that refute this thought?**

   _____

   _____

   _____

   _____

4. **Is this negative thought distorted and can you come up with a more accurate restructured one? (See Chapter 6 for more information on negative thoughts and distortions in thinking.)**

   _____

   _____

   _____

   _____

Worksheet 17-14	My Reflections

Chapter 18

Promoting the Positive

- -

- -

Throughout this book, we focus on ways to help you overcome depression and defeat anxiety. We know that working through the exercises and developing the strategies provides an excellent opportunity for you to substantially improve your mood. You deserve to feel better, and if you're already feeling pretty good, then this is the chapter for you.

In this chapter, we go beyond depression and anxiety and head towards real authentic happiness. Research shows that not only does happiness feel good, but also happy people have better immune systems, live longer, have lower blood pressure and feel more empathy for others. They're generally more productive, successful and satisfied with life. That's a pretty convincing list to support the value of this authentic happiness stuff!

But if happiness is so great, what is it that makes people happy? Although happy people are frequently more successful financially, research shows that money alone doesn't lead to more happiness. Unless you're in extreme poverty where your survival is at stake, studies indicate that wealth in its varied forms isn't directly related to your level of happiness and life satisfaction. Even winning a big lottery payout doesn't necessarily lead to long-lasting happiness. And, surprisingly, having power, youth and good looks also don't seem to contribute much to people's reported happiness either.

Basically rich, gorgeous, young and powerful people are as likely to experience anxiety and depression – and may feel just as miserable – as anyone else. That's not to say you should give away all your money, neglect your appearance and quit your job! It's just that having all those things doesn't automatically lead to nor ensure happiness.

So what does lead to authentic happiness – the real thing? In Chapter 11, we talk about the value of seeking out what we call healthy pleasures. Simple healthy pleasures are very helpful for kick-starting mood improvements, but they're somewhat transitory. In this chapter, we present ideas for achieving deeper longer-lasting satisfaction and well-being.

Developing an Attitude of Gratitude

You may have heard the advice about counting your blessings. Or as the song goes, 'Accentuate the positive. Eliminate the negative.' It's actually pretty good advice. Truth is, concentrating on the good things in your life and becoming acutely aware of what fills you with a sense of gratitude can be surprisingly helpful to developing your sense of well-being.

Keeping track of things that make you grateful

Studies show that keeping a record of what you appreciate or are thankful for improves mood, sleep and health. It's really amazing just how easily you can enhance your life-satisfaction with this technique, also known as counting your blessings.

Jane had a bout of depression and recovered a few months ago. She carefully monitors herself for signs of relapse (see Chapter 17) and feels grateful that she seems to have beaten the blues. Before finishing counselling, her counsellor suggests that Jane count her blessings for a while. So Jane starts keeping a Gratitude Diary; Worksheet 18-1 shows her first week's efforts.

Worksheet 18-1	Jane's Gratitude Diary
Day	*What I Feel Grateful For*
Monday	1. I chose the fastest queue at the supermarket. 2. Got on the scales and found I'd lost another pound. 3. Work went pretty well today. 4. Had a great walk in the park with my dog. 5. The kids were really helpful today – I do so love them (well, most of the time!)
Tuesday	1. My favourite spot in the car park was waiting for me. 2. The weather was glorious today. 3. Saw the first pink blossom trees in bloom. 4. The kids did their homework without me having to nag. 5. I'm really grateful for my good health. 6. Traffic to and from work was delightfully light.
Wednesday	1. It's great to have finished decorating the bedroom. 2. Dinner was delicious. 3. I'm beginning to balance the family finances. 4. Washed the car – it really looks better for it. 5. My new shampoo's made my hair more manageable.
Thursday	1. We didn't argue over leaving the house on time. 2. Just managed to slow down for that speed camera. 3. Enjoyed my aerobics class. 4. Michelle popped over for coffee, which was great. 5. My partner called me gorgeous and said how much I'm loved.
Friday	1. It's Friday! YIPPEE! 2. Looks like I've escaped this round of redundancies. 3. The bedroom's looking so much better than it did before. 4. Invited my parents over for dinner – they were thrilled. 5. My partner cooked and the kids washed up. 6. The DVD I chose was really good.
Saturday	1. Minded my neighbour's baby so she could catch up. 2. The gas man turned up when they said he would. 3. The boiler's fixed, and it was cheaper than I'd feared. 4. I'm not feeling low. 5. The daffodils are all in full bloom.
Sunday	1. Had a lie-in this morning. 2. The birds are really loving their new bird feeder. 3. The kids went to play with friends – it was so peaceful! 4. I'm getting the hang of this cognitive behavioural therapy stuff. 5. The neighbour's baby gurgled and smiled at me. 6. Began dreading Monday – but I short circuited the spiral down.

Jane is surprised at how good it feels to record and review what makes her feel grateful for a few weeks. She starts doing more of what works, like increasing the amount she exercises, and she feels a deepening sense of satisfaction with her life.

With Jane's Gratitude Diary as your guide, fill out your own Gratitude Diary in Worksheet 18-2.

1. **On each day of the week, think of five things you feel grateful for that happened on that day.** The things your write down can be great or small, ranging from easily finding a parking space to excellent test results.

2. **At the end of each day, read through the five items and think about how appreciative you feel that day.**

3. **At the end of the week, use Worksheet 18-3 to reflect on what you've learned following the process of recording and reviewing what makes you feel grateful.**

Continue with this exercise for a solid month and then go back to completing your Gratitude Diary from time to time in the future.

Worksheet 18-2	My Gratitude Diary
Day, Month and Year	*What I Feel Grateful For*
Monday	
Tuesday	
Wednesday	
Thursday	
Friday	
Saturday	
Sunday	

Download as many copies of this exercise as you need for your personal use at www. dummies.com/go/adwb.

Worksheet 18-3	My Reflections

_____

_____

_____

_____

Thanks-Giving

One strategy that helps you focus on what you're grateful for was developed by psychologist Dr Martin Seligman. Dr Seligman conducted some research on the thanks-giving technique and found that participants generally felt much more positive after completing it.

Duraid has a lot to be grateful for. He conquered his social anxiety more than a year ago. His school friend, Jake, invited him to join the band he was forming, and performing music was instrumental in helping Duraid overcome his anxiety. Now both Duraid and Jake are students at a music college. One of their lecturers has studied positive psychology and suggests the following project: each student chooses someone who's made a real difference to his or her life and then writes a 'thank you' letter to that person. They person needn't even still be alive. And the students have free choice of whether they actually send the letter to the person, read it out to other students, keep it or even destroy it. In Worksheet 18-4, you can read what Duraid writes about Jake.

Worksheet 18-4	My Thanks-Giving: To Jake

Dear Jake,

I've chosen you as someone who has made a huge difference to my life. It feels quite strange writing this, but I know I don't even have to show it to you if I decide against doing so. I don't think I've ever told you how much I appreciate what you did for me in helping me overcome my social anxiety.

That first year when we went from middle to secondary school was utterly horrendous. I was teased and bullied something rotten and had never felt so low. But you heard me talk about my passion for keyboards and invited me to join your band. Rehearsing and composing occupied all my spare time, and then some! You encouraged me, even including some of my stuff in our gigs. You got me to do the things I'd been dreaming of, but which I didn't think I could. You were quite a role model for me, showing me how to talk to girls and how to stand up to bullies. We sure had some pretty good times, didn't we? Sometimes, I felt it was all too much, and just wanted to crawl away and hide, but you wouldn't let me, would you? You threatened to kick arse! Then you kept going on and on that I needed to get counselling. That was the last thing I wanted to hear. But you were so right. That whole first year completely turned my life around. I give you credit for so much.

Mates just don't get any better than you. Your friendship's really important to me. And now before I go all gooey, I think I'll stop here. But seriously, I can't even begin to tell you how much I appreciate all you did – and are continuing to do.

Your best mate,

Duraid

Use Worksheet 18-5 and the following instructions to complete your own Thanks-Giving.

1. **Choose someone from your life who has made a real, positive difference in your life.** Ideally, the person you choose isn't someone you're romantically involved with because hopefully you already tell that person what they mean to you. (See Chapter 15 for more about romantic involvement.)

2. **Write at least two or three paragraphs expressing your gratitude and telling the person specific things that he or she did for you.** Write your thank you letter out in longhand – the process and end result usually feel much more personal.

3. **If you feel it's appropriate, decide whether you want to post the letter, give it in person, or, if the person is no longer living, read it to a supportive person, someone in a support group, a counsellor or do none of the above.**

4. **In Worksheet 18-6, reflect on this exercise and what it's taught you about the good people and things in your life.**

Worksheet 18-5	**Thanks-Giving: A Big Thank You**

Dear

Worksheet 18-6	My Reflections

_____

_____

_____

_____

Doing Good Does You Good

A powerful way of achieving happiness is through helping others. Being kind to others not only helps them, but also helps you in two ways: firstly, you're likely to enjoy the feeling you get from it. Most of us experience a lovely, warm, fuzzy feeling when we help others. Secondly, doing something nice for another person enables you to move your focus away from your own problems, provides relief from your worries for a while and can lead to a whole new perspective.

Worksheet 18-7 lists some ideas you can try in order to help others. (This strategy works even better if you come up with your own list of things that are important to you; for more ideas, check out www.actsofkindness.org.)

Worksheet 18-7	Good Deeds

❑ Check out the volunteer work available locally – even a few hours a month.

❑ Offer to help an elderly neighbour.

❑ Smile and say 'Good morning' to a stranger.

❑ Assist someone struggling with something heavy, if you're able to do so.

❑ Welcome the next person you see moving in near you and offer assistance.

❑ Smile and signal your thanks if another driver is nice to you.

❑ Let another car into your lane.

❑ Give blood.

❑ Have a clear out. Take what you no longer use or wear to a charity shop.

❑ Make a phone-call or write a thank-you note for a meal or a gift you enjoyed.

❑ Offer your seat on public transport to someone who seems to need it more than you do.

The following exercise helps you discover the personal benefits of small acts of kindness. Through these small gestures, you make the world a better place while simultaneously enhancing your own well-being.

1. **Brainstorm a list of at least 20 small acts of kindness – things you could do almost anytime.** Write them in the left-hand column of Worksheet 18-8.

   The key is to think of ideas that are truly gifts, for which you don't expect anything in return. If you want to include any bigger gestures, that's fine, but do remember, the frequency of your actions – not the size – is what really makes the difference.

2. **After you compile your list, start acting on it!**

3. Note each act of kindness in the right-hand column, recording the date you did it.

4. After several weeks, reflect on how this exercise affects you in Worksheet 18-9.

Worksheet 18-8	My Good Deed Diary
Acts of Kindness	*When I Did It*

Worksheet 18-9	My Reflections

Letting Go

One way people spoil their own happiness is by nursing grudges. Holding on to resentment, anger and rage doesn't do you any favours. When you've been wronged, you naturally feel upset. Anger can be useful, at least for a while. It can help you defend yourself when attacked. You can get all fired up and energised to right a perceived wrong.

But holding onto anger for too long can start to poison you, body and soul. Chronic anger can lead to high blood pressure, emotional disturbance and a decrease in common sense. When you're angry, you simply can't be happy.

Knowing the toxic side of anger is one thing; what you do about it is quite another matter. Letting go of chronic anger isn't easy. You must do something that feels rather counterintuitive: somehow find forgiveness for those who have wronged you.

Certain wrongs may not be forgivable, realistically. For example, you may find yourself unable to forgive acts of severe violence or abuse. In that case, an alternative approach is to let go of the anger and rage by finding acceptance. See Chapter 8 for ideas on achieving acceptance. If you find that anger is embittering your life, seek professional assistance from a psychologist or counsellor.

In Worksheet 18-10, we guide you through a series of steps for finding forgiveness and the serenity that comes along with it.

Worksheet 18-10	Finding Forgiveness

1. **Write down what has happened to you to make you angry.** Be specific. Try to avoid using words of rage and retribution. Instead, describe the person and event in terms that are as objective and dispassionate as you can. Review what you write over and over until your feelings about it begin to lessen. You may decide to repeat this exercise over several days, because changes in feelings can take some time.

   _____

   _____

   _____

   _____

2. **Try to empathise and understand the other person's perspective.** See if you can find a reason why the person behaved like that towards you. Was it out of fear – or was the person perhaps misguided, depressed, defensive, lacking judgement or purposefully hurtful? Write down your ideas.

   _____

   _____

   _____

   _____

3. **Think of yourself as a forgiving person, not a victim.** Describe how your life may be different when you learn to let go of your anger and forgive.

   _____

   _____

   _____

   _____

4. **When thoughts of revenge come into your mind, write down reasons for letting them go.** Remember that in the long run, anger and rage harm you more than the perpetrator.

   _____

   _____

   _____

   _____

5. **Consider writing a letter of forgiveness.** Jot down ideas of what you could include in the space below. You can then get a separate sheet of paper and draft a letter, if you want. While you certainly don't have to send it to the person concerned, you may find it helps you to discuss it with others.

_____

_____

_____

_____

Forgiving isn't the same as saying that the wrong was okay. Forgiveness helps restore the peace that you had before the event occurred. And letting go of your anger allows you to regain your previous happiness.

Exercising Self-Control: Less Is More

When pursuing happiness, avoiding the quick fix is very important. *Quick fixes* come in all shapes and sizes – alcohol, drugs, chocolate, a new car, a better house, new clothes, to name but a few. While fine in moderation, none of them ensure lasting happiness.

Numerous studies demonstrate that in the long run, self-control and the ability to delay gratification lead to better adjustment and greater satisfaction with life. Yet the world promises and encourages instant gratification – and even suggests that you should be happy at all times. These expectations can easily set you up for disappointment. The truth is that:

- People aren't always happy.
- Meaningful goals require effort and patience.
- Overindulgence leads to satiation and corresponding decreases in pleasure.
- People who expect instant gratification are inevitably frustrated and disappointed.

Worksheet 18-11 starts you on the path to achieving greater self-control. Even small steps in this direction enhance your sense of well-being. You certainly don't have to make major changes all at once, but most importantly, devote some serious time to this exercise to get the best results.

Worksheet 18-11	Strengthening Self-Control

1. **Write a brief description of an area in your life in which you've given in to impulses or expected instant gratification.**

_____

_____

_____

_____

2. **Write your reflections on how increasing self-control in this area of your life may improve your long-term satisfaction.**

_____

_____

_____

_____

3. **Based on what you've written, develop a goal for change. (Take a look at Chapter 3 for more on change and goal-making.)**

_____

_____

_____

_____

4. **Record your reflections on how your life would change for the better if you were to achieve this new goal.**

_____

_____

_____

_____

Now it's time to put self-control into practice, or in the words of Mahatma Gandhi, 'Be the change you want to see in the world.'

Recognising What's Really Important

What do you value? How much of your time do you devote to activities that are meaningful and consistent with your values? And do you live your life according to those values? If not, you're probably not as happy as you could be.

Use Worksheet 18-12 to identify and clarify your values. You'll find this understanding can enable you to focus on what's really important to you. After you complete it, you can then redirect your life plan towards more meaningful goals.

1. **Read through all the values listed in Worksheet 18-12.**

2. **Circle the eight items you prize most highly.**

3. **Of those eight, pick your top three and write them in Worksheet 18-13.**

Worksheet 18-12	**Values Clarification Quiz**
Money	Donating time or money to others
Pleasure	Cleaning up the environment
Independence	Political activism
Risk-taking and/or excitement	Competition
Creativity	Leisure time
Recognition	Honesty
Achievement	Competition
Variety	Family life
Entertainment	Recreation
Close friends	Status
A loving partner	Designer stuff
Spirituality	Intellectual pursuits
Health	Looking good
Good food	Satisfying work
Having happy kids	Showing kindness
Art	Mental or physical stimulation
Economic security	Safety
Influencing others	Predictability
Appreciation of beauty/aesthetics	Delight in learning
Compassion	Kindness
Curiosity	Loyalty
Dependability	Listening skills
Empathy	Loving nature
Generosity	Perseverance
Helpfulness	Sense of humour
Honesty	Trustworthiness

Worksheet 18-13	**My Top Three Values**
1.	
2.	
3.	

Consider how you've spent your time in the past month. Estimate the time and energy you've devoted to activities that are in line with your top three values (see Worksheet 18-13). If you notice a discrepancy between what you value and what you're actually doing, consider reprioritising how you spend your resources. In Worksheet 18-14, note how you plan to reallocate your time and energy and alter your activities to better reflect what you deem important. Making these changes is likely to improve your long-term life satisfaction.

Worksheet 18-14	My Reflections

_____

_____

_____

_____

Composing Your Swansong

You may well think that your funeral is a rather odd place to find meaning in your life. And you may wonder why a book purporting to provide help with emotional distress is asking you to think about dying! Well, give us a minute, and hear us out.

Finding meaning and purpose in life is about connecting with ideas and concepts that pertain to things larger and deeper than just you. For many, religion and spirituality are the primary channels for finding such meaning. But regardless of your spiritual beliefs, giving serious consideration to what you want your life to be about, in other words, the legacy you want to leave behind, can be an enlightening exercise.

In this section, we ask you to think about your memorial service and the thoughts and feelings that people there may experience when contemplating your life. What do you want people to remember about you and your life? The following exercise helps you identify the traits, characteristics and values you hold most dear. By reminding yourself that from now onwards, you intend to live the rest of your life in line with these, the chances are you'll feel more enriched and fulfilled.

Rowan begins writing the following Swansong exercise in an effort to enhance the sense of meaning and purpose he's getting from his life. As he tackles the task, Rowan becomes uncomfortably aware that he hasn't been living his life in a manner that reflects how he wants to be remembered. He perseveres, identifying what he wants people to think of him and to remember about his life after he's gone (see Worksheet 18-15).

Worksheet 18-15	Rowan's Swansong

We're here today to say goodbye to our friend and family member, Rowan. Rowan was a wonderful father and husband. He loved and enjoyed spending time with his family. Rowan's children grew up to be successful and happy. He loved and cherished his wife throughout their marriage. He was careful to keep the romance alive, even until the end. Rowan was a true friend to many of us here today. When someone needed help, Rowan was the first to offer. His door was always open. He not only gave of what he had – he also gave of himself, and did all he could to make the world a better place for us all.

Rowan sees a painful contrast between the life he's been living and the one he wants to be remembered for. In his wildest imagination, he can't see anyone singing a Swansong that sounds anything like the one he's dreamed up! Looking at his life, Rowan realises that he spends far too much of his time working and buying unnecessary 'stuff'. He doesn't want people to remember how he boasted that he was one of the first within his group of friends to get a plasma television or that he changed his car every year. He vows that in the future, he'll spend more time with his friends and family, and he makes a plan for contributing more to his community. After all, he cherishes these values far more than all the material prizes in the world.

Use the space in Worksheet 18-16 to write your own Swansong. Remember to be honest about how you'd like to be remembered, regardless of your current activities and behaviours.

1. **Sit back and relax for a few minutes.**

2. **Ponder how you would like to be remembered at the end of your life.** Think of loved ones and friends – what do you wish they would say or think about you?

3. **Write down your thoughts.** Your Swansong should reflect the things you value most, in other words, what you want the rest of your life to be about.

Worksheet 18-16   **My Swansong**

_____

_____

_____

_____

_____

A renowned man who made his fortune through dynamite and explosives is said to have read his mistakenly published obituary in astonishment. He railed against the notion of being remembered as a war-mongerer. Posterity records that he did something about this situation – Alfred Nobel founded the Nobel Peace Prize!

Starting from this very moment, right now, you're beginning the rest of your life. Think about it for a moment. This really is the first day and night of the rest of your life. So what are you going to do with it? Whatever your age, whatever you have or haven't done before, the time is never too late to start living a life with meaning and purpose.

Part VII
The Part of Tens

'. . . that's Ragnar the Bloodaxe's, that's Sven the Bonecrusher's, and this one's Eric the Anxious's . . .'

In this part . . .

We provide you with some very useful quick references in the grand *For Dummies* tradition. First, we offer lists of resources that you can turn to for extra assistance; you're likely to find at least one if not more of these resources helpful. Then, we look at what you can do when you're not overwhelmed, but merely somewhat out of sorts. We provide ten quick strategies for successfully combating mild to moderately distressing feelings.

Chapter 19

Ten Helpful Resources

We certainly hope and expect that you find this book useful, though the strategies we share here are by no means all there is to overcoming difficulties. Most people benefit from multiple sources of help. This chapter contains our recommended resources for accessing additional support if you're facing anxiety or depression.

Browsing Through Self-Help Books

Bookshops and libraries display a bewildering array of self-help books, not all of which are based on scientifically validated treatments. Here's a short list of books that give solid help based on well-researched strategies for alleviating emotional distress. Obviously, these aren't the only good books out there; however, these are ones we most frequently recommend.

- ✔ *Addiction & Recovery For Dummies*, by Brian F. Shaw, Paul Ritvo, Jane Irvine and M. David Lewis (Wiley, 2004)

- ✔ *The Anxiety & Phobia Workbook*, by Edmund J. Bourne (New Harbinger Publications, Inc., 2005)

- ✔ *Authentic Happiness: Using the New Positive Psychology to Realize Your Potential for Lasting Fulfillment*, by Martin E. P. Seligman (Free Press, 2004)

- ✔ *Changing For Good: A Revolutionary Six-Stage Program for Overcoming Bad Habits and Moving Your Life Positively Forward*, by James O. Prochaska, John C. Norcross, and Carlo C. DiClemente (William Morrow & Co., Inc., 1994)

- ✔ *Choosing to Live: How to Defeat Suicide Through Cognitive Therapy*, by Thomas E. Ellis and Cory F. Newman (New Harbinger Publications, 1996)

- ✔ *Feeling Better, Getting Better, Staying Better: Profound Self-Help Therapy for Your Emotions*, by Albert Ellis (Impact Publishers, Inc., 2001)

- ✔ *The Feeling Good Handbook*, by David D. Burns (Plume, 2000, second edition)

- ✔ *Full Catastrophe Living: How to Cope with Stress, Pain and Illness Using Mindfulness Meditation, 15th anniversary edition*, by Jon Kabat-Zinn (Piatkus, 2001)

- ✔ *Fly Away Fear: Overcoming Fear of Flying*, by Elaine Iljon Foreman and Lucas Van Gerwen (Karnac, 2008)

- ✔ *Love Is Never Enough: How Couples Can Overcome Misunderstandings, Resolve Conflicts, and Solve Relationship Problems Through Cognitive Therapy*, by Aaron T. Beck (HarperCollins, 1989)

✔ *Mastery of Your Anxiety and Panic*, by David Barlow and Michelle Craske (Oxford University Press, 2007)

✔ *Mind Over Mood: Change How You Feel by Changing the Way You Think*, by Dennis Greenberger and Christine A. Padesky (Guildford Press, 1995)

✔ *Mindful Recovery: A Spiritual Path to Healing from Addiction*, by Thomas Bien and Beverly Bien (Wiley, 2002)

✔ *Overcoming Anxiety For Dummies*, by Elaine Iljon Foreman, Charles H. Elliott and Laura L. Smith (Wiley, 2008)

✔ *Overcoming Depression For Dummies*, by Elaine Iljon Foreman, Laura L. Smith and Charles H. Elliott (Wiley, 2008)

✔ *The Seven Principles for Making Marriage Work*, by John M. Gottman and Nan Silver (Three Rivers Press, 2000)

✔ *Why Can't I Get What I Want?: How to Stop Making the Same Old Mistakes and Start Living a Life You Can Love*, by Charles H. Elliott and Maureen Kirby Lassen (Davies-Black Publishing, 1998)

Sampling Suitable Websites

The Internet gives you access to incredible amounts of information, good and bad, accurate and downright inaccurate, so you need to take care about what you read and attempt to put into practice. The following specifically selected websites all contain high quality, reliable information and advice of proven validity, so you're highly unlikely to come a cropper if you follow their suggestions.

✔ **BBC Health Conditions: Mental Health** (www.bbc.co.uk/health/conditions/mental_health/) is a useful website with information and self-help tips.

✔ **The British Psychological Society** (www.bps.org.uk) provides information about the treatment of, as well as interesting facts about, depression and other emotional disorders.

✔ **The Centre for Mindfulness Research and Practice** (www.bangor.ac.uk/mindfulness) is an information resource on mindfulness-based approaches and a networking facility for professionals in the field in the UK and Europe.

✔ **Mindfulness Based Cognitive Therapy** (www.mbct.co.uk) provides information about (you guessed it!) Mindfulness-Based Cognitive Therapy.

✔ **National Alliance on Mental Illness** (www.nami.org) provides information about the causes, prevalence and treatments of mental disorders that affect children and adults (US site).

✔ **National Institute for Health and Clinical Excellence** (www.nice.org.uk) reports on research about a wide variety of mental health issues. They also have an array of educational materials on depression. They provide resources for researchers and practitioners in the field.

✔ **No More Panic** (www.nomorepanic.co.uk) provides valuable information for sufferers and carers of people with panic, anxiety, phobias and Obsessive Compulsive Disorder (OCD).

Seeking Support in Numbers

Support from others who currently experience or have experienced problems similar to your own can be very helpful at times. The local library, newspaper and Citizen's Advice Bureau (www.citizensadvice.org.uk) are all likely to have information on active support groups in your area, and so too may the Internet. You'll probably be surprised at how many different groups you find.

 Be careful with many available Internet support groups. Sometimes people using them are trying to convince others how ill they all are and how progress is impossible rather than assisting and encouraging the process of change. Also, some people unfortunately use message boards and chat rooms to attempt to take advantage of vulnerable people.

Feeling Fortified by Family and Friends

Almost everyone turns to friends or family for help from time to time, and we certainly encourage you to do so. Although your friends and family probably don't have the expertise to do more than support and listen to you, such support is invaluable at stressful times.

 Avoid trying to make your loved ones feel responsible for your mental health. Doing so may jeopardise your relationship and is unlikely to help you in the end. You must take ownership of the task of dealing with your difficulties, getting better, maintaining improvements and coping with any relapse.

Getting to Know Your GP

GPs certainly have some training in the treatment of emotional disorders, although they don't specialise in the manner of a mental health professional. Your anxiety and depression may well be caused by physical problems, and your GP is the person to first rule that out and then refer you to the most appropriate mental health professional if necessary.

Contacting a Counsellor

Most counsellors have Master's degrees in counselling or psychology and have been trained in the treatment and diagnosis of emotional disorders. Before you begin a treatment program, make sure that your counsellor is familiar with scientifically validated psycho-therapeutic techniques.

Consulting a Psychiatrist

Psychiatrists have extensive training in diagnosing and treating mental disorders. Most psychiatrists primarily utilise medication in treating these disorders, and they are well placed to manage medications' side effects. (See Chapter 14 for more information about treatment with medication.) Psychiatrists also have a certain amount of specialised training in psychotherapy techniques, such as those we cover in this book. Some psychiatrists have more training, experience and interest in using psychological therapy than others, so feel free to ask your psychiatrist about his or her therapy techniques if that's the kind of help you're looking for.

Seeing a Clinical Psychologist

Clinical psychologists have a doctoral qualification, for which they've undertaken extensive training in the understanding and treatment of mental disorders. They primarily utilise psychological therapy, which involves one-to-one or group sessions where you work together on overcoming your difficulties. For the best results, make sure your psychologist is familiar with scientifically validated therapies, such as those we cover in this book.

Working With a Social Worker

Social workers typically have Master's degrees in social work. They often specialise in helping people access community resources, but many are trained in psychotherapy as well. Before you begin a treatment programme, inquire as to your social worker's knowledge about scientifically validated psychotherapies.

Checking Out Community Mental Health Centres

New government initiatives are underway. Additional people are being trained to provide basic psychological therapy interventions, at less intensive levels, for a greater number of people than has been available via the mental health professionals we mention in the preceding sections. Ask your doctor or local health care provider for details about the Improving Access to Psychological Therapies (IAPT) programme.

Choosing What's Right for You

Take some time to reflect on which of the preceding resources you want to pursue. In Worksheet 19-1, write down the ones you are going to try. The sooner you start, the sooner you're likely to experience improvement. When working out what and when you want to have a go at, you can record notes in Worksheet 19-1 regarding your own investigation of these resources.

Worksheet 19-1	Resources I'm Investigating

Chapter 20

Ten Terrific Tips to Boost Your Mood

∙ ∙

In This Chapter

▶ Lifting your mood quickly when you're in the dumps

▶ Enjoying different activities

∙ ∙

The ideas in this chapter are designed to lift your spirits when you're feeling a little down or uptight. They're not for dealing with really deep depression or intense anxiety – that's a job for the rest of the book! But if you're feeling not quite yourself, not as good as you know you can be, turn to one – or several – of these handy hints.

Pause for Breath

Typically, when you're experiencing distress, your breathing both quickens and becomes shallower. These changes then add to your stress, making you even more uncomfortable. The following effective breathing technique is an excellent countermeasure to employ:

1. **Place one hand on your abdomen and the other on your chest.**

2. **Breathe in slowly, concentrating on inflating your abdomen first and then your chest.**

3. **Exhale slowly, quietly saying the word 'relaxxxxxxxxx' as the air goes out.**

4. **Repeat steps 1 to 3 for at least ten breaths.**

Talk It Over

People are social creatures. When you connect with others, you're likely to feel better. If you're feeling down, call a friend and talk through what's bothering you. Or phone or visit someone just for a chat about anything, even unrelated to the issue. Whatever the reason you make that connection, it's likely to help.

Wash It Away

Sitting in a warm bath or standing in a hot shower can comfort the body by loosening all those muscles that tighten up when you're stressed. (Saunas and steam-rooms at the gym can also be effective.) As you feel the moisture and heat, imagine that you're wrapped up in a warm blanket. You can let yourself feel safe, soothed and serene.

Chill Out for a Bit

This technique sounds pretty weird, but it works. When your distress feels intense, fill a sink or large bowl with ice water (that's right, ice water), take a deep breath and dunk your face in the water for 30 seconds or so. Believe it or not, the experience isn't as awful as it sounds!

This calming technique is believed to work because it elicits what's known as the body's *dive reflex.* When you're in ice-cold water, your body slows its metabolism in order to protect vital organs. A slowed metabolism reduces tension, so when your face is immersed in ice water, your metabolism slows, your tension decreases, you fret far less about the things that are bothering you and your negative mind chatter decreases too. Though it sounds weird, why not give it a try?

Pinpoint and Unpick Your Thoughts

To work out exactly what's bothering you and consider it in relation to the big picture of your life's events, answer the following four questions. Note: this quick strategy works best if you first read Part II of this book.

1. **What's bothering me?**

   _____

   _____

   _____

2. **How important will this issue be to me in one year?**

   _____

   _____

   _____

3. **Do I have any evidence that suggests my thoughts about the event are incorrect?**

   _____

   _____

   _____

4. **Is there a more reasonable way of looking at what happened?**

   _____

   _____

   _____

Exorcise through Exercise

The body responds to upset by producing stress hormones. However, you can begin burning up those hormones by exercising for at least 15 to 20 minutes. Try something aerobic such as running, jogging or brisk walking. If it's a nice day, going outside gives you the added benefit of sunshine and fresh air. Or if it's more convenient, go to the gym and do your own work out or take part in an exercise class.

Merge with the Music

Sound influences your mind and body, in positive and negative ways. It can jar, startle, upset or soothe you. When you feel distressed, try listening to music that you find relaxing, whether classical, swing, jazz, Latin, hard rock or even heavy metal. Or you may listen to meandering New Age music or recordings of nature's sounds.

Get a Pet

Studies have shown that having a pet is linked to both an improvement in mood and health. Watching animals play can be delightful, and petting them often soothes both petter and pet! In fact, one study suggests that petting dogs even helps reduce blood pressure. So if you don't have a pet, consider getting one or visit a friend who has one.

Initiate Alternative Activities

When you're upset, usually the only thing on your mind is what's bothering you. Focusing on that and on how awful you feel only makes things worse. We're not advocating putting your head in the sand, but if you need quick relief of minor stress and distress – and if there's nothing you can do about the issue at that point – consider involving yourself in alternative activities such as:

✔ Reading a good novel

✔ Going out to a film, the theatre or renting a DVD

✔ Watching television

✔ Surfing the Internet

✔ Playing a game

Recognise the Here and Now

Most of what upsets you has to do with the past or the future. You may feel guilty and depressed about events from the past – or anxious about events that have not yet occurred (and often never will).

To escape this trap, focus on what's actually happening around you right now. Notice your breathing. Feel your feet on the ground. Notice the firmness of your chair. Pay attention to the temperature and the natural movement of air around you. Look around and observe. Don't judge. Just observe, breathe and concentrate on all the feedback from all your senses.

Find What Works for You

1. **Take a few moments to reflect on how the various techniques in this chapter have worked for you in the past.**

2. **In Worksheet 20-1, note the techniques that have helped you and how you felt when you used them.**

3. **Glance through the chapters again and pick out any tip or technique you haven't yet tried and give it a go.** If it works for you, add it to the successful steps recorded in Worksheet 20-1. Make a note of your reflections in Worksheet 20-2.

Worksheet 20-1	Tips and Techniques List
Techniques that have Helped Me	*How I Felt when I Used Them*

Worksheet 20-2	My Reflections

_____

_____

_____

Index

• Q •

• R •

FOR DUMMIES®

Do Anything. Just Add Dummies

UK editions

BUSINESS

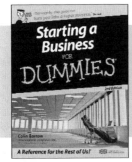
978-0-470-51806-9

978-0-470-99245-6

978-0-7645-7056-8

FINANCE

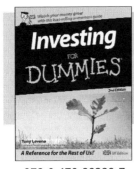
978-0-470-99280-7

978-0-470-99811-3

978-0-470-69515-9

PROPERTY

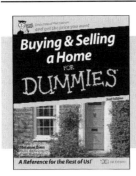
978-0-470-99448-1

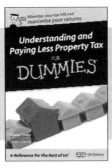
978-0-470-75872-4

978-0-7645-7054-4

Arthritis For Dummies
978-0-470-02582-6

Backgammon For Dummies
978-0-470-77085-6

Body Language For Dummies
978-0-470-51291-3

British Sign Language
For Dummies
978-0-470-69477-0

Business NLP For Dummies
978-0-470-69757-3

Children's Health For Dummies
978-0-470-02735-6

Counselling Skills For Dummies
978-0-470-51190-9

Digital Marketing For Dummies
978-0-470-05793-3

eBay.co.uk For Dummies,
2nd Edition
978-0-470-51807-6

English Grammar For Dummies
978-0-470-05752-0

Fertility & Infertility For Dummies
978-0-470-05750-6

Genealogy Online For Dummies
978-0-7645-7061-2

Golf For Dummies
978-0-470-01811-8

Green Living For Dummies
978-0-470-06038-4

Hypnotherapy For Dummies
978-0-470-01930-6

Available wherever books are sold. For more information or to order direct go to www.wiley.com or call +44 (0) 1243 843291

FOR DUMMIES®

A world of resources to help you grow

UK editions

SELF-HELP

978-0-470-01838-5

978-0-7645-7028-5

978-0-470-75876-2

HEALTH

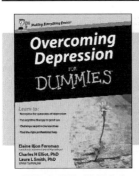
978-0-470-69430-5

978-0-470-51737-6

978-0-470-71401-0

HISTORY

978-0-470-99468-9

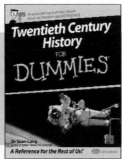
978-0-470-51015-5

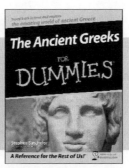
978-0-470-98787-2

Inventing For Dummies
978-0-470-51996-7

Job Hunting and Career Change
All-In-One For Dummies
978-0-470-51611-9

Motivation For Dummies
978-0-470-76035-2

Origami Kit For Dummies
978-0-470-75857-1

Personal Development All-In-One
For Dummies
978-0-470-51501-3

PRINCE2 For Dummies
978-0-470-51919-6

Psychometric Tests For Dummies
978-0-470-75366-8

Raising Happy Children For
Dummies
978-0-470-05978-4

Starting and Running a Business
All-in-One For Dummies
978-0-470-51648-5

Sudoku For Dummies
978-0-470-01892-7

The British Citizenship Test
For Dummies, 2nd Edition
978-0-470-72339-5

Time Management For Dummies
978-0-470-77765-7

Wills, Probate, & Inheritance Tax
For Dummies, 2nd Edition
978-0-470-75629-4

Winning on Betfair For Dummies,
2nd Edition
978-0-470-72336-4

**Available wherever books are sold. For more information or to order direct go to
www.wiley.com or call +44 (0) 1243 843291**

FOR DUMMIES®

The easy way to get more done and have more fun

LANGUAGES

978-0-7645-5194-9

978-0-7645-5193-2

978-0-471-77270-5

MUSIC

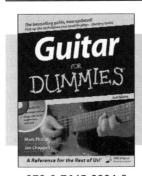
978-0-7645-9904-0

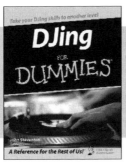
978-0-470-03275-6
UK Edition

978-0-7645-5105-5

SCIENCE & MATHS

978-0-7645-5326-4

978-0-7645-5430-8

978-0-7645-5325-7

Art For Dummies
978-0-7645-5104-8

Baby & Toddler Sleep Solutions
For Dummies
978-0-470-11794-1

Bass Guitar For Dummies
978-0-7645-2487-5

Brain Games For Dummies
978-0-470-37378-1

Christianity For Dummies
978-0-7645-4482-8

Filmmaking For Dummies,
2nd Edition
978-0-470-38694-1

Forensics For Dummies
978-0-7645-5580-0

German For Dummies
978-0-7645-5195-6

Hobby Farming For Dummies
978-0-470-28172-7

Jewelry Making & Beading
For Dummies
978-0-7645-2571-1

Knitting For Dummies, 2nd Edition
978-0-470-28747-7

Music Composition For Dummies
978-0-470-22421-2

Physics For Dummies
978-0-7645-5433-9

Sex For Dummies, 3rd Edition
978-0-470-04523-7

Solar Power Your Home For Dummies
978-0-470-17569-9

Tennis For Dummies
978-0-7645-5087-4

The Koran For Dummies
978-0-7645-5581-7

U.S. History For Dummies
978-0-7645-5249-6

Wine For Dummies, 4th Edition
978-0-470-04579-4

FOR DUMMIES®

Helping you expand your horizons and achieve your potential

COMPUTER BASICS

978-0-470-27759-1   978-0-470-13728-4   978-0-471-75421-3

DIGITAL LIFESTYLE

978-0-470-25074-7   978-0-470-39062-7   978-0-470-17469-2

WEB & DESIGN

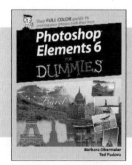  

978-0-470-19238-2   978-0-470-32725-8   978-0-470-34502-3

Access 2007 For Dummies
978-0-470-04612-8

Adobe Creative Suite 3 Design Premium
All-in-One Desk Reference For Dummies
978-0-470-11724-8

AutoCAD 2009 For Dummies
978-0-470-22977-4

C++ For Dummies, 5th Edition
978-0-7645-6852-7

Computers For Seniors For Dummies
978-0-470-24055-7

Excel 2007 All-In-One Desk Reference
For Dummies
978-0-470-03738-6

Flash CS3 For Dummies
978-0-470-12100-9

Mac OS X Leopard For Dummies
978-0-470-05433-8

Macs For Dummies, 10th Edition
978-0-470-27817-8

Networking All-in-One Desk Reference
For Dummies, 3rd Edition
978-0-470-17915-4

Office 2007 All-in-One Desk Reference
For Dummies
978-0-471-78279-7

Search Engine Optimization
For Dummies, 2nd Edition
978-0-471-97998-2

Second Life For Dummies
978-0-470-18025-9

The Internet For Dummies, 11th Edition
978-0-470-12174-0

Visual Studio 2008 All-In-One Desk
Reference For Dummies
978-0-470-19108-8

Web Analytics For Dummies
978-0-470-09824-0

Windows XP For Dummies, 2nd Edition
978-0-7645-7326-2

Available wherever books are sold. For more information or to order direct go to www.wiley.com or call +44 (0) 1243 843291

Printed and bound by CPI Group (UK) Ltd, Croydon, CR0 4YY